Success Strategies
for Teaching Kids With
AUTISM

Wendy
Ashcroft, Ed.D.,

Sue Argiro,

and Joyce
Keohane

PRUFROCK PRESS INC.
WACO, TEXAS

Library of Congress Cataloging-in-Publication Data

Ashcroft, Wendy, 1953-
 Success strategies for teaching kids with autism / Wendy Ashcroft, Sue Agriro, and Joyce Keohane.
   p. cm.
 Includes bibliographical references.
 ISBN 978-1-59363-382-0 (pbk.)
 1. Autistic children--Education. I. Agriro, Sue, 1948- II. Keohane, Joyce, 1954- III. Title.
 LC4717.A75 2010
 371.94--dc22

                    2009038375

Copyright © 2010, Prufrock Press Inc.
Edited by Lacy Compton
Cover and Layout Design by Marjorie Parker

ISBN-13: 978-1-59363-382-0
ISBN-10: 1-59363-382-3

Printed in the United States of America.

At the time of this book's publication, all facts and figures cited are the most current available. All telephone numbers, addresses, and Web site URLs are accurate and active. All publications, organizations, Web sites, and other resources exist as described in the book, and all have been verified. The authors and Prufrock Press Inc. make no warranty or guarantee concerning the information and materials given out by organizations or content found at Web sites, and we are not responsible for any changes that occur after this book's publication. If you find an error, please contact Prufrock Press Inc.

Prufrock Press Inc.
P.O. Box 8813
Waco, TX 76714-8813
Phone: (800) 998-2208
Fax: (800) 240-0333
http://www.prufrock.com

Success Strategies
for Teaching Kids With
AUTISM

CONTENTS

124343

ACKNOWLEDGMENTS

Our loving and encouraging family members, including Tommie Ashcroft, Barbara Ashcroft, John Argiro, Tony Argiro, Amy Daniels, Joe Keohane, Theresa Smith, Josh Keohane, and Kyle Keohane, have been patient and tolerant throughout this project. We love them and thank them as this project would not have been accomplished without their support.

We extend our sincere gratitude to the many colleagues who have shared their expertise with us throughout the years. Team members who have helped us by contributing ideas and information for the book include: Jo Bellanti, Terry Browning, Mary Coleman, Angie Delloso, Michelle Haney, Cathy Henderson, Gretchen Jones, Rick Marcus, Dee Dee Mitchell, Sandra Ourth, Anne Marie Quinn, Michele Seiler, and Anne Troutman.

There are countless others who have helped shape our careers and ultimately this book. Our students and their parents have taught us, our mentors have educated and motivated us, and our friends have encouraged us. We are especially grateful to Catherine Grossner whose friendship and support made this project possible.

We are grateful to Lacy Compton and other Prufrock Press support staff for having confidence in us and allowing us this opportunity. We appreciate the many hours they invested in helping us develop this book.

This project was developed with the intention of providing information on teaching children with ASD. Every effort has been made to provide credit to the originators of the ideas in the book. Any mistakes or omissions in the book are entirely unintentional or unconscious and we apologize if we have erred.

Finally, we would like to dedicate this book to the memory of Dr. Sam Ashcroft, an internationally known pioneer in special education. He believed strongly in the value of education and the importance of teaching children with disabilities. His knowledge of the history of special education provided us insight, his passion for his career inspired us, and his analytical, problem-solving wisdom has enriched us.

INTRODUCTION

We love children and we love teaching. We find children with autism to be particularly delightful and we have found great satisfaction in helping them learn. We have discovered many effective strategies for teaching children with this intriguing condition, and our goal for this publication was to compile them into a practical, useful resource book for the many conscientious and dedicated teachers and parents of children with special needs.

In this book we explain educational approaches that we believe contribute to the successes of children with autism. We have spent many years working with parents and other professionals to develop Individualized Education Programs (IEPs), the documents at the basis of educational planning for students with special needs. In our experiences, we have learned that the best partnerships with parents are developed through discussions of effective, evidence-based strategies. We work continuously to keep in touch with the ongoing research, and we constantly are assessing our interventions with each child.

Through both our research and our experience, we have come to believe that all instructional programs for children with autism should be based on applied behavior analysis (ABA). In this book we'll explain ABA and some of the methodologies and strategies that have been developed using ABA principles. In some cases, we have included strategies not generally considered to be behavioral approaches, but, as behaviorists ourselves, we explain and implement the strategy from a behavioral perspective. For example, we observed one of our students, Carter, responding to activities such as singing, playing instruments, and dancing to music. Carter often laughed and requested repetitions of those activities, so they were immediately incorporated into his school day as reinforcers for his more academic work. So, although a therapist may aim to develop new neural pathways through Music Therapy, our goal as teachers is to use music activities to change observable behavior and accomplish IEP objectives. These are the kinds of strategies we'll be discussing—ones teachers can implement in their own classrooms.

As public school teachers and consultants, we have worked with many families, teachers, behavior specialists, and related service professionals (e.g., speech-language pathologists [SLP], occupational therapists [OT], physical therapists [PT], and vision and hearing specialists). In IEP team meetings, we developed many unique, but effective, individualized programs by adding strategies such as visual supports, work systems, sensory or music activities, and many other techniques to more traditional ABA programs. We believe that, with careful planning and training, all of these strategies can be implemented using principles of ABA. We'll show you throughout this book how to utilize multiple techniques to your advantage when working with children with autism.

We believe that continuing to learn is the best way to develop our skills as teachers. In addition to gaining information about the methodologies and documenting the results of implementing them, we feel it is important to experience learning through them. Our training sessions often include opportunities for adults to use ABA methods to teach other adults skills they do not know. We believe effective teachers should continuously practice how it feels to be in the learner's role. For example, Figure 1 shows teachers at a recent training session using ABA to teach one another a new, challenging topic—the nautical flag alphabet. This is a skill that many of us would be unfamiliar (and maybe even uncomfortable) with, reminding us how children with autism can feel as they are learning new, challenging skills. By keeping our thoughts about learning something new and difficult clearly in mind, we can remember to be patient, encouraging, and positive in our teaching.

FIGURE 1. Staff members using principles of applied behavior analysis to teach each other the nautical flag alphabet.

We know that every child with autism is unique and that each child needs a truly individualized program implemented by a team of supporters. We hope this book will be helpful to all of us as we reach out to teach children with autism.

CHAPTER

I

WHAT IS AUTISM?

parent of a child with autism, in an anonymous posting on the Internet, describes autism as:

Always
Unique,
Thoroughly
Intriguing, and
Sometimes
Mysterious.

In the same passage, the author states that autism has brought **A**nger and rage, **U**nbelief and denial, **T**ears and sadness, **I**solation and loneliness, and then **S**olace and peace. The author ends with thoughts of rejoicing in the child's successes and delighting in the child's **M**agic smile (Let's Beat Autism Now, n.d.; see http://www.letsbeatautismnow.com/Poems.html for similar parent writings on this disorder).

In our experiences as teachers, we have found children with autism to be wonderful and fascinating. We have been privileged to participate in the many amazing achievements of our children and we have celebrated with their families. But, we also have shared in some of the pain, sorrow, and frustration experienced by the families and, perhaps most importantly, we have learned much from the challenges of helping children with this puzzling condition.

Autism is a complex spectrum disorder characterized by impairments in social interaction, communication, and behavior. The label autism spectrum disorder (ASD), an umbrella term, frequently is used to describe a continuum of features ranging from mild to severe. Each person with a diagnosis of ASD has a unique combination of characteristics related to verbal and nonverbal language (communication), interacting with others (social skills), and repetitive, narrow, and restricted interests (behavior). In individuals, these characteristics are presented in varying degrees of severity and result in different levels of functioning.

Autism spectrum disorders are considered to be neurobiological and generally are diagnosed by a team of professionals, including medical personnel. They also are described as developmental disabilities, meaning they usually are evident by 3 years of age. These neurobiological, developmental diagnoses of ASDs have lifelong influences on how individuals communicate their ideas and feelings, how they develop relationships with others, and how they participate in their environments.

The term ASD often is used interchangeably with Pervasive Developmental Disorder (PDD). PDD also is an umbrella term (see Figure 2) encompassing the five disorders in the text revision of the fourth edition of the *Diagnostic and Statistical Manual* (*DSM-IV-TR*; American Psychiatric Association, 2000). Sometimes, ASD is used to refer only to three of the disorders: autism, Asperger's syndrome, and Pervasive Development Disorder-Not Otherwise Specified (PDD-NOS). The prognosis for each of these three disorders is quite favorable in that, with effective treatment, individuals make significant progress. Other times, ASD also is considered to encompass two other disorders: Rett syndrome and childhood disintegrative disorder. Both of these are progressive disorders, describing individuals who start with a period of typical development and then enter a regressive phase. The prognosis for these two disorders is not as promising.

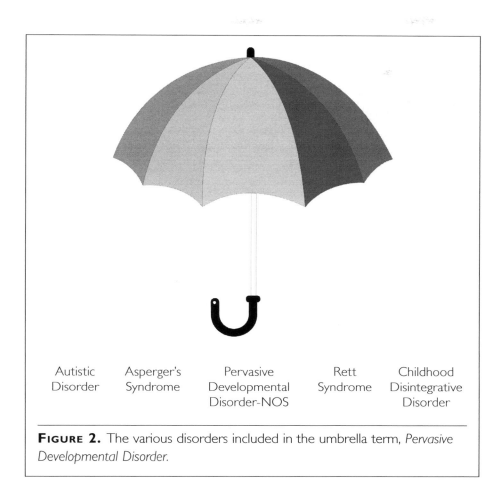

| Autistic Disorder | Asperger's Syndrome | Pervasive Developmental Disorder-NOS | Rett Syndrome | Childhood Disintegrative Disorder |

FIGURE 2. The various disorders included in the umbrella term, *Pervasive Developmental Disorder.*

In the following pages, additional information is provided for each of the five disorders. Descriptions of children are presented to help explain how the disorder may affect individuals.

AUTISM

Autism (also called autistic disorder) is a complex condition diagnosed by observation and analysis of a person's behavior patterns. It is a spectrum disorder, meaning it includes individuals with widely varying abilities and unique combinations of behavioral deficits and excesses. A complete evaluation of language, cognition, and behavior, as well as physical and neurological assessments, are necessary for a formal diagnosis. A good evaluation process involves consultations from a physician, psychologist, and speech-language pathologist, and parent information regarding developmental history and current functioning.

There is general agreement that autism is a neurological disorder affecting brain functioning and that it is a developmental disorder, usually diagnosed before the age of 3. People with autism often have difficulty with verbal and nonverbal communication and social interactions along with restricted interests, repetitive behaviors, and resistance to change.

Case Study of Autism: Mark

Mark was diagnosed with autism at age 2. From birth he had typical development, sitting at about age 6 months and walking at about a year. At 14 months he was consistently imitating sounds and actions, verbalizing while pointing to things he wanted and babbling. He clearly asked for mama, daddy, ball, and play, and occasionally put two words together like "Daddy go." By 18 months he was walking on his tiptoes, wringing his hands, and crying instead of communicating. He no longer used understandable words and he stopped interacting with people.

When Mark was diagnosed, he had significant delays in social interaction such as avoiding eye contact and running away from people. Not only did he lose his ability to communicate with others, he showed no understanding of spoken language. He did not follow even simple directions. Between the ages of 2 and 3, Mark developed very frequent hand movements such as wringing his hands and twisting his fingers. His interest in toys was limited to waving them in front of his eyes.

At age 3, Mark began receiving intensive Discrete Trial Training (DTT) and quickly regained his ability to follow directions. He also learned to match and to name objects and pictures. In spite of intensive interactive instruction, Mark continued to show little interest in communicating with people. His restricted interests limited his opportunities to play with his brothers and yielded even fewer activities with neighbors and schoolmates. By age 6, Mark's expressive vocabulary was more than 1,000 words; however, he still had little interest in interacting with others and often communicated with whining and crying rather than talking.

Today, Mark is improving in his abilities to listen to and communicate with others. His interests are widening as he has developed a passion for watching movies and playing video games. His ability to read words is providing his teachers an opportunity to use many of the strategies in this book to help him increase his interactions with others.

ASPERGER'S SYNDROME

The diagnosis of Asperger's syndrome is made with a thorough analysis of the history of the person's development of social and language skills and assessments and observation of an individual's behaviors. A true diagnosis of Asperger's syndrome (also called Asperger Disorder) is made when there is impairment in social interaction and unusual patterns of behavior along with no significant delay in language or cognitive development.

The impairment in social interaction is characterized by difficulties with tasks such as understanding nonverbal social cues, peculiarities in speech and language, recognizing and communicating emotions, making friends and maintaining peer relationships, and sharing enjoyment, interests, and achievements with others. The patterns of behavior can include restricted interests and activities; preoccupation or obsession with a particular subject; strong dislike for change and inflexible adherence to routines or rituals; unusual sensitivity to sound, light, or touch; or awkward, repetitive mannerisms.

People with Asperger's syndrome may demonstrate clumsy and uncoordinated motor movements and repetitive behaviors or rituals. Sometimes, people with Asperger's syndrome have an impaired ability to be empathetic with other people and can be thought of as egotistical, selfish, or uncaring.

Case Study of Asperger's Syndrome: Michael

Michael's language developed early and quickly, but his motor milestones were slightly delayed. At age 2, he was speaking in complete sentences with a remarkably advanced vocabulary. By age 3, he was reading first-grade-level books and adding and subtracting double-digit math problems. These academic tasks became his favorite activities, and he often would whine or scream when he was interrupted from them. He would spend some time interacting with others while playing with his extensive collection of trains; however, whenever free to choose, he spent both his academic and play time alone.

Michael was very anxious in unstructured situations and quite uncooperative during group play times in his daycare program. Rather than interact with others, he played by himself and shouted at children who attempted to play with him.

Michael did not respond appropriately to social cues. For example, he talked when it was quiet time and often stayed silent when asked a question. In addition, his tone of voice frequently did not match the situation. When he was 5 years old, he spoke like an adult and his vocabulary and intonation indicated to others that he was much older, almost adult-like.

Michael was very sensitive to smells and it was difficult for him to eat in the cafeteria. He was very anxious, even fearful, of situations like elevators or escalators and hated most art projects. Michael seemed uncomfortable conversing with classmates and happiest when working on the computer. He did not seem to know how to approach small groups of children to join an activity and although he had plenty of language skills, he often was unsuccessful in beginning and ending conversations. He seemed most comfortable talking about trains and would talk about trains as long as anyone would listen.

Today, Michael is achieving well in school. His teachers and parents have used the strategies in this book, and Michael is becoming more comfortable interacting with others.

PERVASIVE DEVELOPMENTAL DISORDER- NOT OTHERWISE SPECIFIED

The third disorder under the PDD umbrella is Pervasive Developmental Disorder-Not Otherwise Specified (PDD-NOS). PDD-NOS is a diagnosis that sometimes is referred to as atypical autism or atypical personality development.

The diagnosis of PDD-NOS is used when a child does not have the complete features of autism or a more clearly defined pervasive developmental disorder. The relatively broad definition for this mixed group of children presents problems for diagnosing this condition and results in a very heterogeneous population. In PDD-NOS, there is noticeable impairment of social interaction, communication, and/or stereotyped behavior patterns, usually recognizable before a child is 3 years old. However, in children with PDD-NOS, the deficits may not be as severe or the impairments may not occur in configurations that would meet the criteria for an autism diagnosis. For example, one child may receive a diagnosis of PDD-NOS due to having only a few mild symptoms. Another child might have very significant language or social impairments, but not have the unusual behavior patterns necessary for a diagnosis of autism. In addition, while a child's profile might seem to fit the criteria, many of these behaviors are developmental and, for some children, the symptoms might just be part of a slightly unusual growth pattern, rather than PDD-NOS.

Case Study of PDD-NOS: Mindy

Mindy was the oldest of two children. She was a difficult baby who was not easy to console, but her developmental milestones for both communication and motor skills seemed appropriate. She enjoyed social interaction but was easily overstimulated. As a toddler, Mindy exhibited high sensitivity to sounds, smells, and touch and at times of excitement engaged in hand flapping.

Her parents sought evaluation when she was 4 years of age because of difficulties in preschool. Her communicative and cognitive functions were within the normal range and she did not have the full features of autism. Mindy received a diagnosis of PDD-NOS due to her social problems with peers and her insistence on routines. When upset by changes in her environment, Mindy was slow to respond to her parents' reassurances and often would stay agitated for hours at a time. Mindy was enrolled in preschool where she made significant gains in social skills and continued her academic success. Throughout elementary school, problems with peer interactions persisted and her academic progress slowed. Mindy resisted changes to her routine by continuing to follow the previous pattern of activity. When asked to change or to do something new, Mindy would hum, rock, and spin while refusing to comply with instructions. In elementary school, Mindy continued to have difficulties with social interaction, tended to enjoy solitary activities, and described herself as a loner.

Today, Mindy is using many of the strategies in this book to communicate and interact with others. She seems happier and more comfortable in school and plays with friends in structured play groups at home.

CHILDHOOD DISINTEGRATIVE DISORDER

Children with childhood disintegrative disorder typically show normal development for at least the first 2 years of life. This includes typical development of motor skills, verbal and nonverbal communication, social interaction and play skills, and self-care skills. Before the age of 10, there is regression in the ability to say words or sentences (expressive language), the ability to understand verbal and nonverbal communication (receptive language), and the ability to interact with others (social skills). There also may be loss of motor skills, bowel and bladder control, and self-care skills (adaptive behavior). These changes may occur suddenly and quickly, possibly in a few days or weeks, or they may occur gradually over a period of several months.

The loss of communication skills may include a reduction in spoken language, a decrease in the ability to initiate or sustain a conversation, an increase in repetitive use of language, and a decline in imaginative or make-believe play. The loss of abilities in social interaction skills may include impairment in the ability to respond appropriately to the nonverbal behaviors of others, failure to develop peer relationships, and a lack of social or emotional reciprocity. In this stage, children often have an inability to recognize, understand, and respond to social cues and feelings of others. The loss of motor skills involves a declining ability to move the body in a purposeful way. This may be accompanied by the development of repetitive and stereotyped patterns such as hand flapping, rocking, and spinning; the development of specific routines and rituals; difficulty with transitions or changes in routine; maintaining a fixed posture or body position; and preoccupation with certain objects or activities.

Case Study of Childhood Disintegrative Disorder: John

John's early history was within normal limits. By age 2 he was speaking in sentences and his development appeared to be proceeding appropriately. He was a cheerful toddler—smiling, developing language, and using the toilet. Then, gradually, he began losing interest in other people and his use of language seemed to decrease. He developed self-stimulating behavior such as flapping his hands and rocking and stopped using the bathroom.

Previously, John accepted hugs as reassurance from his parents, but eventually lost the ability to be consoled and tensed his muscles every time he was touched. At age 30 months John stopped all attempts at communication and was no longer toilet trained. He no longer showed interest in social interaction and his self-stimulatory actions became almost constant. A comprehensive medical examination failed to reveal any physical conditions to explain his regression and all medical notes described features of autism. At age 9 he occasionally spoke single words, pulled away from hugs and touch, and spent all unengaged time in self-stimulating behaviors.

Today, John is responding to visual supports recommended in this book. Although he is still uncomfortable with too much touch, he allows and tolerates interactions that are predictable to him. He responds well to routines and is particularly responsive to high-five gestures from others.

RETT SYNDROME

Rett syndrome (also known as Rett's disorder) is characterized by an initial period of normal development followed by a loss of communication skills and deliberate hand movements. It is the only one of the PDD conditions that has a period of rapid deterioration followed by stabilization and sometimes includes periods of increases in eye contact and reductions of stereotypical hand movements. Because of these periods of stabilization, most experts now agree that it is a developmental disorder, rather than a degenerative disorder. Rett syndrome often is mistaken for autism, cerebral palsy, or mental retardation, so a precise developmental history is critical to an accurate diagnosis.

Rett syndrome occurs almost exclusively in females and occurs in a variety of racial and ethnic groups worldwide. In earlier times it was thought that males with Rett syndrome did not survive long enough to be born. Researchers have now identified a genetic flaw in some children with Rett syndrome. Although the great majority of these have been girls, a few boys have been identified to have this same gene mutation. Researchers recommend that Rett syndrome remain a clinical diagnosis that should not be dismissed for boys.

Children with Rett syndrome often engage in repetitive hand movements such as hand wringing, hand clapping, and hand mouthing. Sometimes, children with Rett syndrome have some shakiness of their bodies and tremors in their arms and legs. Some children have scoliosis and may lose the ability to walk. Those children who are able to walk may walk on their toes and may walk by rocking sideways with a wide-based, stiff-legged gait.

Case Study of Rett Syndrome: Sarah

Sarah progressed normally through the milestones of sitting, walking, and speaking in two- and three-word phrases. At age 18 months, her communication and socialization abilities regressed. She stopped using words she previously said with ease, and she became uninterested in interacting with children who had once been her playmates. A specialist diagnosed her with autism at age 3. At that stage she had many characteristics of autism, including fear of change, fixation on certain objects, a fascination with books and magazines, intolerance to touch, lack of sleep, crying episodes, and loss of eye contact. At age 4 she was unable to hold things independently and started twisting her hands and wringing them together. At age 4 ½ she received the more appropriate diagnosis of Rett syndrome.

At school, Sarah was provided with instruction in using a one-step communicator and was given assistive devices to help her hold musical, vibrating toys. However, she eventually started to have seizures and began developing scoliosis. She started in physical and occupational therapy to slow down the loss of strength in her legs and to prevent further loss of balance. She loved music, videos, TV, and all sensory activities such as riding in a wheelchair, bouncing, and swimming.

Today, Sarah is receiving homebound instruction characterized by gentle sensory activities. Her teacher and therapists watch closely for signs of her preference for activities and encourage her to use eye gaze and her one-step communicator to express her desires. They work through physical activities designed to maintain her strength and range of motion. Sarah shows signs of enjoying her activities by smiling and making sounds and is maintaining her voluntary movements to use the communicator.

WHAT IS THE EDUCATIONAL DEFINITION OF ASD?

The Individuals with Disabilities Education Improvement Act (IDEA, 2004) defined autism as:

> a developmental disability significantly affecting verbal and nonverbal communication and social interaction, generally evident before age three, that adversely affects a child's educational performance. Other characteristics often associated with autism are engagement in repetitive activities and stereotyped movements, resistance to environmental change or change in daily routines, and unusual responses to sensory experiences. (Part 300.A.300.8.c.1.i)

IDEA is a federal law, requiring each state that receives federal funds to have a corresponding law regarding, among other things, nondiscriminatory evaluation procedures. These laws vary from state to state, so the definition of autism might be slightly different in each state.

The most unique aspect of the IDEA definition is that to become eligible for services under IDEA in the category of autism, the child's educational performance must be adversely affected. If the child can succeed in general education without special education, a team of professionals may decide that a particular child does not meet the criteria in that particular state to be identified as having autism.

WHAT CAUSES AUTISM SPECTRUM DISORDERS?

There are many theories about the causes of ASDs, but most experts agree autism is probably caused by a combination of genetic and environmental factors. Researchers have been studying a wide range of possible causes, including, but not limited to, genetics, allergies, infectious disease, the mercury-based preservative called thimerosal (used in some vaccines), irregularities in brain development, abnormal levels of neurotransmitters, immune deficiencies, and malnutrition. For most of these, there is no consensus that they actually cause autism. Recent studies suggest that some people have a genetic predisposition to autism (Autism Genome Project Consortium, 2007; Gupta & State, 2007; Zhao et al., 2007).

In families with one child with autism, the risk of having a second child with the disorder is greater than the risk for the general population. Researchers are looking for clues about which genes contribute to this increased susceptibility. In some cases, parents and other relatives of a child with autism show mild impairments in social and communicative skills or engage in repetitive behaviors. Evidence also suggests that some emotional disorders, such as manic depression, occur more frequently than average in the families of people with autism (National Institute of Health, n.d.; see http://www.ninds.nih.gov for more information).

In the past, some researchers had suggested that autism was the result of poor parenting skills on the part of the mother. This belief has caused parents of children with autism unwarranted feelings of pain and guilt, when actually, the inability of the child to interact appropriately is one of the key symptoms of this developmental disorder. There is agreement that there is no causal link between parenting and autism.

Recent research (Offit, 2007) has indicated that there also is no causal link between the MMR vaccine and autism or between thimerosal and autism. This was further verified by three special federal court cases that reviewed extensive expert testimony and widespread research. All three cases concluded that the combination of the thimerosal-containing vaccines and the MMR vaccine are not causal factors in development of autism (*Cedillo v. Secretary of Health and Human Services*, 2009; *Hazlehurst v. Secretary of Health and Human Services*, 2009; *Snyder v. Secretary of Health and Human Services*, 2009).

It seems likely, given the research so far, that several factors combine to cause autism (Happé, Ronald, & Plomin, 2006). For example, it may be that certain children have a genetic predisposition and are more susceptible to certain environmental triggers such as food allergies or toxins.

Interest in and funding for autism research is on the rise, so new and better information should be forthcoming in later months and years. Until we have more definitive answers, it seems to make sense for teachers to focus on effective educational methodologies and to support researchers as they learn more about the causes of autism.

HOW COMMON IS AUTISM?

Autism is diagnosed among all racial, ethnic, and social groups; all family income levels and lifestyle choices; and all educational levels, and can affect any family and any child. The incidence of autism generally is consistent around the world, however, ASD is four times more prevalent in boys than in girls (Washington State Department of Social & Health Services, n.d.).

Based on data collected on 8-year-olds from various areas of the United States, the Centers for Disease Control and Prevention (CDC, 2008) estimated that one in 150 children is diagnosed with a disorder on the autism spectrum (for more information, see http://www.cdc.gov/ncbddd/autism/faq_prevalence.htm). The CDC also stated that more children are being classified as having autism spectrum disorders. The increase may be partly due to increased awareness and changes in how we identify and classify ASDs in people as well as a true increase in prevalence.

More children than ever before are receiving special education services for autism. It is possible that some of the growth in the number of children receiving special education may be caused in part by the addition of autism as a special education category when the separate classification of autism was added to IDEA in 1990. In 2006, 224,594 children ages 6–21 and 35,111 children ages 3–5 were served under the autism classification for special education services (Data Accountability Center, n.d.). These numbers most likely are a significant underestimate of the actual prevalence of ASDs in schools as some children with ASDs might receive special education services under another disability category such as language impaired or developmentally delayed.

WHAT ARE THE CHARACTERISTICS OF INDIVIDUALS WITH AUTISM SPECTRUM DISORDER?

There is a common saying in the autism community that if you've met one person with autism, you've met one person with autism. We have found this to be very true in our extensive experience—we've yet to encounter any two children who are alike. However, there are some common characteristics of people with autism. Each individual with a diagnosis of an ASD will have a unique combination of some of the characteristics listed below.

Characteristic 1: Individuals With ASD Often Have Difficulty Communicating With Others, Both in Understanding What Others Say and in Conveying Their Needs and Desires

Communication is a two-way process involving the transfer of information, usually thought of as an exchange of thoughts, feelings, or ideas through gestures, body language, speech, or writing. This process involves both giving and receiving information.

As a group, children with ASD have a variety of communication abilities ranging from those who have no vocal communication skills to those who have highly advanced vocabularies and articulate speaking abilities. Some children may have no noticeable communication skills (i.e., actual intent to exchange information with others) or they may have unusual methods of communication, such as speaking without looking at a person or using unexpected words, sounds, or body language.

In addition, most children with diagnoses of ASD have some difficulty understanding what others say. This can range from difficulties understanding complex verbal messages to an inability to understand even simple directions.

From birth to age 3, Emma showed no response to her name or to verbal instructions and she made no attempts to interact with people to get what she needed. When she began to speak words, she spoke them in isolation, unrelated to the situation and without eye contact or proximity to adults. For example, one day, while playing alone with a puzzle, she clearly said "Emma." From across the room, her teacher heard her and spent nearly an hour trying to get Emma to repeat her name. Emma continued to play with items, but did not look at her teacher or verbalize in any way.

On the other hand, Michael, at age 12, was able to speak with highly sophisticated language clearly related to the topic. Once, when asked if he thought a classmate liked him, he responded, "There's a better chance of being struck by lightning on a cloudless day than there is that she would like me. And in fact, there's a better chance of being bitten by a shark 1,000 miles up the Mississippi River than there is that she would like me."

Sometimes, children with ASD have large vocabularies but don't use words and sentences to communicate their needs. Mark, for example, had a vocabulary of thousands of words, demonstrated by naming objects and pictures for hours at a time. However, when his tape recorder wouldn't work, he would throw it across the room in anger rather than requesting help to replace the batteries.

Other people with autism are able to speak hundreds of words even though they don't understand their meanings. Keith knew every word to every verse of the song "Seventy-Six Trombones" and could clearly articulate such phrases as "copper-bottomed tympani" and "big bassoon" with absolutely no understanding that these words were describing musical instruments.

Sometimes people with autism have the vocabulary words and the ability to communicate to others, but cannot articulate clearly enough to communicate. For example, it took Emma's mother days to understand that "nunna neeno" meant "want a Cheeto®."

Characteristic 2: Individuals With ASD Frequently Have Deficits in the Area of Social Skills, Making It Challenging to Develop and Maintain Meaningful Relationships

Social skills are characterized by the ability to interact with others in appropriate and expected ways. Sometimes known as people skills, social skills include basic skills such as taking turns, listening to others, saying positive things, receiving help from others, giving help, and sharing. It is not uncommon to see children with autism walking or pacing the perimeter of the playground instead of joining with the class for a social game. In the classroom or community, individuals with autism often retreat into their own comfort zone, shutting out others.

Joseph was an enthusiastic and active 7-year-old who had a tendency to ignore social expectations. Not interested in the games most other boys of his age played, he preferred simpler stories and TV programs, such as "Sesame Street®" and "Barney®." He spent hours looking at books, playing with stuffed animals, drawing pictures, reciting complicated stories, and playing solitary games involving these characters. His classmates were long past their interest in these activities, and they often described the characters as babyish. They tended to ignore Joseph when he was around, especially when he was engaging in activities centered on these preferred characters. When his peers did try to interact with him and play with his toys, Joseph would growl or screech in order to express his frustration.

Emily seemed to lack empathy toward others and to disregard their feelings. She often appeared rude in social situations, refusing to acknowledge others, say hello, or answer questions. She frequently muttered "Shut up" and said "I hate you" directly to her teachers or friends. Emily used much of her free time to ride on scooters and bicycles, but preferred to go off on her own, speeding dangerously down steep hills and going far from home. She also was interested in art, but rarely interacted with others during art projects.

George spent his entire school day alone even though there were many boys from his neighborhood in his class. He was loud and immature in his communication and other children seemed to be uncomfortable around him. The few that did interact with him often said and did things to provoke George. They knew that George was obsessed with cameras so they often would say, "Hey George, want to take a picture?" knowing George would repeat the words "Say cheese" loudly and repetitively. Although George was interested in current music and television, he didn't initiate conversations about these topics. When someone else introduced a topic for discussion, George took over the topic with a monologue of teaching and preaching. At these times, the other children quickly moved away from George.

Characteristic 3: Individuals With ASD Usually Display Stereotypic Motor Movements and/or Have Ritualistic, Odd, or Inappropriate Behaviors Generally Considered Socially Unacceptable

Although people with autism are unique individuals, there often are distinctive motor movements or patterns that are similar among different children. These movements, such as hand flapping, spinning, repetitive verbalizations, and rocking, can interfere with acceptance among typical peers. Of course, many people show emotion and react by clapping, jumping up and down, verbal shouts, or repetitive tapping of a pen, but these behaviors seem to be exaggerated in individuals with autism.

For example, at age 3, Mark walked on his tiptoes everywhere he went. He would rub his fingers together and wring his hands. Nearby, at another school, Steven, who was 8 years old at the time, was engaging in nearly identical finger rubbing and hand wringing. And, while walking around the track at the community center, Paul would flex his hands and twist his wrists. Although these movements are similar in some ways, a closer look reveals unique actions and different timing of the movement. Yet, for each child, the behavior appears to be unrelated to the other activities and is usually inappropriate in that setting.

Other children engage in ritualistic activities. Derek spent his entire playtime sorting toys by color and putting them in lines and other geometric patterns. When others rearranged his patterns, he showed his displeasure by crying, screaming, and yelling. Whenever Parker approached a stranger, he immediately leaned in to smell the person's shoulder and feel the texture of the clothes the person was wearing. When he was anxious, he rubbed his first two fingers together and put them up to his nose.

George developed a ritual for changing classes. He would avoid the crowded hall and covered walkway that led from one building to the next and instead would exit the front door of the first building and use the outside sidewalk to get to the front door of the next building. However, immediately after he exited the first building, he would stop at the sidewalk intersection and tap his bag three times on the ground. He would then turn left and bolt to the end of the walkway to the main building. There, he would tap his bag three times on the ground, turn left, run a few steps and enter the building. In many child-teacher conferences, George agreed to stop this ritual and use the inside hallway to change buildings. However, each time the bell rang, George would dash quickly toward the front door and engage in his unusual routine.

Characteristic 4: Individuals With ASD Typically Like Routines and May Have Significant Anxiety About Changes in Their Environment

Change can be upsetting to many people, but for children with ASD, changes to established routines can cause unease, worry, and even fear. Children with ASD often notice small variations in schedules, settings, people, and instructional materials. Sometimes, even changes from less preferred activities to more favored activities can be distressing just because it breaks the routine.

Mindy followed the same route to the cafeteria each day. Upon entering, she would go directly to the far wall and touch it before getting in line to get her food. She would then touch her chair with each hand before sitting down. Mindy got very upset whenever these routines were disrupted. For example, when her teacher directed her to get in line immediately upon entering, Mindy pushed past the teacher to go to the wall. As the teacher tried to block this movement and redirect Mindy to the line, Mindy began to scream and cry.

Russell had a written daily schedule with places to check off each completed activity throughout the day. At the end of each day, checks were exchanged for a chance to participate in the preparation of a frozen drink and the opportunity for a snack of cookies or crackers. Highly motivated by these rewards, Russell conscientiously kept up with his clipboard and checkmarks. On the day before

Thanksgiving, his class had the opportunity to join with another class to cook biscuits in a toaster oven and make butter by shaking whipped cream in the empty milk cartons left over from lunch. As this fun and exciting activity began, Russell started saying what sounded like "vacations . . . guests." His teacher tried to understand his communication by repeating it and asking questions like, "Are you having guests over for Thanksgiving?" and "Are you going on a vacation with your guests?" These questions escalated Russell's frustration as he repeated his phrases, increasing his volume and speed. As the situation continued, Russell began hitting himself in the head and screaming. His frustrated teacher tried in vain to understand his communication until she finally said, in exasperation, "Don't tell me; show me." Russell, still hitting his head and screaming, got his clipboard and his teacher realized he was trying to say, "vocational skills," the next activity on his schedule. Russell's attempts to communicate were eventually rewarded with a demonstration and explanation that a check would be provided in the vocational skills section for the biscuit and butter activity, but he continued to show anxious behaviors such as fidgeting and squirming the rest of the day.

Characteristic 5: Individuals With ASD May Focus on Specific, Sometimes Irrelevant Details, Possibly to a Degree That May Result in Undergeneralizing, Overgeneralizing, and/or Even Prevent Complete Understanding of a Concept or Situation

Generalization occurs when behaviors learned in one setting are demonstrated in another setting over time with a variety of people and materials and not just in the original setting with the original teacher (Alberto & Troutman, 2009). Part of the skill in generalizing appropriately is related to noticing the conditions that indicate that it is time to perform (or not perform) the behavior.

Typical children learn to focus on important and relevant conditions while children with diagnoses of ASD often focus on specific details that are not pertinent to understanding the situation. In addition, many children with ASD have difficulty continuing to use skills they have learned when conditions change. These children, who are undergeneralizing, do not perform the skill when the setting, materials, or people are different. They may not notice the similarities in conditions that indicate that it is appropriate to use the skill. Other children use the skills they learn in too many situations. These children, who are overgeneralizing, perform the behavior whether the situation calls for it or not. They may not notice conditions indicating that it is not appropriate to act in a certain way. Or, they may notice an irrelevant condition indicating to them that it is time to perform the skill.

Once when Aisha's class was involved in a Circle Time language activity, the teacher had placed an object under each child's chair. The activity involved providing each child a turn to pick up the object, show it, label it, and answer questions about it. When it was Aisha's turn, her teacher directed her by gesturing and saying, "Aisha, get your object from under the chair." Aisha bent over to look under her chair and picked up a small dust bunny instead of the large blue cup her teacher had placed under her chair.

When Robby's behavior consultant arrived in his room, she was wearing a light-colored jacket and her nametag. Her silver sunglasses were hanging from her nametag lanyard. Robby immediately pulled up his shirt. After a moment or two of analyzing this unexpected behavior, his behavior consultant realized that Robby assumed she was a doctor arriving with a stethoscope to examine him. Without regard for the overall situation, his focus on her jacket and hanging silver sunglasses prompted him to assume she was a doctor.

Eric's teacher felt confident that he had mastered identifying the numerals one to five by labeling them as she held up index cards. No matter the order presented, he was always accurate in labeling each one. However, Eric was unable to identify these numbers in a number book checked out from the library. Upon further investigation, his teacher was surprised that he could not identify numbers in any other situation. She tried games, blocks, and flashcards to no avail. Yet, Eric was still able to identify each number correctly when presented his original set of index cards. After a week of experimenting, his teacher finally realized that Eric was using smudges and folds on the well-used index cards as his clues and was truly unable to identify the actual numbers.

Maria's teachers required all children in the classroom to raise their hands before speaking. Whenever children spoke out, they were prompted to stop, raise their hands, and repeat their communication. The most common situation in which this occurred was when one of the teachers was talking to another child. Instead of raising their hands, children often would just call out the teachers' names. As good behaviorists, the teachers would delay calling on children who hadn't raised their hands and respond enthusiastically to those who had. Children quickly learned that to get the teachers' attention, it was more efficient to raise their hands first, rather than be last to get the teachers' response. Maria developed a habit of raising her hand every time she wanted to speak, even outside the classroom setting. Once, Maria even raised her hand in a department store when she and her mother unexpectedly encountered one of her teachers!

Characteristic 6: Individuals With ASD Might Experience Difficulty With Auditory Processing and Thus Learn Best When Visual Supports Supplement Verbal Instruction

Auditory processing involves recognizing and interpreting sounds. Ordinarily, children learn to discriminate among sounds and respond to them appropriately. This involves listening (tuning in) to important information and screening out distracting information. Children with auditory processing difficulties may have difficulty following verbal directions, remembering information presented orally, and carrying out directions with multiple steps.

Providing visual support creates learning opportunities for those who experience difficulty understanding verbal communication. Pictures, symbols, visual schedules, photos, objects, and choice boards stay in place after the verbal words are said and gone. Because they stay in place, these visuals also allow the child to gain independence when supported in daily routines.

Erica mastered matching quickly. With very few discrete trials, she quickly became accurate at matching colors, shapes, numbers, letters, and words. Although Erica didn't speak at all, she followed routines easily and consistently. Erica had difficulty with receptive language tasks such as following one-step directions and responding to requests to pick out objects and pictures. She was particularly inconsistent in identifying colors receptively. Erica's teacher wrote the words "Give me red" on a blank sentence strip. She wrote the word red with a red magic marker and wrote the rest of the words in black. Her teacher pointed to and read each word to Erica and held out her hand near a red piece of construction paper. Erica immediately handed her teacher the red piece of paper. Continuing with the process, Erica was flawless in responding to the written directions that were paired with the verbal instructions and color prompt. Over the next several days, Erica's teacher faded the color prompt for the full word to the first letter of the color word and then to a colored dot on the first letter of the color word. When the color prompts were faded completely, Erica's teacher was pleasantly surprised that Erica responded with 100% accuracy to the written directions. Even more surprising, within a few days, Erica's teacher withdrew the written prompts and Erica was able to respond correctly to the verbal instructions alone.

In third grade, Benjamin participated consistently in a reading program that allowed children to progress to higher levels contingent on accurate performance in written tests. Benjamin had successfully accomplished grade levels 3.1 through 3.7 and was particularly proud of his work, looking forward to his goal of getting to the fourth-grade levels. Shortly after this point, Benjamin's third-grade teacher brought him to his consulting special education teacher because Benjamin was crying inconsolably. Benjamin had completed level 3.9 and was expecting to start immediately on level 4.0 when his teacher discovered that he had inadvertently skipped level 3.8. The more his teacher tried to explain the situation to Benjamin, the more upset he became. When they found his consulting teacher, she took a scrap of paper and made a list of the levels. She said, "Look, Benjamin, you finished 3.5, 3.6, 3.7, and 3.9." She put a check by each of the levels as she listed them. Then she said, "Do 3.8 and then you can do 4.0." Benjamin immediately calmed down and quickly went to accomplish his goal.

Characteristic 7: Individuals With ASD May Be Hypersensitive or Hyposensitive and Thus React Atypically to Input From the Five Traditional Senses (Sight, Hearing, Touch, Smell, and Taste) as Well as the Vestibular and Kinesthetic Senses

Reactions to sensory input range widely among people, but most people generally are able to tolerate the sights, sounds, smells, and tastes they experience. Typically, people regulate their movements and automatically interpret the sensory input and focus and control their energy in appropriate ways.

Children with autism often have unusual reactions to sensory input, creating challenges when attempting to process sensory information (Ayers, 1979). Some children seek out high levels of vestibular (movement), proprioceptive (sense of body in space), or kinesthetic (tactile) activities. These include activities that involve motion related to moving through space, bouncing, swinging, and spinning. Other children might smell or taste a high percentage of objects or persons they encounter. Still others may manipulate objects by waving, spinning, or twirling them in front of their eyes. Other individuals with hyperactive sensory systems might attempt to avoid sights, sounds, smells, foods, and touch that they find aversive.

Whenever occupational therapy (OT) was on Joseph's schedule, he would run to the OT room and go quickly to the large rubber balls or swing. He constantly sought movement and often used objects creatively to add variety to his activities. For example, he taped chip clips to his shoes and said he was going skating.

Robby sought opportunities to smell things. When entering a room, he walked around picking up objects and putting them close to his nose. If he encountered something too big to pick up, Robby would lean in close to get a good smell.

Ella was constantly moving, making noises, fidgeting, touching, mouthing, or chewing objects. She also frequently dropped an assortment of items on the floor, listening intently to the sound each object made. The only time Ella was still was when she played with an interactive toy with moveable parts, sounds, or lights.

Phillip would scream loudly whenever he heard the swishing sound of a person crossing her legs. He showed signs of anxiety such as excess movement and tensing of his muscles when he heard the humming of the computer or the buzzing of the florescent lights. In the same classroom, John rarely reacted to loud noises or sudden movements. John seemed to have such a high threshold for environmental stimuli that it often was difficult to get him to respond at all.

Mindy's muscles tensed whenever she approached the school gym or auditorium. When encouraged to enter, she covered her ears. Within a few minutes, Mindy would begin crying and yelling until she left the area.

Emma had a restricted diet due to her dislike of food except Nacho Cheese Doritos® and Cheetos®. She would gag at the sight or even smell of other foods. Foods with soft textures actually caused her to vomit.

Characteristic 8: Individuals With ASD Often Struggle to Understand the Perspective of Others, May Have an Impaired Ability to Read and Interpret the Emotions of Others, and Might Have Difficulty Understanding Social Cues

People who are successful social thinkers are those who can regard the point of view of others as they consider the thoughts, emotions, and beliefs of someone other than themselves (Winner, 2005). Most people begin developing these skills from birth and improve them by observing the social practices of others and analyzing the results of their social interactions. Effective social interaction involves more than just knowing the right words to say. It includes controlling body language, facial expressions, intonation, and voice volume and cadence. In addition, successful social interaction involves skills related to recognizing emotions in others. Human emotions are complex and have many degrees and subtleties. There is not always a direct correlation between body language and emotion. Understanding the context of a situation often is critical to accurately interpreting it.

Even when children with autism learn appropriate words to say, they may display unusual body language when communicating. For example, they might not engage in or maintain eye contact or face their communication partner. Their intonation, voice volume, and cadence may be unusual and may not match the situation. Sometimes, their impaired ability to understand the context of a social interaction will cause them to react in unexpected ways.

On one occasion, when Elijah's family and staff were celebrating a recent accomplishment, Elijah's mother began to cry with tears of joy. Elijah attended to this closely. Subsequently, Elijah tried various actions to get others to repeat this crying action. Through trial and error, Elijah realized that if he hurt someone, the person would usually cry. For a long time, Elijah was obsessed with the crying behavior of others and unfortunately spent time trying to hurt others to get a crying response.

Often children with autism display no appreciation for the feelings of others. Typical peers and many adults unaware of the characteristics of ASD would probably characterize Michael as rude and disrespectful. Michael continually gave his unrestrained opinion of the fashions, hairstyles, or mannerisms of those he observed in his surroundings. When approached by a staff member who had recently dyed her hair, Michael loudly remarked, "Oh, Miss Beverly, that dye job you got is just too much. Even the gray looked better than that!"

Juan, a high school child diagnosed with autism, would engage in many behaviors to gain attention from adults. When he entered a classroom, he announced his arrival in a loud voice and followed up with assorted compliments to the female staff members, remarking about their beauty and grandeur while being totally oblivious to the fact that he had disturbed the classroom instruction.

Characteristic 9: Individuals With ASD Might Demonstrate Predominantly Concrete Thinking and Thus Make Literal Interpretations of Statements and Situations

Some people with autism understand language in a very literal way, characterizing them as concrete thinkers. Concrete thinking is characterized by a person's own specific, immediate experiences, rather than general examples, abstract concepts, or the experiences of others. For example, while concrete thinkers can think about specific objects, abstract thinkers can reflect on categories of objects, common attributes, and relationships. For concrete or literal thinkers, sayings such as "A bird in the hand is worth two in the bush" or "It's raining cats and dogs" often cause confusion. Children with autism might actually look for the bird in the hand or for the cats and dogs falling from the sky. Once when Liam's teacher was explaining a complex math concept to the children, she looked out and saw blank faces. She said, "Let's back up a minute," and Liam immediately scooted his chair back from his desk.

At a birthday party, Sammy was taking pictures with a digital camera. His teacher wanted to take photos of the people sitting at the table and asked Sammy for the camera. However, what she said was, "You can take more pictures as soon as I take pictures of the table." Sammy said, "I'll do it" as he bent down to take a close-up shot of the actual table rather than the people sitting around it.

Although Ian was quite a loner in high school, he seemed to be coping in all of his classes. He was somewhat clumsy in gym classes, but consistently participated as much as he could. Rather suddenly, he announced that he would no longer be attending gym class. When asked why, he explained that the coach didn't like him any more. Exploration into the situation determined that the coach had been giving Ian a congratulatory fist bump at the end of each class. Ian misinterpreted this positive interaction and gesture, thinking the coach was hitting him.

When Benjamin's class was discussing the topic "What's cool about school?" Benjamin answered, "Air conditioning." He then drew a detailed, to-scale picture of the 26 air conditioning units positioned on top of the school building to illustrate what was cool about school.

Isaac had been discussing idioms with his speech-language pathologist. Later that day, at home, he put a huge bunch of grapes in his mouth and proudly said, "I think I've bitten off more than I can chew."

Characteristic 10: Individuals With ASD Could Have Executive Functioning Challenges Such as an Impaired Ability to Initiate Tasks, Difficulty Stopping One Task and Starting Another, and an Inability to Organize Complex Tasks Independently

Executive functions include a set of mental processes or cognitive abilities that regulate behavior. They are necessary for goal-directed behavior and include the abilities to initiate and stop actions, to monitor and change behavior as needed, and to plan future behavior when faced with novel tasks and situations. Executive functioning is involved in performing activities such as planning, organizing, and paying attention to and remembering details. Executive functions allow us to anticipate outcomes and adapt to changing situations. In addition, thinking abstractly and forming concepts are executive functioning abilities.

Seth's high school teacher gave his class directions for a writing assignment and directed the class to get started. Seth sat still for a few minutes, manipulated his paper and pencil for a while and, as a result, started about 5 minutes later than the rest of his classmates. Within a few minutes of his beginning, the teacher interrupted the class to give an additional direction. Seth did not stop to attend to the teacher's direction, even when she called his name. His teacher called his name again and walked over closely and said, "I need to tell you something important about your work." Seth said, "I need to finish this before I can listen."

A gifted cellist, Benjamin played his parts flawlessly as a part of his middle school orchestra. However, in rehearsals, he was frequently frustrated with the orchestra director who would start and stop the group to practice certain sections. Often, Benjamin would finish a passage, playing long after his peers stopped playing.

Joey's class was practicing for the spring group achievement tests and he sat quietly while everyone else started to work. His behavior consultant slipped quietly to his side and directed him to begin the test. He looked up and continued to stare into space. His behavior consultant took a scrap of paper and wrote the word "read" and the numbers 1–10, drawing a box by the word and by each number. After quietly explaining to Joey that he needed to read and answer the questions, mark the answer in his practice book, and then check off the number on the paper, Joey went to work. He completed his questions with 80% accuracy.

A Mixture of Characteristics

Children with ASD have a mixture of the above characteristics and each child will be unique. It is important to keep the characteristics of each individual child in mind when developing an effective educational program. The challenge for educators often is how to create successful programs when presented with such a range of characteristics. Our next chapter will outline the components of an effective program for children with ASD.

2

WHAT MAKES A SUCCESSFUL EDUCATION PROGRAM FOR CHILDREN WITH A DIAGNOSIS OF ASD?

WHAT DOES THE LAW REQUIRE?

Since 1975, when Congress enacted the Education for All Handicapped Children Act (EHA), public schools that receive federal funds have been required to provide a free appropriate public education (FAPE) to children with disabilities, including autism. At first, the law required schools to serve children from ages 3 to 21, but in 1986, the law was amended to add children from birth to age 3.

The 1990 Amendments to EHA changed the name to the Individuals with Disabilities Education Act (IDEA) and added autism as a separate category of disability. Prior to 1990, children diagnosed with autism often were served under the law in eligibility categories such as language impaired or developmentally delayed. The most recent amendments to IDEA (2004) changed the name to the Individuals with Disabilities Education Improvement Act, and still required FAPE for every child, no matter the extent of the disability. One of the major modifications of IDEA (2004) was to require teaching methods based on scientific research to the highest extent possible.

The act includes six major principles (Turnbull & Turnbull, 2000):

1. *Zero reject:* The right of every child, no matter how severe the disability, to receive FAPE.
2. *Nondiscriminatory classification:* The right of every child to receive a complete and fair evaluation so correct placements and programs can be developed.
3. *Appropriate education:* The right of every child to a meaningful education designed to meet his or her unique needs.
4. *Least restrictive environment:* The right of every child to be educated with nondisabled children to the maximum extent appropriate.
5. *Parent participation:* The right of every child to have the family involved in making educational decisions.
6. *Due process:* The right of every child to challenge any aspect of his or her education program.

The original EHA has been amended numerous times and has resulted in several significant changes over the years. However, these six principles have remained intact throughout all of the versions of the legislation (Turnbull, Huerta, & Stowe, 2006). For each new version of the law, the U.S. Department of Education has developed regulations to provide direction to schools in implementing the spirit and letter of the law. Each state also has a version of the law that must require adherence to all aspects of the federal law, but can implement them in varied ways. State departments of education develop state regulations to provide guidance and direction to local education agencies in implementing the law. Once the state regulations have been developed, each board of education develops policies, procedures, and guidelines for their schools and teachers.

In addition, many issues have been decided in court to clarify the requirements. One of the most complex issues is determining what constitutes an appropriate education. It generally is agreed that under IDEA, schools are required to give children the chance to make educational progress, but that the law does not require them to educate children to their absolute highest level or maximize their potential. The 2004 addition of the requirement for schools to implement scientifically proven instruction to the extent practical is generating increased interest in determining not only which methodologies are effective but even how to determine whether a methodology has sufficient evidence to justify its use.

WHAT DO RESEARCHERS SAY?

Providing an effective program for children with autism requires knowledge of the most current information on research and practice. There is a tremendous amount of information on the education and treatment of children with autism. A Google search in March 2009 for the term *autism* produced 18,100,000 hits. "Education and autism" produced 574,000 sites, "best practices and autism" resulted in 560,000 hits, and "evidence-based practices and autism" yielded 348,000 results. There were 902,000 entries for autism news articles and 1,360,000 for autism journals.

This continuously increasing, constantly changing information puts teachers and parents in the difficult position of making judgments about educational methodologies and strategies. It is easy to say that choosing effective, evidence-based treatments is the best way teachers and parents can help children with autism achieve their highest potential. But, sifting through the available information, identifying and analyzing research studies, and determining their relevance to teaching can be a challenging task even for experienced professionals.

Complicating the situation further, increased demands on schools to document progress and additional pressures resulting from the reported recovery of individuals with autism have added to the challenge of choosing effective programs for children with autism. The pressure is particularly strong as parents and advocates are reading about autism recovery and cure on the Internet.

In the past several decades, there has been a tremendous increase in the number of interventions claimed to be effective in spite of a lack of objective evidence. These often are highly subjective, biased reports offering easy, quick, or effective treatments and claiming to be supported by research. Parents often are frustrated that no cause or cure for autism has been found and can be drawn to claims of quick, easy treatments. Teachers must help parents consider risks and benefits and to help them focus on evidence-based practices rather than taking a chance on trying something new and unproven.

Educators are accountable for progress and success and thus, it is vital to study and implement educational practices that are based on good research. Teachers and parents of children with ASD must resist the enticements of treatments that have no evidence to support them. When searching for effective treatments for their children, they must find and use sound data.

Realizing that some treatments have empirical evidence showing their effectiveness and that others do not is a good first step. But then it is important to learn how to interpret the research and make judgments related to the degree of effectiveness of particular interventions. Educational practices that are likely to be effective are those found to be successful in research studies that have been replicated and reviewed by professional peers in the field. In addition, the best research analyzes the effect of a methodology on groups of children rather than just on individuals. Good research also compares the effect of different interventions on matched groups or compares the effect of an intervention on an experimental group to a control group.

Considering the tremendous amount of information available and the massive task of reviewing the literature and analyzing the research, it makes sense for teachers and parents to monitor reviews and practice guidelines. In this section, we will present five reviews related to best practices, evidence-based practices, and scientific research. They are presented in chronological order.

Dawson and Osterling (1997)

Dawson and Osterling (1997) described eight examples of early intervention programs for children with autism, reviewing the programs to assess their effectiveness and determine whether the effectiveness of the intervention was related to the philosophy of the intervention or to characteristics of the child, such as IQ or verbal ability. They started their review with the assumption that, based on outcome research, children make substantial gains in their early intervention programs. Many of these children are able to be included in a general education classroom when they enter elementary school.

Dawson and Osterling (1997) stated that seasoned clinicians and researchers, in spite of their philosophical differences, are shaped by the common experience of working with these children and come to share basic beliefs and methods. After reviewing these eight programs, they listed the essential features of an early intervention program for children with autism. They described a successful program in autism as one that requires highly individualized assessment of a child's emerging skills, strengths, interests, and needs. They found that, despite considerable differences in the philosophical approaches and implementation of the various methodologies, certain key elements are common across programs, including:

- The curriculum content typically emphasizes five basic skill areas:
  - attending to elements of the environment,
  - imitating others,
  - comprehending and using language,
  - playing appropriately with toys, and
  - interacting socially with others.

- There are needs for:
    - supportive teaching environments and generalization strategies,
    - predictability and routine,
    - functional approach to problem behaviors,
    - transition to new settings and new personnel, and
    - family involvement.

U.S. Surgeon General's Report on Autism (1999)

The U.S. Surgeon General's report on autism (1999) stated that 30 years of research has demonstrated the efficacy of Applied Behavioral Analysis (ABA) in reducing inappropriate behavior and in increasing communication, learning, and appropriate social behavior in children with autism. The Surgeon General mentioned the highly significant research study that was carried out by Dr. Ivar Lovaas of UCLA (Lovaas, 1987; McEachin, Smith, & Lovaas, 1993). In this landmark study, 19 children with autism were treated for 2 years with intensive therapy (an average of 40 hours a week) based on ABA. The progress of the children was compared with two control groups. Children in the experimental group made highly significant gains including increases in intelligence quotients (IQ). By first grade, 9 of the 19 children (47%) were found to be indistinguishable from typical peers on measures of IQ and adaptive behavior. Follow-up studies of the experimental group were done in first grade, in late childhood, and in adolescence. These found that nearly half of the experimental group, but almost none of the children in the matched control group, were able to participate in regular school classes. Attempts to replicate these results are in progress and several have shown significant improvements in children with autism who participate in intensive ABA therapy (Cohen, Amerine-Dickens, & Smith, 2006; Sallows & Graupner, 2005).

The Surgeon General (1999) also mentioned several uncontrolled studies of comprehensive center-based programs that have been conducted, focusing on language development and other developmental skills. For example, a comprehensive model, Treatment and Education of Autistic and related Communication Handicapped Children (TEACCH), demonstrated short-term gains for preschoolers with autism who received daily TEACCH home-teaching sessions, compared with a matched control group (Ozonoff & Cathcart, 1998). The Surgeon General concluded that of the many methods available for treatment and education of people with autism, ABA has become widely accepted as an effective treatment.

The New York State Department of Health–Clinical Practice Guidelines: Report of the Recommendations (1999)

The New York State Department of Health (NYSDOH, 1999) recruited a panel of experts to develop clinical practice guidelines for working with young children with autism. The panel reviewed 32 articles that reported using behavioral and educational approaches in children with autism and 68 articles from a comprehensive review on single-subject design studies. The report used a rating system to judge claims as being supported by strong evidence, moderate evidence, or limited evidence. In some cases, the panel came to a consensus of opinion on important issues that do not have clear, objective research.

In the foreword of the report, Michael Guralnick described the document as an extraordinarily thoughtful and balanced presentation of critical issues in assessment and intervention. He stated that it is the result of a methodologically sound approach to accurately gather and summarize information based on the available evidence.

Among the claims that were found to be supported by strong research were that:

- principles of ABA and behavior intervention strategies should be included as an important element of any program for young children with autism;
- parents should be included as active participants in the intervention team to the extent of their interests, resources, and abilities;
- parent training in behavioral methods should be extensive and ongoing and include regular consultation with a qualified professional;
- target behaviors for each individual child should be clearly identified and defined with developmentally appropriate measurable criteria for mastery; and
- appropriate supervision of paraprofessionals and coordination of efforts should be provided to accomplish intervention goals.

Similar to the findings of Dawson and Osterling (1997), and in part due to them, the NYSDOH (1999) found strong evidence to support:

- using a curriculum specifically designed for autism with emphasis on attending to environment, imitation, social and play skills, language, and communication;
- individualizing instruction for a child's strengths and needs;
- providing a highly structured and supportive environment;
- providing a high degree of routine and predictability;

- involving families in intervention planning; and
- using a functional approach (understanding function of behavior), implementing positive behavior supports, changing antecedents, and teaching replacement skills.

Taking this a step further, it is recommended that parents and professionals consider the following factors when selecting a comprehensive intervention program:
- content and emphasis of the program's curriculum,
- strategies for using a functional approach for problem behaviors,
- strategies for providing a highly structured and supportive teaching environment with a high degree of predictability and routine,
- strategies for taking skills learned in more structured settings and generalizing them to more complex natural environments,
- strategies for transitions from one activity to another during the day,
- long-term strategies for transition between intervention settings, and
- opportunities for family involvement.

With regard to using principles of ABA for interventions, the NYSDOH found strong evidence to support:
- including principles of ABA and behavior intervention strategies as an important element of any intervention program for young children with autism;
- including a minimum of approximately 20 hours per week of individualized behavioral intervention using ABA techniques (not including time spent by parents); and
- considering factors such as the child's age and health considerations, severity of autistic symptoms, rate of progress, tolerance of the child, and family participation in determining the number of hours of behavioral intervention.

The NYSDOH (1999) review pointed out that the precise number of recommended hours for behavioral intervention varies depending on a variety of child and family characteristics. It further explained that in deciding upon the frequency and intensity of a behavioral intervention, it is important to recognize that effective interventions based on ABA techniques used between 18 and 40 hours per week in the studies reviewed and that based on the then-current scientific evidence, it is not possible to accurately predict the optimal number of hours that will be effective for any given child. Finally, the report stated that it is recommended that the number of hours of intensive behavioral intervention be periodically reviewed and revised. Monitoring the child's progress may lead to a conclusion that hours need to be increased or decreased.

The NYSDOH (1999) report also included interventions that are without scientific evidence and support. In some cases, the reports found only limited evidence and in other cases, found no evidence at all. The report explains that without evidence from controlled studies demonstrating effectiveness, interventions cannot be recommended for young children with autism. In some cases, the panel found evidence against particular treatments. For example, the NYSDOH cautioned readers about the dangers of treatment such as auditory integration therapy and facilitated communication.

The National Research Council (2001)

The National Research Council (NRC, 2001) found that effective models follow several common universal best practices. This report is especially useful because eclectic models can vary widely, as they are tailored for individual children and it is difficult to isolate variables for empirical research. The NRC developed a section summarizing the research on 10 comprehensive early intervention programs for children with autism. After reviewing the 10 programs, the NRC recommended that effective programs for children with ASD:

- begin as early as possible;
- are intensive in nature (25 hours per week, 12 months per year);
- involve families actively in the intervention;
- provide staff who are highly trained and specialized in autism;
- provide ongoing objective assessment of a child's progress;
- have curricula that provide systematic, planned teaching;
- provide highly supportive physical, temporal, and staffing environments;
- use a curriculum focusing on communication, engagement, social skills, play, cognitive skills, self-help, behavior, and motor goals;
- use carefully planned, research-based teaching procedures that include plans for generalization and maintenance of skills;
- use individualized intervention plans to adjust for the wide range of children's strengths and needs;
- plan and support transitions from preschool to school. (pp. 151–165)

Perry and Condillac (2003)

Perry and Condillac's (2003) study is a summary of assessment and intervention approaches for children and adolescents with ASDs sponsored by

Children's Mental Health Ontario. To develop the guide, the authors, working with an advisory committee and expert panel, reviewed empirical research and literature reviews and summarized best practices in assessment and intervention.

The purpose of this guide was to provide a summary of empirically based assessment and intervention approaches for children and adolescents with ASDs and best practices for supporting families. Perry and Condillac (2003) stated that evidence-based treatment guidelines are especially important in the field of serving children with diagnoses of ASD. They pointed out that many widely promoted new approaches have no empirical support, and that it is extremely difficult for parents and practitioners to critically evaluate the tremendous amount of information available today. They warned that new treatments, although they may be promising and worthy of investigation, also may be unhelpful or even harmful.

This guide described and evaluated interventions as to whether they were evidence-based, meaning that there is convincing evidence of their effectiveness, or empirically disconfirmed, meaning that there is convincing evidence they are not effective or harmful. The guide also included a third category for those interventions that cannot be recommended because there is insufficient evidence either way.

The social and play-related interventions listed in the Perry and Condillac (2003) guide as somewhat effective were social stories, Peer-Mediated Instruction, Social Script Training, and Theory of Mind Training. The Language and Communication-Based Interventions that were demonstrated as effective for individuals with an ASD included Augmentative Communication, Picture Exchange Communication System (PECS), and the Verbal Behavior Approach.

The comprehensive program that has strong evidence of effectiveness, although individualized evaluation is a necessary component to ensure the best match of the curriculum to the child's needs, is Intensive Behavioral Intervention (IBI). This is the use of ABA in an approach similar to the Lovaas program in intensity of services and concentration on behavioral principles.

The following interventions were included in a list of those having inadequate scientific evidence. The guide recommended that they only be used in conjunction with proven therapies, with careful evaluation, and if they do not interfere with proven therapies. The interventions included:

- sensory integration therapy,
- sensory diet (sensory summation approach),
- deep pressure,
- "squeeze machine" or "hug machine,"

- touch therapy/massage,
- patterning,
- physical exercise,
- Auditory Integration Training (AIT),
- Irlen lenses, and
- oculomotor exercises.

The Perry and Condillac (2003) guide provided more than 100 recommendations related to interventions for challenging behavior. The following four points are especially critical when intervening and developing plans for children with challenging behaviors.

- A large body of evidence provides empirical support for the use of positive behavioral supports as the first course of treatment for problem behavior.
- If necessary, medication should be used as an adjunct to behavioral treatment or to treat specific behavioral/psychiatric disorders (e.g., OCD, ADHD).
- Direct-care staff should be trained in crisis intervention procedures approved by their settings and consistent with facility guidelines.
- Intrusive behavior reduction procedures should be considered only as a last resort, and should be used under careful supervision, with proper documentation.

The Perry and Condillac (2003) guide included a section on family support and on recommending, designing, and/or implementing intervention plans. It recommended carefully considering the level of scientific evidence and putting evaluation procedures into place to monitor the effectiveness of the intervention and any potential side effects. It also recommended informing parents and individuals with diagnoses of an ASD of the degree to which procedures are proven or experimental and ensuring they understand the importance of objective evaluation of the intervention as it is implemented for the particular individual.

Summary of the Summaries

It is clear from these reviews that a successful program in autism requires research-supported practices that include individualized assessment of a child's skills and strengths, interests, and needs. It also is evident that effective interventions are characterized by intense treatment, low adult-child ratios, and highly structured and individualized intervention programs.

There is general agreement that children with autism need an ABA approach to become more responsive to their environments and the people they encounter. However, variations of ABA programs handle interactions with children differently. Some programs intrude directly into the child's world, while others enter gently, following the child's interests.

The goal of education for children with ASD is to improve and increase the child's social and language skills as well as to reduce or minimize behaviors that interfere with the child's functioning and learning. This requires an approach that incorporates strategies and techniques that are individualized and customized to meet the needs of each individual child.

In the remainder of the book, we'll describe methodologies and strategies that are recognized in the research as ones that are proven to succeed with young children who have ASD. We'll start with an explanation of applied behavior analysis and then discuss its principles along with examples related to teaching children with ASD.

3

WHAT IS ABA?

Applied behavior analysis (ABA) is a science that allows us to analyze behavior, explain why it might be happening, and predict its patterns in the future. In addition, ABA provides us with a set of principles or teaching tools to change behavior.

More formally, ABA is defined as the process of systematically applying interventions based upon the principles of learning theory to improve socially significant behaviors to a meaningful degree, and to demonstrate that the interventions employed are responsible for the improvement in behavior (Baer, Wolf, & Risley, 1968; Sulzer-Azaroff & Mayer, 1991). Applied behavior analysis is different from behaviorism, experimental analysis of behavior, and professional practice of behavior analysis as it focuses on changing human behavior in socially significant ways.

ABA helps us bring about positive change and improve lives whether it is by teaching new skills or reducing interfering behaviors. To use ABA, behaviors need to be defined in observable and measurable terms. This helps us assess changes in behavior over time.

The major tenets of ABA guide teachers in developing ABA-based education programs. To start, we define behavior as any act that is observable (e.g., any act that can be seen, heard, or felt) and quantifiable (e.g., any act that can be counted or measured).

In ABA training sessions, we often ask parents and teachers to list three behaviors. Sometimes, participants will list defiance, noncompliance, or disobedience. That gives us the chance to explain that in using ABA, it is important to describe behaviors using verbs rather than nouns. Descriptions of the behaviors need to be precise enough so that other people can understand the behavior exactly. So, instead of trying to describe behavior with words like defiance, noncompliance, or disobedience, we start with verbs like stomping, screaming, or refusing to follow directions. These verbs paint a clearer picture of the behavior.

Many participants do use verbs and then list such behaviors as hitting, kicking, and pinching. We then point out that it is difficult to get a true understanding of the behavior without knowing its context. In these cases, participants generally are talking about behaviors that are quite undesirable. But, actually, each of those behaviors can be quite useful in other contexts. For example, hitting a drum, kicking a ball, and pinching a button can be very desirable behaviors. In using ABA, it is important to view behaviors in their context and not in isolation. To help us understand why behaviors are happening, it also is important to analyze behavior in relation to the environment to determine what factors are influencing the behavior.

Children with diagnoses of ASD often have excesses of undesirable behavior. For example, they might talk too much, scream too often, or run too frequently. Each of these behaviors can be appropriate in certain settings. Talking a lot is a good skill for preachers, screaming is expected at sporting events, and running is an excellent form of exercise. But, in other contexts, or at high rates or lengthy durations, these behaviors can interfere with social acceptance. Using ABA, we can measure dimensions such as the frequency, rate, and duration of behaviors; analyze the environments in which they occur; and suggest the reasons they occur. With this information, the principles of ABA can help us reduce the occurrences of interfering behaviors.

The analysis of behavior does not include just interfering behaviors. Skills we want children to learn are behaviors as well. These behaviors might be saying hello, shaking hands, reading a word, solving a math problem, buttoning a coat, or cooking a meal. Children with diagnoses of ASD have deficits, particularly in language and social skills, and ABA gives us the tools to increase (or teach) these behaviors.

Once behaviors are defined, we need to understand that:

All behavior (B) is affected by:
its antecedents (A)—what happens before the behavior
and
its consequences (C)—what happens after the behavior.

Practitioners of ABA say that all behavior, both typical and atypical, is learned and that learning will take place as a result of the consequences of behavior (Alberto & Troutman, 2009). With regard to consequences, behavior that is followed by pleasant consequences generally is repeated and thus learned (Alberto & Troutman, 2009). For example, shortly after babies are born, they emit cries, often resulting in their mothers coming to feed them. It is not long before babies repeat the crying behavior, learning that it results in food. This ABA principle, of course, is called positive reinforcement.

Behavior that is followed by unpleasant consequences usually is not repeated and thus not learned (Alberto & Troutman, 2009). Soon these babies are up and about exploring their worlds. Sometimes they will touch something that hurts and they quickly learn not to repeat that behavior. This ABA principle is called punishment.

In the previous examples, behaviors become associated with the consequences and people learn that their behavior produces such consequences. Behavior also becomes associated with its antecedents. In other words, behavior that occurs close to or at the same time as its antecedent will become associated with that antecedent.

Young children learn language when a word is associated with something that happens at that time. For example, they learn to sit after a few times of hearing the words "sit down" when they are helped to sit in a chair. This ABA principle is called pairing. Antecedents also can become signals that consequences may be available. When toys or food are provided when children are in the chair, they learn that sitting is a signal that toys or food may be obtainable.

With ABA, we can manipulate the antecedents and consequences and thus change behavior. For example, once children reach preschool age, we might arrange the environment so that certain preferred toys only are available when children are sitting at the table. Later, those preferred toys might be provided only after children say, "May I have the toys, please?"

In teaching with ABA, we can accomplish five important goals. We can *teach new skills* with systematic reinforcement. For example, we can teach children to look at a person who is talking, to use words to request food or toys, to comment on things in the environment, and to start and end conversations. We also can *strengthen, improve, or increase behaviors* that already are in the child's repertoire. For example, we can teach children behaviors such as staying on task longer, using longer sentences in speaking or writing, or continuing a conversation. ABA helps us *maintain productive behaviors* that children have. For example, once a child has learned a skill such as raising a hand before speaking in class, we can teach the child to continue doing it even if the teacher doesn't respond every time. We can use ABA to help children *generalize skills* or transfer them to other situations. For example, if the child learns to follow directions at school, ABA can help us teach the child to follow directions at home. And, ABA helps us *reduce interfering behaviors* such as repetitive, self-stimulating behavior, socially disruptive behavior such as blurting out in class, or socially inappropriate behavior such as ignoring a conversation partner. Chapter 4 will address the ways we can accomplish these important goals.

WHAT ARE THE PRINCIPLES OF ABA?

The principles of ABA are the rules or laws we can use to explain, predict, and change behavior (Alberto & Troutman, 2009). They can be viewed as tools we can use to increase, decrease, or maintain behaviors. In the next few sections, we explain tools such as positive and negative reinforcement that will help us teach new skills or increase targeted behaviors. We'll include teaching strategies such as pairing, modeling, shaping, and prompting and fading that will assist us in maintaining behaviors and transferring them to new environments. Then, we'll end with principles such as extinction, punishment, and differential reinforcement that will help us reduce or eliminate interfering or undesirable behavior.

WHAT PRINCIPLES HELP TEACH NEW SKILLS AND INCREASE DESIRABLE BEHAVIOR?

Positive Reinforcement

The term *positive reinforcement* also can describe the consequence itself that is provided to maintain or increase the chance that the behavior will be repeated in the future. When a behavior is reinforced, the child is likely to repeat it so that the good things that happened will happen again.

Positive reinforcement can be provided continuously—immediately after every targeted behavior occurs. Or, it can be provided intermittently—only after some of the times the behavior occurs.

> **Definition of the Principle:** Positive reinforcement is the principle that describes the probable increase in the future occurrence or frequency of a behavior due to the consequence that immediately followed the response.
>
> **Tool:** To increase the chance a behavior will happen again, arrange for an immediate reward to follow the behavior.

TOOLS FOR POSITIVE REINFORCEMENT

Tool: *Continuous Reinforcement:* To establish a new behavior, reward the behavior every single time it occurs.

Tool: *Intermittent Reinforcement:* To encourage a learner to continue performing an established behavior with few or no rewards, gradually decrease the frequency with which the correct behavior is rewarded.

Tool: *Pairing:* To reinforce a learner with a previously ineffective reward, present it just before the time you present the more effective reward.

The consequences that act as positive reinforcers can be primary or natural, that is, they initially and immediately increase the chance the behavior will occur again. Examples of primary reinforcers may include food, sensory activities, or for some children, attention. Consequences that act as positive reinforcers also can be secondary or artificial. Secondary reinforcers are those that initially have no effect on the behavior. For example, very young children have no understanding that a sticker or happy face is a good thing. They come to react to stickers and happy faces only after they become associated with primary reinforcers such as attention, food, or toys.

The only consequences that are considered positive reinforcers are ones that cause behavior to be repeated or strengthened. It is not correct to say that candy, toys, attention, and sensory activities are always positive reinforcers. They may act as reinforcers for the behavior of some children and not for others. For example, some children don't like certain foods. If a child's action is followed by a disliked food, the action is not likely to be repeated, and thus, the food, no matter how good it sounds to others, did not act as a reinforcer. And, while the disliked food itself may not act as a reinforcer for one child, it might be a favorite food and a positive reinforcer for another child.

Although it is always important to know the preferences of children, it especially is critical to individualize the reinforcers used with children who have diagnoses of ASD. They often have unique patterns of likes and dislikes and these can be quite strong. Even when effective reinforcers are identified, reinforcer assessments should be ongoing, as most children will become satiated when presented the same item over and over. To keep consequences powerful in changing behavior, continuous evaluation of the effect of the consequence is necessary.

Some examples of items that could be reinforcers include:

- food (special treats, not meals);
- desired objects such as toys, games, or computers;
- preferred activities with items such as puzzles, clay, music, and swings;
- verbal praise and nonverbal gestures such as high fives, shoulder pats, and OK or thumbs-up signs; and
- privileges such as special jobs or opportunities to run errands.

Reinforcement Assessments

It is critical to know what serves as reinforcement for each particular child. Consequences are not reinforcers unless they increase the probability that the child will repeat the behavior.

Reinforcement menus are helpful tools for finding a variety of interests for the child. In some cases, these may involve checklists of things to let children explore so observations can be made about what the children like. In other cases, the reinforcement assessment may include an opportunity for children to complete a survey or answer questions from an interview guideline regarding their preferences.

Reinforcement Schedules

Once we have an idea about potential reinforcers, we begin to evaluate when that reinforcer should be given or presented. The pattern of timing for delivery of the reinforcers is known as schedules of reinforcement (Alberto & Troutman, 2009).

Continuous reinforcement provides reinforcement after every correct response and strengthens the bond between the instruction and the response. This schedule often is used when teaching new tasks.

Intermittent reinforcement provides reinforcement for some, but not all, correct responses. This can prevent a child from becoming satiated with the reinforcer, lessening its effect. Moving from continuous reinforcement to intermittent can keep motivation at a high level as the child is not sure when the reward will be delivered.

The process of decreasing the rate of reinforcement is called thinning the schedule. Thinning should happen gradually and systematically. One purpose of thinning the schedule is to allow for higher rates of responding. However, care should be taken not to thin too quickly. This may result in a lower rate of responding.

Differential Reinforcement

Some people use the term *differential reinforcement* to describe the process of providing a level of reinforcement that will most likely increase that behavior. It is differential because the level of reinforcement varies depending on the child's response. The term differential reinforcement also can be used to describe procedures that decrease behaviors. In these cases, reinforcement is provided for an alternative behavior, for the absence of a behavior, or for low rates of behavior.

It takes great skill to use reinforcement effectively. A major goal in using reinforcement is for the child eventually to respond appropriately under the most natural schedules of reinforcement (intermittent) with the most natural types of reinforcers (social).

Shaping

Shaping can be used to develop behaviors that don't already exist in the child's repertoire of skills. It also can be used to increase the frequency of behaviors that occur less often than desired.

One way to use shaping is to reinforce behaviors that resemble or approximate the desired behavior. For example, if a child says "ba," we can reinforce the approximation of the word "ball" and provide ball-playing time. As this behavior becomes more consistent, we can model the entire word and hold the reinforcement

> **Definition of the Principle:** Shaping is the process of using repeated reinforcement for successive approximations (small steps) toward a target behavior.
>
> **Tool:** To teach a new behavior, reward a series of steps toward the final behavior.

Tips for Using Positive Reinforcement

1. Tell or show the child what to do in order to receive the reinforcement. A cue card with "first _____, then _____," is helpful to show a child what to do and to help the child make a connection between the behavior and its consequence. Children with autism often need the visual support of a picture or object along with instructions.

2. Provide the positive reinforcement immediately after the appropriate response or behavior occurs to help the child see the relationship between the response and the positive feedback.

3. Deliver reinforcement continuously (reinforcement after every occurrence of a behavior) in the early stages of learning. Later, thin the schedule by providing reinforcement only after some occurrences of the behavior. If behaviors weaken or decrease in frequency, provide a more frequent schedule of reinforcement for a while before attempting to thin the schedule again.

4. Describe the acceptable behavior such as, "Yes, that's red," or "Thanks for participating in class," rather than repeating, "Good job" multiple times. This gives the child informational feedback linking the behavior to the positive reinforcement.

5. Deliver social praise paired with edibles or tangible objects. Giving the social praise first, with rewards close behind, allows the child to focus on the praise prior to delivery and to link it with the more tangible reward. Reward small steps to shape simple behaviors into more complex skills, especially in the beginning. Gradually increase the length, complexity, or difficulty of the expected response by providing repeated reinforcements of a series of approximations (successive approximations) of the target behavior.

6. Provide a high rate and quick pace of reinforcement. When the appropriate behavior is exhibited, notice it right away and reward it!

7. Model the positive behavior to be imitated and reinforce peers when they engage in the appropriate behavior.

8. Over time, attempt to move toward more social praise and fewer tangible reinforcers.

until there is an approximation of the /l/ sound. This approximation might even be an attempt to raise the tongue at the end of the word, even if the /l/ sound isn't clear.

Shaping also can involve gradually modifying the existing behavior of a child into the desired behavior. For example, consider a young boy who hits his pet dog. His parents can shape his behavior by blocking the hit and guiding his hand to turn the hit into a stroking motion every time he interacts with the dog. This should be paired with attention and praise such as, "It's great when you pet gently!"

Some examples of using the principle of shaping are:

* When a baby begins to say "mama," his parents respond with attention and excitement, encouraging the continuation of utterances and shaping the desired response of "mommy."

- To teach a child to write the number "1," the teacher begins to reinforce marks on paper, then scribbles, then slightly curving lines, gradually shaping the behavior into straighter lines.
- When teaching a child to look at an object, the teacher says, "Look!" and reinforces the child to turn in the direction of the item by giving it to the child for a brief period.
- To teach a child to play on the playground, the teacher first provides praise and attention when the child stands close to the equipment, then when the child touches the equipment, next when the child stands on it, and finally when the child plays on it.
- When teaching a child to sit still in a chair for music class, the teacher reinforces the child's sitting behavior by providing happy faces for each 30-second period of sitting. At the end of 2 minutes, the four happy faces are exchanged for time to play with toys. Gradually, the teacher requires longer periods of sitting for each happy face and more happy faces for toy time.

TIPS FOR SHAPING

- Complete a task analysis by breaking down the skill into small steps.
- Focus instruction on one specific step, prompting and continuously attempting to fade the prompts.
- Establish consistent, fluent responding at one stage before moving onto the next step.
- Collect data on each step in the shaping process to help determine if the move to the next task is appropriate.
- Move back to the previous level in the task analysis if the behavior begins to break down.
- Keep the ultimate goal or objective in mind while moving through the steps in the process. When there are multiple steps in the process, it's often easy to lose track of the desired final outcome.
- If progress is extremely slow, determine whether or not the final objective is realistic for the child or if the child has the necessary prerequisite skills to perform the task.

Modeling

Modeling is the term that describes the process of teaching through demonstrations. Just a few minutes of watching children play confirms that people learn by watching the behavior of others around them. Any person's behavior, good or bad, can serve as a model. Imitation is the response of matching the behavior of a model. Imitation is basic to most learning because much of what we learn comes from watching others.

Models can be actual or symbolic demonstrations (Bandura, 1977). Actual modeling may involve providing a demonstration of a task such as putting on a coat in front of the child. Symbolic models are presented in media such as pictures in books and actors on movies or television.

Teaching children with diagnoses of ASD to imitate is extremely important to their development. Whereas typically developing children learn easily to imitate for social reinforcement, some children with ASD need powerful positive reinforcement to learn the benefits of imitation. Imitation is an important skill for learning how to learn. Once children learn to imitate, opportunities for learning expand exponentially. It is important, of course, for them to learn which behaviors they should imitate and which they shouldn't imitate.

> **Definition of the Principle:** Modeling is the process of providing an antecedent stimulus that is identical (or at least similar) to the behavior the teacher wants imitated. The term *model* often is applied to both the individual demonstrating the behavior and the behavior that is demonstrated. Models can be considered a prompt or can be considered the stimulus itself.
>
> **Tool:** To teach a new behavior, present demonstrations of the desired behavior and reinforce the behavior when it occurs.

TIPS FOR USING MODELING

- Complete a task analysis by breaking down the skill into small steps.
- Identify one specific step and instruct the child to watch and do. In the early stages, give a quick "Do this!" along with the model. Later, say things like "Do what I do" or "Watch me and then you do it."
- Provide reinforcement for the child's attempts to imitate.
- Use shaping to develop the child's accuracy and fluency.
- Collect data on each step to help determine when to move to the next step in the task analysis.
- Move back to the previous level in the task analysis if the behavior begins to break down.
- Keep the ultimate goal or objective in mind while moving through the steps of the task analysis. It's often beneficial for children to see a demonstration of the whole task. Then, practicing a particular step may have more meaning.

Videotaped Self-Modeling

Peter Dowrick (1999) described videotaped self-modeling (VSM) as repeated observations of oneself on videotapes that are edited to show only desired target behaviors. To use VSM, a child is videotaped engaging in behaviors to be learned. This might involve editing out undesired behaviors and creating ways to get the child to perform on tape. For example, Miguel was a child whose mother had been frustrated when taking Miguel on shopping trips. Miguel would run ahead of her, dash to the toy section, grab various toys, and scream when asked to put them back. Miguel was taken to the store and the trip was videotaped. Miguel only walked with his mother for a few seconds, but when the final videotape was made, his running ahead to the store was removed. Once in the store, he was taped looking at toys. To get some tape of him putting toys back on the shelf, he was handed toys that he didn't like. As the tape was rolling, he put them back on the shelves while his mother said things like, "Let's put that back—it's too expensive." Although Miguel screamed and cried in the checkout line, the audio was erased and replaced with a narration of Miguel giving the item to the cashier, paying for the item, and getting the item back in a bag. The final movie, "Shopping With Miguel," showed him walking into the store, looking at toys, putting items back on the shelves, selecting one item, paying for it, leaving the store, and giving a high-five to his teacher.

Watching a short 3- to 5-minute movie such as this has great potential for helping a child see how positive his behavior could be, especially when the video includes reinforcers like captions with the child's name and sounds of applause. VSM sometimes involves feedforward, in which children view themselves doing something they've never done before. More information on VSM and feedforward can be found at http://www.creating-futures.org.

Prompting

A prompt can be used to teach a new skill or to build positive behavior momentum during periods of stress or anxiety. In the early stages of teaching, many teachers use "errorless learning" by providing enough prompts to prevent the child from making a mistake. This allows the child an opportunity to perform the skill from start to finish with assistance and success. Prompts gradually are faded until the child can perform the task independently.

> **Definition of the Principle:** A prompt is an added stimulus used to help the child achieve a desired response (Alberto & Troutman, 2009).
>
> **Tool:** To help elicit a correct response, help the learner by providing a verbal or physical hint.

Wolery and Gast (1984) listed the seven types of prompts below. For each prompt, a description and examples are provided.

- A *physical prompt* involves guiding the child to perform the behavior. It is the most intrusive type of prompt as it involves actually touching the child. Physical prompts could include hand-over-hand assistance to write, cut with scissors, or put pieces in a puzzle. Physical prompting could involve placing a hand on the child's back to encourage him to walk down the hall or lifting a child's foot to assist in putting on a shoe.

- A *visual prompt* provides a picture, a written word(s), or an object to assist the learner in providing the correct response. Simple visual prompts might include a word such as "stop" on the door or perhaps pictures of footprints on the floor indicating where to stand in line. More complex visual prompts could include a checklist of tasks to do to complete an assignment. For example, a visual checklist could be developed as a prompt to color, cut, and paste pictures.

- A *gestural prompt* involves actions such as pointing, nodding, looking in the direction of the correct answer, and shrugging. Common gestural prompts include pointing to a chair while saying, "Sit down, please," or pairing a "Come here" sign when calling the class. Other gestural prompts might include pointing to the correct answer on a worksheet or pairing the sign for "stop" with a verbal command to wait at the door.

- A *positional prompt* involves the placement of items or objects to increase the chance that children will perform a task correctly. The chance that children will use soap for washing their hands increases when the soap is positioned in reach, and children are more likely to remember to take home their backpacks that are placed on their desks when it's time to go. In errorless learning procedures, the correct answer in a field of objects or pictures can be placed closest to a child, providing an increased chance that he or she will choose the correct item when directed.

- A *verbal prompt* involves the use of expressive language to cue the behavior. It may be a word, phrase, or sentence used to direct or model the expected answer (see Figure 3). As the prompt is faded, it may consist of only the first word or sound. Verbal prompts might be used to prompt interaction ("Say 'Hi!'"), to cue requests ("Ask your friend to play"), or to provide correct answers ("It's blue").

- *Demonstration prompts* (or modeling) involve performing the desired behavior in order to obtain an imitative response of that behavior. For example, in teaching shoe tying, the initial instruction might be "cross the laces" accompanied by a demonstration of the action.

- An *instructional prompt* uses previously mastered responses to prompt a new one by building positive behavior momentum. When a child has difficulty finding the color red, the teacher may say, "An apple is also red. Find red," giving an added stimulus to help her choose the correct color.

FIGURE 3. A child completes a paper with verbal prompts from the autism consultant.

TIPS FOR PROVIDING PROMPTS

- Fading should occur gradually to avoid a disruption in the desired behavior.
- Make certain that all team members are aware of the prompt level for a particular skill so that the intensity of assistance is consistent.
- Systematically fade the prompts before considering that the skill is mastered.
- Collect data on the various prompt levels to gather critical information to determine the rate of skill acquisition and the timing of the prompt fading procedure.
- Use visual scripts in social situations to outline what a child should say to a peer during a greeting or other interactions. This allows the child to interact without adult intrusion.
- When using positional prompts, be sure to change the position of the item to the more natural position over time.
- Remember that a visual prompt outlining steps to a task such as steps involved in unpacking and packing the child's backpack must be faded to consider the skill mastered at an independent level.
- Take care to fade verbal prompts as quickly as possible as they often are the most difficult to fade.

Stimulus Control

Once a behavior consistently follows a cue, signal, prompt, instruction, or model, it is said to be under stimulus control. This means that each time that particular stimulus is presented, there is a high probability that the behavior will be exhibited. The antecedent (cue, signal, prompt, instruction, or model) also is called a discriminative stimulus (S^D). This is the specific stimulus we want to signal the occurrence of the behavior.

To bring behaviors under stimulus control, the behaviors need to occur consistently in response to a particular antecedent. For efficient teaching, the antecedent should be carefully chosen. For example, when teaching young children to identify colors, it often is efficient to start by saying the word "red" and prompting the child to touch the red paper when it is the only paper on the table. Prompts should be faded gradually and once the child independently and consistently touches red in response to the S^D (the spoken word "red"), a distracter is introduced. This allows the child an opportunity to learn to discriminate between papers of two colors and to touch the red one in response to the S^D.

Although the child may be experiencing success in touching red in response to the spoken word, the behavior may not truly be under stimulus control. For complete stimulus control, the behavior of touching red should not occur in response to other stimuli. For example, if the child touches the red paper in response to the word "green," the behavior is not under control of the stimulus "red."

Understanding that behavior is affected by its antecedents can help teachers increase desirable behavior. The following tips are designed to increase the chance that a behavior will occur in response to an antecedent:

- Provide clear and consistent cues or directions to signal that behavior

Definition of the Principle: When a behavior occurs consistently after a stimulus, the behavior is said to be under stimulus control. This means each time the stimulus is present, there is a high probability that the behavior will be exhibited.

Tool: To teach a learner to discriminate (i.e., act in a particular way under one set of circumstances but not another), help him to identify the cues that differentiate the circumstances and reward him only when his action is appropriate to the cue.

Tool: To get a behavior under stimulus control, fade (decrease) the prompts until the behavior occurs consistently after the discriminative stimulus.

Tool: To teach a learner to remember to act at a specific time, arrange for him to receive a cue for the correct performance just before the action is expected, rather than after he has performed incorrectly.

should occur. For example, turning off the lights can become a signal for children to return to their seats.

- ◆ Follow the occurrence of appropriate responses to the cues and signals with rewards. When first teaching children to return to their seats when the light is turned off, they should be provided attention, praise, or treats for responding correctly.
- ◆ Use visual cues as reminders. For example, to teach Kyle to ask for permission to leave the room, teach him to stop when shown a stop sign and to say, "Water, please" when shown a picture of the water fountain. Once these behaviors are consistent, place a cue card with a picture of a stop sign and water fountain on the inside of the classroom door to remind him to ask before bolting out of the classroom.

Understanding the concept of stimulus control also can help teachers analyze why a behavior is occurring and take steps to reduce or eliminate it if it is maladaptive. For example, Mariah would cry and shake at parties. An analysis of this behavior indicated that it only occurred in parties where she saw a camera. Knowing that Mariah was afraid of thunderstorms, it was eventually determined that it was an association of the camera flash and lightning that caused the crying and shaking behavior. Once an understanding such as this is achieved, the situation can be managed in two possible ways. One might involve reducing Mariah's crying and shaking at parties by eliminating cameras in her presence. Another might be reducing crying and shaking by pairing a camera closely with food and fun activities, gradually desensitizing her to them. For example, at first the camera might be on a high shelf in the party room. At the next party, it might be on a table near the food. Later, she might even hold the camera and finally use it to take a picture of the cake.

> **Tool:** *Desensitization*: To help a learner overcome his fear of a particular situation, gradually increase his exposure to the feared situation while he is otherwise comfortable, relaxed, secure, or rewarded.

Fading

Billingsley and Romer (1983) suggested four major categories when systematically fading the prompts. Once a prompt is provided, a plan should be in place to gradually fade the prompt. Procedures used to fade prompts include:

> **Definition of the Principle:** Fading describes the process of gradually removing prompts until the child performs the behavior independently.
>
> **Tool:** To get a behavior under stimulus control, decrease the prompts gradually until the behavior occurs consistently after the discriminative stimulus.

- *Decreasing assistance* (most-to-least prompts) describes the process of starting with full prompts and fading to partial and minimal prompts before eliminating prompts entirely. Ideally, with this errorless learning approach, the child is successful on every attempt. Fading procedures are related to the types of prompts provided. For physical prompts, hand-over-hand assistance may be faded to hand on elbow assistance or a firm touch may be faded to a light touch. Gestures may be faded from large and exaggerated gestures to small movements or expressions. Visual prompts may be faded from large and noticeable photographs to smaller line drawings or symbols. Verbal directions given in sentences may be faded to phrases, then words, and then sounds. Remember, verbal prompts often are the most difficult to fade.
- *Increasing assistance* (least-to-most prompts) describes the process of letting children attempt to respond without prompts and providing the least amount of prompting necessary for a successful response. Fading is still necessary when using a least-to-most prompting procedure. Once the prompting level necessary for success is determined, the fading procedures described above should be implemented.
- *Time delay* fading describes the process of adjusting the timing, rather than the form, of delivering the prompt. The time delay can be a constant delay. In this instance, every time the instruction is given a defined amount of time passes (e.g., waiting 3 seconds) before a prompt is provided. A progressive time delay involves waiting for a longer interval of time after each response. For example, on the first response waiting 3 seconds before a prompt is provided and for the next response waiting 5 seconds before a prompt is provided. Correct responses should be provided before increasing the wait time. If there is a series of incorrect responses, the wait time for prompting should be decreased.
- *Graduated guidance* is used when fading physical prompts. As much physical assistance as necessary is provided. Gradually the physical touch and pressure is reduced. Moving from the physical area that is prompted to another part of the body can facilitate this reduction. Hovering close by if needed can provide support as the prompt is faded.

Continually prompting children without proper fading procedures can produce prompt-dependent behavior. With children who are prone to prompt dependence, it may be more effective to begin prompting with the least intrusive prompt possible. In all cases, care should be taken to fade prompts as efficiently as possible. Remember that for an objective to be considered mastered, the child must be able to perform the skill without any prompts.

Negative Reinforcement

Negative reinforcement has been incorrectly thought of as a punishment procedure. Punishment weakens a behavior because a negative condition is introduced or experienced as a consequence of the behavior. In contrast, negative reinforcement strengthens a behavior because a negative condition is avoided as a consequence of the behavior. In the above examples, the behaviors are strengthened as a result of the termination of the aversive conditions. This procedure is called negative only in the sense that the behavior removes a stimulus rather than producing a consequence.

For example, to use the principle of negative reinforcement to teach a child to say "No thanks," offer the child a plate of something you know the child doesn't like.

> **Definition of the Principle:** Negative reinforcement occurs when an aversive stimulus is removed as a result of a behavior and when the chance that the behavior will occur again is increased. The principle of negative reinforcement can explain the reasons that behavior is repeated, increased, or strengthened. For example, when the act of buckling the car seatbelt eliminates the aversive beeping sound, there is an increased chance that a person will buckle the seatbelt in the future.
>
> **Tool:** To encourage a learner to perform in a particular way, arrange for him to perform the desired behavior in order to terminate a mildly aversive situation.

As soon as the child says the words, take away the undesired item. The behavior of saying "No thanks" is reinforced by the removal of the undesired food.

Understanding the principle of negative reinforcement helps us explain why behaviors occur. For example, we leave the school building when the fire alarm rings. Going out of the building helps us avoid the aversive sound. We go inside to a warm house on winter days and thus avoid the discomfort of cold and wet snow. In each instance, the responses occurred because of past negative reinforcement. The negative stimulus was removed contingent upon the response. As a result, there is a greater chance that if similar stimuli are presented in the future, the behavior will occur again. Although a positive reinforcer strengthens any behavior that it follows, a negative reinforcer strengthens any behavior that reduces or terminates it.

Probably the most common use of negative reinforcement in schools is the use of an aversive teacher's glare to motivate children to get to work on an assignment. The children learn to terminate the glare by beginning to work and later get to work immediately on assignments to avoid the glare in the first place. A major disadvantage of relying on this technique is that it doesn't really teach children what to do. Even if it were true that all children want to avoid glares, some children don't know what it is they are expected to do.

Another common interaction in schools also is an example of negative reinforcement. This example involves teachers who nag children to go to their seats. When children go to the seats in order to stop the nagging, negative reinforcement has occurred. Children are likely in the future to go to their seats to avoid the nagging.

If a teacher finds loud talking in the classroom to be disruptive, the teacher might reprimand the class. If the reprimand terminates the loud talking, it is more likely that he will reprimand the children again. However, if the children continue to talk loudly in the future, the teacher's statement or attention may serve as a positive reinforcer for the loud behavior.

In reality, there may be more instances of children effectively using negative reinforcement with teachers. Children who scream when presented with schoolwork demands often escape from the work as the teacher terminates the screaming by removing the demand. Similarly, if a screaming child is placed in time-out and gets quiet, the teacher avoids the screaming. Caution is in order here as the child's behavior of screaming to escape an activity might be strengthened, although the teacher is reinforced with a quieter room. A similar situation can occur when children want to avoid difficult activities. For example, if Jill wants to avoid the reading lesson and begins to scream loudly and the teacher removes the reading lesson to stop the aversive screaming, Jill's behavior of screaming to escape reading will be strengthened.

Disadvantages of using negative reinforcement include:

- ◆ It is possible that if negative reinforcement is used too often, individuals will simply avoid situations or settings in which aversive stimuli are present.
- ◆ Aggressive or emotional behaviors might be directed at the source of the aversive stimulus (the teacher or the parent).

Combining positive approaches with negative reinforcement procedures can minimize these disadvantages.

WHAT PRINCIPLES HELP DECREASE UNDESIRABLE BEHAVIOR?

Differential Reinforcement

The following are examples of how differential reinforcement can be used in the classroom:

- *Differential reinforcement for the omission of behavior* (DRO): John screams loudly when he is near people who are talking or laughing. In order to reduce John's screams, his teacher decided to use DRO. She set up a plan to provide a reinforcer for periods of time during which John did not scream. His teacher began the intervention with 3-minute intervals. If the screaming did not occur, John was rewarded with a blue ticket. After earning five tickets, John was able to spend 10 minutes on the computer. If the screaming did occur, the timer was reset for 3 minutes and John was told that his time started over. This DRO program reduced John's screaming behavior and his teacher began to set the timer for longer periods of time. Over a period of years, John's screaming behavior has been reduced tremendously using the principles of differential reinforcement.

- *Differential reinforcement for low rates of behavior* (DRL): In the above example, John's teacher

Definition of the Principle: Differential reinforcement for:

- The *omission of behavior* (DRO) describes the process of decreasing undesired behaviors by providing positive reinforcement for the omission (absence) of a behavior targeted for change. With this principle, teachers reinforce children when they are not engaging in the target behavior the teacher wants to reduce or eliminate.

- *Low rates of behavior* (DRL) describes the process of providing reinforcement for low rates of behavior. In this case, the teacher reinforces children when they engage in fewer instances of a previously high-frequency behavior.

- *Alternative behavior* (DRA) or *incompatible behavior* (DRI) describes the process of reinforcing an incompatible behavior. This is a behavior that cannot be performed at the same time as the behavior the teacher wants to eliminate.

Tool: *Differential Reinforcement:* To help a learner reduce a misbehavior, create a system that rewards the learner as he decreases or eliminates the misbehavior.

Tool: *Reinforcement of Incompatible Behavior:* To stop a learner from misbehaving, reward an alternative action that is inconsistent with or cannot be performed at the same time as the undesired behavior.

could start with a plan to provide reinforcement if John screamed only one time in each interval.

- *Differential reinforcement of alternative/incompatible behavior*: John would pace, jump up and down, and run out of the room whenever his schedule changed. John's team decided to implement a relaxation procedure, teaching him an alternative or replacement behavior that was incompatible with pacing, jumping, and running. This procedure involved standing still, taking three deep breaths, counting to 10, and checking to see if he was calm. As long as John was following the procedure, he couldn't engage in the above behaviors. More details on relaxation procedures can be found in Chapter 6.

Some important factors to consider before implementing differential reinforcement procedures are (Alberto & Troutman, 2009):

- True DRO requires that reinforcement be delivered if children do not perform the target behavior, no matter what other behaviors they exhibit.
- Because DRO reinforces the absence of a behavior, care should be taken in situations where children do not display a range of appropriate behavior.
- The effectiveness of a differential reinforcement procedure may depend on the power of the reinforcer selected. To identify appropriate reinforcers, it is helpful to conduct a reinforcement survey. This survey helps the team examine many items that might serve as reinforcers. Teachers, parents, and caregivers can assist in identifying items to use as reinforcement. Primary or secondary reinforcers may be provided depending on the needs of the individual child. It's critical to deliver reinforcers that are meaningful and appropriate according to the child's functioning level. (Examples of primary reinforcers are foods, liquids, sensory items, or activities. Secondary reinforcers can be badges, stickers, stars, privileges, play activities, computer time, tokens, points, credits, and social reinforcement.)

Extinction

Implementing an extinction program is extremely challenging because it often is difficult to prevent children from receiving reinforcement for the targeted behavior. This sometimes is thought of as planned ignoring and used in instances of aiming to eliminate behavior such as nagging or crying. In such examples, a teacher or parent may decide not to respond to repeated requests knowing that if the behavior is not reinforced, it will decrease.

A major problem is that behaviors such as repetitive requesting have been reinforced for a long period of time and it can take an extremely long time for these kinds of behaviors to become extinct. A second problem is that it is common to respond to such requests with attention even if the request is not granted. This attention can serve to provide intermittent reinforcement of the behavior, making it even more resistant to extinction. A third problem is that it often is impossible to control other kinds of reinforcement such as attention or responses from others. Each time a behavior is reinforced, whether intentionally or not, that behavior is strengthened and becomes more resistant to change. Yet another problem is that even when extinction successfully eliminates a behavior, the extinction, by itself, doesn't teach children what to do.

> **Definition of the Principle:** Extinction occurs when no reinforcement is given to a behavior that was previously reinforced (Alberto & Troutman, 2009). This principle explains why behaviors go away, whether they were appropriate behaviors or inappropriate behaviors. We generally think of extinction as a possible strategy to help reduce or eliminate inappropriate behavior, but it is helpful to understand that an appropriate behavior that does not result in reinforcement may become extinct as well.
>
> **Tool:** To stop a learner from misbehaving, arrange conditions so that he receives no rewards following misbehavior.

For example, Mattie previously has been reinforced with books or toys when she engaged in tantrum behavior such as screaming and crying. Although able to make simple requests, Mattie would yell or whine, resulting in unlimited access to her favorite books. A carefully planned program of ignoring tantrums was combined with several preventive measures to decrease Mattie's tantrums. First, a visual support, in the form of a picture, was used to prompt Mattie to request items and make choices when the schedule allowed time for books and toys. A schedule of time for books and toys was developed. Books and toys also were given to peers engaged in requesting behavior. Verbal praise was paired with requesting behavior. These proactive measures decreased the frequency of tantrums and when they did occur, Mattie's tantrums were ignored. Other children were directed to request books and toys and, without any overt attention to Mattie, her picture prompts were surreptitiously moved closer to her. During brief moments of quiet, Mattie was prompted to use the picture to request preferred books and if she complied, she was reinforced with the books. If she screamed or cried, the adults turned away from her and did not respond. Consistent implementation of this combination of approaches resulted in significantly fewer tantrums and greatly increased requesting behavior.

TIPS FOR IMPLEMENTING AN EFFECTIVE EXTINCTION PROCESS

- Be prepared for the behavior to get worse before it gets better. The child's behavior may escalate in order to attempt to regain reinforcement. There often is an increase in the rate, duration, and/or intensity of the behavior because the child is not conditioned to the new intervention.
- Be careful not to reinforce the behavior. When an ignored behavior is reinforced, even with nonverbal attention, it will be maintained. Intermittent or periodic reinforcement makes behaviors even more resistant to extinction.
- Be prepared for a possible spontaneous recovery of the behavior. That is, once the behavior has been extinct for a period of time, the behavior may resurface. Children often test adults to see if their behavior will be reinforced.
- Be ready for the possibility that other children will begin to imitate the behavior that is being ignored. Try to prevent this by providing attention to the children in the class who are behaving appropriately.
- Behaviors changed by extinction often are not generalized to other settings. Extinction should be implemented in all settings in which the targeted behavior is observed.
- When a child engages in a behavior because "it feels good" or "is fun to do," sensory extinction may be used to change the behavior. Teachers or parents using sensory extinction would attempt to remove reinforcement a child gains when engaging in undesired behaviors. For example, a padded helmet might be used to reduce face slapping or head banging (Alberto & Troutman, 2009).

Teachers and parents should consider the following questions before implementing an extinction program (Benoit & Mayer, 1974):

- Can the frequency of the behavior be tolerated temporarily when it is ignored?
- Can an increase in the behavior be tolerated?
- Is the behavior likely to be imitated by peers?
- Does the team know what is reinforcing the behavior to keep it going?
- Can the reinforcement be withheld?
- Has the team identified an alternative plan for reinforcement?

Punishment

An important point about possible punishers is that they affect different people in different ways. For example, it is possible that a teacher might use time-out as a behavioral intervention for two children who frequently call out in the classroom. One child stops calling out almost immediately. For this child, time-out clearly is a punisher. The second child persists in calling out, despite being placed repeatedly in time-out. For that child, time-out has no effect and is not a punisher at all.

Because punishment tends to rapidly stop problem behaviors, teachers often are positively reinforced for using it. On the surface, punishment may appear to be a powerful and attractive behavior management strategy. However, there often are undesired side effects to using punishment procedures.

Before using any punishment techniques, teachers and parents should consider the following points.

- If the child's behavioral problems are caused by a skill deficit, they should be taught to do the skill rather than receive a negative consequence for not performing the skill. For example, a child who is chronically disorganized and always arrives late to class with no writing materials should be taught a system of organization, rather than be punished for his inability to prepare for class.

- If positive techniques alone can address the behavior, they should be used before any negative consequences are considered. For example, structuring the child's classroom with clear visual

In the field of applied behavior analysis, punishment has a narrow definition. It is described as the presentation (Type I) or removal (Type II) of an event resulting in a reduction in a target behavior. According to this definition, events that decrease an individual's behaviors are considered to be punishers.

In Type I punishment, an event is presented when the child shows an undesired behavior. For example, a teacher may provide a verbal reprimand to a child each time that the child gets up without permission. If the verbal reprimand stops the behavior and decreases or prevents subsequent occurrences of the behavior, the reprimand acted as a punisher.

In Type II punishment, something is removed to decrease the behavior. In this type of punishment, an item or activity is taken away when the child engages in an undesirable behavior. For example, a teacher may take away a toy each time the child bangs it on the table.

Two variations of Type II punishment include time-out from reinforcement and response cost. When implementing a time-out procedure, children are denied the opportunity to receive reinforcement for a period of time. Time-out can be implemented so that a child is removed from the environment or the environment can be engineered to remove reinforcement from the child. When implementing a response-cost procedure, positive reinforcers (e.g., food, toys, tokens, privileges, or activities) are taken away for each instance of an undesired behavior.

Type I: To decrease misbehaviors, arrange for an aversive consequence to follow each occurrence of a specific inappropriate behavior.

Type II: To reduce misbehaviors, remove reinforcement for a period of time.

supports can avoid behavioral triggers that lead to problems. The use of praise and other reinforcers to reward the child for engaging in appropriate behaviors also can prevent behavior problems.

- Punishment techniques, particularly strong forms of punishment such as isolation or seclusion time-out (see section below on cautions for time-out), should not be considered unless a variety of positive strategies have been unsuccessful in improving the child's conduct over a reasonable amount of time. In addition, these techniques should only be used if the behavior is interfering significantly with the child's education and quality of life.

- Punishment often is accompanied by significant negative side effects. Children who regularly experience negative consequences may over time begin to dislike school. The child also may attach negative or punitive thoughts toward the adults who deliver the punishment.

- Punishment shows a child what not to do, but by itself does not tell a child what to do in place of the undesired behavior. If the behavior serves a purpose for the child, teachers and parents must work to provide more appropriate ways to meet those needs. Simply stopping the behaviors through punishment will not teach critical and more desirable behaviors.

- If a child performs a task out of fear of punishment from the staff, chances are that little learning or behavioral change will take place. The constant punitive measures can damage the rapport needed with the child and create negative momentum during daily interactions.

- When children engage in self-injurious behaviors such as pulling out their hair, hitting their head, or biting themselves, briefly holding the children's hands while counting to signal a brief time of refraining from the behavior may be effective in stopping the injurious behavior. After a verbal count up to 10, the child is redirected back to task. In many situations, with intensive, consistent implementation, the self-injurious behavior can be reduced significantly.

Time-Out

Time-out actually is a short name for time away from positive reinforcement. It means a period during which the child does not have access to rewarding experiences. Time-out can be a place to go or a place to sit. For example, time-out can be in a section of the room that doesn't have toys and activities or it can be in a chair facing a wall.

However, when implementing time-out, the child doesn't actually have to go anywhere. Time-out can be a few minutes without access to toys that are placed on a high shelf or it can be a short period without the opportunity to earn points or tokens toward a special privilege.

The purpose of this procedure is to ensure that the child in time-out is not able to receive any reinforcement for a particular period of time. If the child goes to a time-out spot and enjoys looking at pictures on the wall, it is not really time-out. And, if the child stays in a place without toys, but is able to eat a snack, it's not a period away from reinforcement.

It is critical to understand what is reinforcing for the individual child. Even if the child goes to a place where no visible rewards are present, it is important to make sure that the time alone is not reinforcing for the child. If the child enjoys time alone or likes escaping work or interaction, time-out that was intended to reduce behavior may actually act as a reward and increase the behavior. There is an old saying that "Time-out doesn't mean a thing unless the child wants time-in."

What to Do When Using Time-Out

When using time-out areas, the place should be easily accessible and completely visible for supervision. A chair in an empty section of a room is an excellent spot.

Short periods of time for time-out generally are more effective than long periods. Children often forget why they are in time-out and can sometimes begin to think of inappropriate ways to get attention. Preschool children should have time-out periods ranging from 2 to 5 minutes and time-out for school age children might range from 5 to 10 minutes. The child's ability level affects the length of the period as well. Some children learn more from several 15-second time-out periods than one 2 or 3 minute time-out session.

Fouse and Wheeler (1997) described "time-out on the spot" (TOOTS) as a short form of time-out that does not involve moving the child to another place. For example, the child might be required to turn away or put his head down for a short period of time as in the following procedure:

 * The teacher says, "No grabbing—put your head down."
 * The teacher counts silently or sets a timer for a few seconds.
 * The child is then cued to sit up and the activity continues with no further discussion of the inappropriate behavior or the time-out.

TOOTS also can consist of desired objects being placed in time-out. Immediately after an undesired behavior occurs, the teacher might hold a reinforcing object or put the object in a box for 10 or 15 seconds. In another variation, the teacher can turn away (removing attention) for 10 or 15 seconds after each occurrence of an undesired behavior.

Procedures for sending children to a time-out area might include:

1. Immediately after the behavior, tell the child, "Time-out for . . ." and describe the behavior. For example, say, "Time-out for hitting," or "Time-out for grabbing." There should be no further discussion.

2. Use a timer with a beep or bell. Set the timer for the length of the time-out and tell the child he must stay in time-out until the timer beeps.

3. Make sure the child does not have an opportunity to play with toys or engage in conversation with adults or other children.

TIPS FOR USING TIME-OUT EFFECTIVELY

- Implement time-out immediately after the inappropriate behavior is displayed, providing the best chance for children to connect the consequence with their behavior.
- Arrange the environment so that the child receives no reinforcement (including attention) during time-out.
- Control when time-out begins and ends.
- Make sure children don't use time-out to escape from undesired activities by arranging for them to return to and complete tasks they were doing before the time-out.
- Refrain from inadvertently entertaining children with your own emotional outbursts. Instead, remain calm and unemotional when placing children in time-out.
- Adjust your language to meet the needs of children when placing them in time-out. Rather than lengthy explanations, simplify your message with limited words such as, "No hitting. Time-out starts now."
- Implement time-out with items by using a time-out box for reinforcing items (e.g., toys, movies, or treats).
- Make sure time-in is rewarding. When the motivation and reinforcement within the classroom is high, the child will more than likely perform appropriately to be included in the desired activities. If the child is not actively engaged in the learning process, or the daily schedule is unrewarding or boring, time-out may not be an effective strategy to use.

Cautions Regarding Time-Out

No time-out procedure should seclude or confine the child alone in a room or area without supervision. The Council for Children with Behavioral Disorders (CCBD, 2009a, 2009b), a division of the Council for Exceptional Children (CEC), has developed position statements concerning the use of seclusion in school settings that include specifications about the use of time-out. According to CCBD's position, seclusionary time-out occurs when children are placed in a setting where they are alone and prevented from leaving the environment. Seclusion does not include chill-out rooms, destimulation areas, safe places, or cool-down rooms provided as a place for children to be alone when they choose.

Seclusion should be used only "when a student's behavior is so out of control or so dangerous that the student's behavior in the current environment poses a risk of injury to the student or others" (CCBD, 2009a, p. 2). Any use of seclusion that is involuntary confinement should be an extremely rare instance, implemented by trained personnel as a last resort, and only when children are in imminent danger of hurting themselves or others. Seclusion should only last until additional help arrives. Many states and school systems have policies and guidelines on the use of time-out and teachers and parents should know and understand them.

CCBD (2009b) also developed a position statement on the use of physical restraints in schools. Teachers or parents who are considering the use of any restraints should read this position statement and all state and school system guidelines before including it in any child's program. At the minimum, physical restraint should be used only as a last resort and by fully trained personnel.

It is critical to understand the function of the behavior before using time-out with a child with autism. If the function of the behavior were to escape a task, then time-out would reinforce the child for the behavior and possibly strengthen the inappropriate actions. The time spent away from reinforcement will vary from child to child. Once a child is calm and in control, it is critical to begin the task again. Creating positive behavior momentum by a faster delivery of reinforcement or making the task manageable often will help the child calm down and continue to work until a break can be given.

Understanding the child's motivation is critical for the effective use of time-out. Meaningful reinforcement must be available to keep the child engaged and interested in the tasks. Otherwise, the child may choose to engage in disruptive behaviors in order to escape to time-out. Conducting a reinforcement menu to investigate a variety of appropriate reinforcers is in order and will be presented in the next section.

In the next chapter, we will provide descriptions of methodologies and strategies that use principles of ABA. These methodologies will differ in several ways, but they all will provide opportunities to use behavioral principles such as positive reinforcement, stimulus control, shaping, modeling, and prompting. Thus, when used effectively, they will contribute to the success of children with ASD.

CHAPTER

4

HOW CAN ABA PRINCIPLES BE IMPLEMENTED IN EDUCATION PROGRAMS?

t is clear from the research that children with diagnoses of ASD need a program based on applied behavior analysis (ABA). Reviews of the research (see Chapter 2) also indicate that an effective program in autism requires structure, routine, predictability, consistency, and highly individualized, ongoing assessment of a child's emerging skills, strengths, and interests. Successful education programs also are characterized by intense treatment and low adult-child ratios.

As we have mentioned before, professionals agree that education programs must teach children with ASD to become more responsive to their environments, and especially to the people in their lives. However, there are several different approaches or methodologies for accomplishing this. Some methodologies are highly adult-directed and use a stronger, more intrusive way of attaining responsiveness. Other methods are more child-directed and use more gentle and enticing means of accomplishing responsiveness.

This chapter presents methodologies and strategies divided into three categories. We view all three methodologies as ones that:

- ◆ are based on applied behavior analysis,
- ◆ can be individualized, and
- ◆ can be implemented in many educational environments.

It is important for readers to realize that we are recommending that all of the methodologies and strategies in this chapter be viewed through the lens of an ABA approach. For example, although the theoretical basis of sensory integration is that the sensory activities change and build new neural pathways (a view in contrast to the ABA goal of changing observable, measurable behavior), it is our view that sensory activities can be used effectively with certain children as antecedents or consequences to affect behavior.

To explain further, the first thing on Ahmed's school schedule was a Discrete Trial Training (DTT) session on labeling objects and actions. Each morning, upon arriving at school, Ahmed refused to get out of the car. After much coaxing by his teachers, he would slowly and reluctantly walk into the classroom. As an experiment, his teachers changed his schedule so that his first activity would be in a sensory room. He would have about 15 minutes to bounce, swing, jump, and run. He would then go to his DTT work session. After two days of his new schedule, Ahmed starting hurrying into school to get to his sensory activities. After 15 minutes of these sensory activities, he made a smooth transition to his work session.

We explain each of the methodologies, strategies, and procedures below through the antecedent-behavior-consequence model. Rather than reject a strategy or methodology because it was developed without ABA in mind, we adapt it to implement it with principles of ABA.

In all categories of instruction, motivation (M) is a key component. Based primarily on the work of Jack Michael (1982, 2007), many ABA practitioners are viewing the former three-term contingency (the A-B-C model) as a four-term contingency—M-A-B-C. Before Michael's work, motivation often was thought to be the same as reinforcement, and it also was thought that motivation (or lack thereof) meant the presence (or absence) of sufficient, appropriately scheduled reinforcement. But, the effectiveness of the reinforcement depends on the extent of the deprivation or satiation with respect to the reinforcer. In all methodologies and strategies, it is important to observe the effects of our instruction to ensure that we are increasing productive behaviors and decreasing interfering behaviors so the child can be successful at home and school. Much of our success will be tied to the degree to which we are considering the fact that what the child does is related in part to what the child wants. It will be important to keep this in mind as we explore the following categories of instruction.

The first category is *controlled presentations*. These are adult-directed methodologies focused on teaching one small component of a skill with multiple repetitions of practice. Controlled presentations emphasize clear, concise antecedents and specific consequences. The second category includes *naturalistic teaching methods* that are child-directed methodologies with an emphasis on motivation and natural consequences. The third category is *environmental engineering approaches* that place emphasis on enhancing the antecedent, including using the physical structure, sensory activities, and visual supports to supplement ordinary antecedents. In the rest of the chapter, each category will be explained in more detail.

CONTROLLED PRESENTATIONS

Our category of controlled presentations includes Discrete Trial Training (DTT), Direct Instruction (DI), and direct instruction (di). DTT, a very structured system of providing many separate learning trials, is the method described by Ivar Lovaas in his 1987 publication on his work with young children with autism. Although DTT often is referred to as ABA therapy, it is only one method based on principles of ABA. In Lovaas' landmark study, children received an average of 40 hours a week of intensive DTT. After treatment, almost half (47%) of those children attained scores in the normal range for IQ and adaptive and social skills (Lovaas, 1987). DTT is the methodology often referred to in programs using Intensive Behavioral Intervention (IBI).

Direct Instruction (DI) also is based on principles of applied behavior analysis. Effective DI involves carefully planned instruction provided in small learning increments. DI is adult-directed, fast-paced, and provides constant interaction between the children and the teacher. Direct Instruction (DI) refers to a specific method of teaching that focuses on both the design of the curriculum and specific teaching techniques while direct instruction (di) refers to more general teaching methods.

The following list of key characteristics of controlled presentations helps us explain what DTT and di have in common. Later in the chapter, each of these two methodologies will be explained in more detail. Key characteristics of controlled presentations include:

- breaking down complex tasks into their component skills;
- eliciting frequent responses;
- providing specific, immediate, corrective feedback;
- providing positive reinforcement;
- providing mass practice until mastery is reached;
- maintaining rapid pacing;
- providing systematic review of learned material;
- using rapid transitions to intersperse new material with mastered material;
- using teacher scripts;
- eliciting choral group responses;
- facilitating responses by using teacher signals; and
- providing opportunities for group and independent work.

Discrete Trial Training

Discrete Trial Training (DTT) is a method of teaching that uses multiple trials or Antecedent-Behavior-Consequence (A-B-C) chains to teach student behaviors. An example of an A-B-C chain follows:

Antecedent (A)	The teacher says, "Sit down."
Behavior (B)	The child sits.
Consequence (C)	The teacher says, "Thanks for sitting!"

Each A-B-C chain is a trial and each trial should be separate (or discrete). To make the A-B-C chains discrete, a break is provided after each one. In the above example, the teacher could provide a break between trials by taking the child to another section of the room for a few seconds, walking back toward the chair, and then beginning a second trial. An example of a complete trial with a break might be:

Antecedent (A)	The teacher says, "Show me the ball."
Behavior (B)	The child points to the picture of the ball.
Consequence (C)	The teacher says, "Hooray! You found the ball!"
Break	The teacher removes the pictures.

After each antecedent, it is possible that the child might respond correctly, respond incorrectly, or not respond at all.

In the case of an incorrect response, an example of a discrete trial is:

Antecedent (A)	The teacher says, "Touch your head."
Behavior (B)	The child claps.
Consequence (C)	The teacher says, "No. Try again."
Break	The teacher pauses for a few seconds.

In the case of no response, an example of a discrete trial is:

Antecedent (A)	The teacher says, "Touch your head."
Behavior (B)	The child does nothing.
Consequence (C)	The teacher says, "Try again."
Break	The teacher pauses for a few seconds.

In each case, the pause (or intertrial break) makes it clear that the next antecedent is the beginning of another trial. This often is critical for children who don't learn in more natural ways. They have a better chance of making a connection between their responses and the feedback when breaks are used between trials.

When the child makes an error, an error correction procedure should be implemented. To do this, the next trial includes a prompt (an additional stimulus) added to ensure the child makes a correct response. For example:

Antecedent (A)	The teacher says, "Touch your head" and immediately provides a prompt by taking the child's hand and putting it to the child's head.
Behavior (B)	The child allows the teacher to assist.
Consequence (C)	The teacher says, "Good touching your head."
Break	The teacher pauses for a few seconds.

A major characteristic of effective DTT is making each A-B-C chain clear and distinct. In many other teaching sequences, such trials don't have clear beginnings and endings. Teachers often say, "Sit down . . . I said, sit down . . . Please sit down . . . Come on sit . . . you sat yesterday when I asked you . . . Sit down, sit down, sit down . . ."

During this time, the child might be walking around, standing still, wiggling, or spinning. Whatever the child's behavior is at the time, it is unlikely that the child will associate the words "sit down" with the action of sitting.

In effective DTT, the teacher paces the instruction so that the antecedent is never provided more than once per trial. This requires allowing time for the child's response, the teacher's feedback, and the break before providing the antecedent again. If the child is not responding, prompts are provided so that the child never makes more than one or two errors in a row.

The more often the antecedent and the child's correct response happen closely in time, the more likely the child is to learn the correct response. To add to the above example, the more often the words "sit down" immediately precede the action of sitting down, the more likely the child is to associate the words and actions and thus learn the meaning of the words.

DTT is sometimes referred to as discrimination training because children are taught specific responses to the teacher's antecedents. For example, in learning colors, the teacher might put out one red piece of paper and say, "Point to red." It is likely that a child who has a pointing response will point to red as it is the only thing on the table. (If the child does not point to red, a prompt should be provided.) Once the child consistently points to red, a distracter piece of paper is introduced. The child is asked to point to red, but now the child has to discriminate between the two colors and choose the correct one. As language builds, the child soon can respond correctly to thousands of requests, each request requiring discrimination from among the many behaviors in the child's repertoire.

Young children with diagnoses of ASD often have difficulty developing language in a natural way. When they are not discriminating appropriately, they might point to "red" when the teacher asks for "blue" or even touch their heads when the teacher asks for ball. It's likely that they have been reinforced in the past when the teacher said, "touch your head," and also when the teacher said, "find blue." Because each behavior has resulted in pleasant consequences in the past, the children might try that response. It is sometimes called scrolling when children try a number of different behaviors, searching for the one that results in a positive outcome. Effective DTT provides enough trials so children make a clear association between a behavior and that particular antecedent.

In behavioral language, the discriminative stimulus (S^D) is the antecedent (instruction or cue) that sets the occasion for the response (R). Any stimulus may become an S^D when it is consistently associated with a response. The S^D

for a particular response could be an object, sound, motion, facial expression, signal, word, or sentence.

Discrete trial chains are designed to teach (increase or strengthen) behaviors, so consequences are designed to provide positive (S^{R+}) or negative (S^{R-}) reinforcement. To make the trial discrete, an intertrial interval is provided. This break between trials may involve a pause, rearrangement of materials, or even another brief activity.

Consider the examples below.

S^D (Discriminative Stimulus)	Response
Teacher says, "Sit down"	Child sits down
Traffic light turns red	Driver stops the car
The phone rings	Person answers

When teaching, the S^D may be in forms such as:

* a command,
* an instruction or direction,
* a question, or
* a gesture.

The response (R) is the behavior that follows the S^D. Responses may be correct or incorrect. (When a child does not respond, that is considered incorrect.) Consider these examples:

S^D (Discriminative Stimulus)	Correct Response	Incorrect Response
Teacher says, "Sit down"	Child sits down	Child doesn't move
Traffic light turns red	Driver stops the car	Driver speeds up
The phone rings	Person answers	Person leaves the room

The consequence is the stimulus following the response. Consequences may increase the chance that the response will occur again (reinforcers) or decrease the chance the response will happen again (punishers). Of course, as we mentioned in the beginning of this chapter, motivation is not the same as consequences. So, in some cases, the consequence may not affect whether the behavior occurs again or not. In these cases, it is important to understand the motivating operations of the child and make efforts to find effective consequences.

In behavioral language, the consequence may (a) increase the probability the behavior will occur again (SR), or (b) decrease the probability the behavior will occur again (SP). Consider these examples:

S^D (Discriminative Stimulus)	Correct Response	Consequence
Teacher says, "Sit down"	Child sits down	Teacher says, "Thanks!"
Traffic light turns red	Driver stops the car	Driver avoids ticket
The phone rings	Person answers	Phone stops ringing

These consequences have the potential to increase the chance that the behavior will occur again in response to the discriminative stimulus. In the first example, the teacher's response is intended to act as a positive reinforcer, that is, it is a pleasant consequence that will hopefully cause the behavior to be repeated. The other two examples are instances of negative reinforcement, that is, an aversive consequence is avoided as a result of the behavior. However, the consequences can't truly be called reinforcers until it is determined that the behaviors actually are increased. Consider these examples for incorrect responses:

S^D (Discriminative Stimulus)	Correct Response	Consequence
Teacher says, "Sit down"	Child jumps around	Teacher says, "No, try again!"
Traffic light turns red	Driver speeds up	Driver gets ticket
The phone rings	Person ignores phone	Phone continues ringing

In each of these cases, the consequence is likely to reduce the probability that the response will occur again. However, the consequences aren't really called punishers until their effect on the behavior is to reduce or eliminate its occurrence.

Implementing effective DTT involves breaking down complex tasks into their component skills. Once a targeted skill is identified, a clear S^D should be chosen. This S^D should be appropriate to the child's level. For example,

TIPS FOR IMPLEMENTING DISCRETE TRIAL TRAINING

- ◆ Pick a clear stimulus that will be consistent from trial to trial.
  - ▪ Give the direction in clear and concise language.
  - ▪ Avoid confusing or changing commands or questions.
  - ▪ Do not use extraneous words.
  - ▪ Do not repeat the direction without giving the child a response.

- ◆ Establish an expected response.
  - ▪ Break down the skill into a small enough segment so a successful response can be elicited.
  - ▪ Define what is expected for the response before you give the S^D.
  - ▪ Give the child 3–5 seconds after the S^D to respond.
  - ▪ Within each discrete trial there will be three possible responses:
    - • Correct response: A response meeting the established response criteria. (Be consistent in what you require for a correct response. Correct response criteria must be consistent among all teachers and assistants.)
    - • Incorrect response: A response not meeting the established criteria.
    - • No response: No response is considered incorrect.

- ◆ Arrange for the response to occur.
  - ▪ Elicit a correct response. Prompt by modeling, telling, showing, arranging the materials, exaggerating, hinting, pointing, touching, or looking at the correct answer.

- ◆ Provide feedback after the response.
  - ▪ Reinforce correct responses or approximations with praise, a wink, eye contact, a head nod, edibles, tokens, puzzle pieces, or blocks.
  - ▪ Correct incorrect responses with an instructional "No, " or "Try again."

- ◆ Pause and/or rearrange the field before beginning the next trial.
  - ▪ Clarify the beginning and end of each trial.

- ◆ Maintain a high success rate.
  - ▪ If a child responds incorrectly two times, elicit a correct response on the third trial by prompting the child.

- ◆ Maintain a high rate of responses.
  - ▪ Break down the skill into small enough segments so a high rate of responses can be maintained.

- ◆ Train a skill to mastery before teaching additional skills.
  - ▪ Define mastery according to the need.
  - ▪ Choose a lower level of mastery for skills that are less critical or that will be practiced continually along with the next skill.

in teaching an early learner, the S^D for putting blocks in a bucket might be, "Put in." For a more advanced learner, the S^D for naming opposites might be, "What's the opposite of hot?"

Before starting, it is helpful to determine what responses will be counted as correct and how the teacher will provide feedback for responses that are unexpected. For example, in response to the S^D, "Put in," the child might put a block back in the box rather than the bucket or in response to the question, "What's the opposite of hot?" the child might say, "Cool." Effective practitioners of DTT provide feedback that is specific, immediate and, when necessary, corrective.

Effective DTT is characterized by frequent, quick, teacher-child interactions. The fast pace keeps children actively engaged and prevents off-task behavior. DTT is designed to provide repetitive practice on skills until they are mastered (performed accurately and independently) and to receive systematic review of previously mastered skills. Because of this and its error correction procedures, well-implemented DTT results in a high percentage of successful responses.

Sequences for Traditional DTT

When a task or skill is introduced in DTT, many repetitive trials are provided. As the child masters the responses expected for a particular stimulus, distracters are gradually introduced so that the child can learn to discriminate. Distracters are added stimuli put in place to require the child to attend and make a decision regarding the correct response. For example, when teaching a child to pick up a cup from among several objects, the teacher might start with a cup on the table and say, "Pick up the cup." Once the child is able to do this easily, the teacher could place both a cup and a spoon on the table and say, "Pick up the cup." The spoon acts as a distracter, requiring the child to attend, rather than just pick up whatever object is on the table. With both objects on the table, the child must make a decision about which object is correct. For further information, see the section on DTT in Chapter 6.

Manipulating Antecedents in DTT

Antecedent control is the manipulation of cues or conditions in the environment in an effort to trigger a behavior. Implementing antecedent control serves to trigger more acceptable responses and helps to minimize inappropriate behaviors. These strategies set the stage for success and can significantly improve the effectiveness of other behavior interventions.

Manipulating antecedents may involve:

+ providing a clear S^D;
+ accompanying the S^D with a clear model of the expected response;
+ defining the expected response as one manageable, achievable step;
+ slowing down the commands or directions;
+ exaggerating the instructions;
+ setting up a signal or cue for when the response is to occur;
+ clearly communicating expectations using visual supports;
+ visually structuring the environment, routines, and tasks;
+ physically structuring the environment or materials;
+ managing stimulation levels; and
+ addressing sensory and attention issues by interspersing physical activities.

Manipulating Consequences in DTT

Using consequences to control behavior involves the manipulation of actions or objects following the behavior. This may involve providing a reinforcer (a consequence that increases the probability the behavior will occur again) or a punisher (a consequence that decreases the probability the behavior will occur again). It also may involve time-out from positive reinforcement or response cost.

Given the repetitiveness of DTT, it is important to ensure variety, not only in the tangible reinforcers (e.g., food, toys, activities) the child receives, but also in the social reinforcers he or she experiences. Many people beginning to use DTT will follow hundreds of correct behaviors with, "Good job," delivered in a very loud and unnatural manner, a consequence that loses power over time.

Manipulating consequences may involve:

+ finding potential reinforcers such as
  - sensory experiences (e.g., music, water, flashlight, bubbles, glittery objects, lotions, powder, shaving cream);
  - vestibular experiences (e.g., swinging, bouncing, riding, rocking);
  - social interactions (e.g., smiling, praising, patting the back);
  - activities (e.g., computer time, taped music, going to get water); and
  - tangible items such as food or toys;
+ providing a reinforcer immediately following the behavior;
+ clearly communicating the availability of the potential reinforcer by showing the reinforcer or a symbol of it;
+ using preferred activities to reward less preferred activities;

- using tokens to reinforce behaviors, beginning with continuous reinforcement and fading to intermittent reinforcement;
- setting up a chart of symbolic or token rewards leading to a more tangible reward;
- providing time-out from positive reinforcement;
- removing a privilege, activity, or token; and
- requiring positive practice.

Concerns About DTT

Programs based on the Lovaas (1987) model have been criticized for their emphasis on teaching children to respond to adult directives and questions, potentially decreasing the spontaneity, initiative, and decision making children develop when they are taught using other methodologies. Because of this criticism, many behavioral programs now modify their instructional planning to include more opportunities for children to choose, lead, and initiate.

Another concern arises when nonprofessional therapists or trainers implement DTT programs. Sometimes, these trainers receive only brief training and have little ongoing contact with professionals. However, there are times when such novice trainers provide much of the direct instruction children receive.

A third concern is the ability of children to generalize their skills from the DTT sessions to their natural environment. Many times, children with diagnoses of ASD have difficulty learning in the natural course of childhood activities without explicit instruction. Although DTT can provide that instruction, it often is done by teaching in isolated settings with specific materials by a small group of people. These children then face challenges using skills in other situations unless their instructional programs provide them extensive practice in doing so.

Effective behavioral programs today include teaching in a variety of functional situations, for example, using language for requesting foods within the context of lunch and practicing words about clothing in the context of putting on a hat and coat to go home. Functional teaching does not replace formal instructional sessions using a DTT format. In the most effective programs, the two should complement and supplement each other to promote generalization.

Direct Instruction

Much like DTT, direct instruction techniques are based on the idea that clear instruction eliminates misinterpretations and improves and accelerates learning. This section will discuss both Direct Instruction (DI) programs and direct instruction (di) methods.

Direct Instruction (DI) is an explicit, systematic, teacher-directed model of effective instruction originally developed by Siegfried Engelmann (1968, 1980; Bereiter & Engelmann, 1966; Engelmann & Carnine, 1982; also see Hunter, 1980, and Rosenshine, 1976, for more information). Engelmann's experiences in teaching his own children shaped his thought that children should learn specific skills carefully designed to help them eventually generalize their learning to new, untaught examples and situations. His approach was intense and involved high numbers of child responses and low amounts of teacher talk. His published programs use teacher scripts and a fast pace to keep the rate of child responses high by the use of choral responding and to decrease teacher talk that reduces the rate of child involvement. When written with capital letters (DI), we are referring to programs developed by Engelmann and his colleagues such as the ones published by Science Research Associates (see http://www.sraonline.com). Popular examples are included below:

- language programs such as Language for Learning, Language for Thinking, and Language for Writing;
- reading programs such as Corrective Reading, Reading Mastery, Reading Mastery Plus, and Horizons;
- math programs such as Connecting Math Concepts, DISTAR Arithmetic, and Corrective Mathematics;
- writing programs such as Basic Writing Skills, Expressive Writing, Reasoning and Writing, and Cursive Writing; and
- spelling programs such as Corrective Spelling Through Morphographs and Spelling Mastery.

Direct instruction (di) refers to a generic set of practices that include systematic, teacher-directed instruction designed to maximize learning of specific, targeted objectives. It includes teaching in small steps with child practice after each step, guiding children during initial practice, and ensuring that all children experience a high level of successful practice. Rosenshine and Stevens (1986) analyzed effective instructional practices teachers used and grouped them into six teaching functions: (a) review, (b) presentation, (c) guided practice, (d) corrections and feedback, (e) independent practice, and (f) weekly and monthly reviews. They called these strategies direct instruction.

Whether it is DI or di, the goal is to accelerate learning by maximizing efficiency in the design and delivery of instruction. The theory behind these methods is that the more direct the instruction, the more effective it is. In addition, supporters of direct instruction believe that more direct instructional time is associated with greater achievement.

Direct instruction (di) methods:

* are teacher directed and fast-paced,
* break down tasks into component parts,
* emphasize repetition and practice,
* require a high level of mastery for each skill, and
* may use teacher scripts.

Both DI and di have tremendous potential for working with children with ASD. Teacher training is highly recommended and the commercially prepared DI materials make it relatively easy to implement well-designed programs for academic instruction. It is somewhat more difficult to become skilled in the use of direct instruction techniques, and we will use the rest of this section to provide examples for the use of di techniques for children with autism.

A typical di lesson includes explicit and carefully sequenced instruction provided by the teacher (model) along with frequent opportunities for children to practice their skills with teacher-delivered feedback (guided practice) and then on their own (independent practice) over time (distributed practice/review).

For example, to teach the concept of opposites, the teacher could select a list of 10 pairs of antonyms. This set should include easy, clear pairs such as hot/cold, up/down, in/out, wet/dry, fast/slow, empty/full, happy/sad, new/old, smooth/rough, and high/low. Words that might have more than one opposite, such as light/dark and light/heavy should be avoided in the first set. A sample lesson with a group of three children is included below:

> **Teacher:** Everybody listen! The opposite of up is down. When I say, "What is the opposite of up?" you say "Down." What is the opposite of up?
> **Children:** Down
> **Teacher:** Great! What is the opposite of up?
> **Children:** Down
> **Teacher:** Terrific! Mark, what is the opposite of up?
> **Mark:** Down
> **Teacher:** Hooray, Mark! Matt, what is the opposite of up?
> **Matt:** Down
> **Teacher:** Super, Matt! Emily, what is the opposite of up?
> **Emily:** Down
> **Teacher:** Woo-hoo, Emily! Everybody, what is the opposite of up?

Children: Down

Teacher: Everybody listen! Here's a new one! The opposite of hot is cold. When I say, "What is the opposite of hot?" you say "Cold." Everybody, what is the opposite of hot?

Children: Cold

Teacher: Super! What is the opposite of hot?

Children: Cold

Teacher: Terrific! Emily, what is the opposite of hot?

Emily: Down

Teacher: Emily, the opposite of hot is cold. Emily, what's the opposite of hot?

Emily: Cold

Teacher: Way to go, Emily! Everybody, what's the opposite of hot?

Children: Cold

Teacher: Matt, what's the opposite of hot?

Matt: Cold

Teacher: Alright, Matt! Emily, what is the opposite of hot?

Emily: Cold

Teacher: Terrific, Emily! Everybody, what is the opposite of hot?

Children: Cold

Teacher: Listen! What's the opposite of up?

Children: Down

Teacher: Hooray, you remembered! What's the opposite of hot?

Children: Cold

Teacher: Listen! Here's a new one! The opposite of in is out. Everybody, what's the opposite of in?

Children: Out

Teacher: Terrific! Matt, what's the opposite of in?

Matt: Out

Teacher: Great, Matt! Everybody, what's the opposite of in?

Children: Out

Teacher: Emily, what's the opposite of in?

Emily: Out

Teacher: Super, Emily! Everybody, what's the opposite of in?

Children: Out

Teacher: Woo-hoo everybody! What's the opposite of up?

Children: Down

Teacher: Terrific everybody! What's the opposite of in?

Children: Out

Teacher: Great everyone! What's the opposite of hot?

Children: Cold

Teacher: Everybody, let's count to 10.

Children: 1, 2, 3, 4, 5, 6, 7, 8, 9, 10

Teacher: Excellent!

Teacher: Everybody, what's the opposite of in?

Children: Out

Teacher: Perfect! What's the opposite of up?

Children: Down

Teacher: Superb! What's the opposite of in?

Children: Out

Teacher: Wow! Terrific! What's the opposite of hot?

Children: Cold

As the lesson progresses, the teacher should rotate randomly and quickly among children and alternate between group and individual responses. Enthusiastic, positive feedback should be given for all correct responses and immediate, corrective feedback should be provided for each incorrect response. New targets should be introduced gradually and previous targets should be reviewed systematically.

Previously mastered material should be inserted periodically to ensure children are attending to the instructions rather than answering without thinking. This also allows the teacher to distribute practice over time. Children are more likely to retain information when they practice it periodically rather than all at once. For example, it is better to distribute 10 opportunities to respond over several sessions (interspersed with responses to previously mastered questions), rather than having children respond to the same question 10 times in a row.

As the teacher gains familiarity with the skills of the group, the number of new targets to be introduced each day can be estimated accurately. Some groups may be able to handle three or four new targets each day while others may be able to manage only one or two. In the beginning, it is especially important to provide reinforcement for every response. Not only does this make the feedback very clear to children, it serves to motivate them to continue attending and responding. Praise was used in the above examples, but sometimes children need more visual, tangible feedback. Good practitioners of direct instruction will monitor the effect of the feedback on the children and will learn what is necessary to keep a high success rate. Sometimes, teachers will need to implement a token system in which correct responses are rewarded with points, checks, plastic chips, or happy faces that can be exchanged for privileges, special activities, free time, or even food.

When the children are experiencing a high rate of success, the teacher can thin the schedule of reinforcement, moving from a continuous schedule (after every correct response) to an intermittent schedule. This means that a reinforcer might be provided after every two, three, four, or more correct responses. Incorrect responses always should be corrected immediately. Children learn that moving onto the next opportunity without correction is essentially feedback that the previous response was correct. This can be especially motivating when children understand that a powerful reinforcer will be provided at the end.

Teachers must be careful not to thin the schedule too quickly or too much so that the attention and response rates deteriorate. To keep children motivated to respond, varying the schedules of reinforcement is helpful. Then the children don't know when the reinforcement will occur.

When children are well practiced in responses to direct instruction, the teacher can take shortcuts to pick up the pace. The teacher might start with complete sentences for directions and questions, and later move to shortened versions. For example, later in the lesson the language might fade as follows (the children's responses are included in parentheses):

"Everybody, what's the opposite of hot?" (cold)
"Matt, what's the opposite of hot?" (cold)
"The opposite of hot is . . ." (cold)
"Hot" (cold)
"Up" (down)
"In" (out)

Sometimes the group will be of mixed ability and the teacher will be asking the group to respond to the targets that are designed for everyone. Then, the teacher should ask individuals to respond to their own individual targets. A mixed-group session might go like this:

Teacher: Everybody, let's count to 10.
Children: 1, 2, 3, 4, 5, 6, 7, 8, 9, 10
Teacher: Super! Shawn, this is a 9. Shawn, what is this?
Shawn: Nine

Teacher: Shawn, read these numbers. (shows 2, 9, 4, 6, 9, 1, 9)

Shawn: Two, nine, four, six, nine, one, nine

Teacher: Terrific, Shawn! Sara, this is a 3. Sara, what is this?

Sara: Three

Teacher: Sara, read these numbers. (shows 2, 1, 3)

Sara: Two, one, _____

Teacher: Three. Say three.

Sara: Three

Teacher: Hooray, Sara! What is this?

Sara: Three

Teacher: Super! Sallie, this is a 5. Sallie, what is this?

Sallie: Five

Teacher: Super! Sallie, read these numbers. (shows 5, 3, 5, 2, 1, 5)

Sallie: Five, three, five, two, one, five

Teacher: Woo-hoo, Sallie!

Teacher: Shawn, read the number. (shows 9)

Shawn: Nine

Teacher: Sara, read the number. (shows 3)

Sara: Three

Teacher: Sallie, read the number. (shows 4)

Sallie: Four

Teacher: Everybody, count to 5.

Children: 1, 2, 3, 4, 5

Teacher: Perfect!

Teacher: Super! Shawn, what is this? (shows 9)

Shawn: Nine

Teacher: Hooray, Shawn. Shawn, read these numbers. (shows 1, 9, 5, 7, 9, 2, 9)

Shawn: One, nine, five, seven, nine, two, nine

Teacher: Great, Shawn! Sara, what is this?

Sara: _____

Teacher: Three. Say three.

Sara: Three

Teacher: Alright, Sara!

Teacher: Sara, read these numbers. (shows 3, 2, 3, 1, 3, 2, 1, 3, 1, 2, 3, 3, 2, 3)

Sara: Three, two, three, one, three, two, one, three, one, two, three, three, two, three

Teacher: Super, super, super, Sara! What is this?
Sara: Three
Teacher: Hooray! Sallie, what is this?
Sallie: Five
Teacher: Super! Sallie, read these numbers. (shows 5, 2, 5, 3, 1, 4, 5)
Sallie: Five, two, five, three, one, four, five
Teacher: Way to go, Sallie! Everybody, count to 10!
Children: 1, 2, 3, 4, 5, 6, 7, 8, 9, 10
Teacher: What great counting!

Direct instruction programs can be designed and used to teach advanced skills as well as beginning skills. It can be used to teach all subject areas. The following guidelines should be observed in di programs:

- **Antecedent:** The teacher's questions, instructions, or cues should be designed to communicate to the children what their responses should be and when they should respond.
- **Behavior:** The child's response should be clearly defined to determine what responses should count as correct. All other responses should receive corrective feedback.
- **Consequence:** The feedback should be designed to provide positive reinforcement for correct responses (increasing the probability that children will respond correctly in the future) and corrective feedback for child errors.

NATURALISTIC TEACHING METHODS

Naturalistic teaching methods (NTMs) refer to teaching approaches that alter the environment in an unobtrusive way to increase the probability that a desired behavior—or some approximation of the desired behavior—will occur. In contrast to teaching procedures that emphasize bringing the child under the adult's control, naturalistic approaches parallel developmentally appropriate practice using procedures that are child-centered, child-directed, and teacher-guided (Bredekamp, 1987).

Child-centered approaches are those that use materials and tasks designed around a child's interest and developmental level. Adults provide support and encouragement while a child's preferences guide the selection of materials. Naturally occurring reinforcers are used to provide the motivation for learning.

For example, the natural reinforcer for putting on shoes is getting to go outside for a child who wants to go to the playground. Teachers often use naturalistic teaching methods to increase the likelihood that what is taught will be functional and will be used to avoid or reduce problems related to generalization.

In this category, we have included methods such as activity-based instruction, natural environment teaching, incidental teaching, and pivotal response training. In each of these methods, we see A-B-C chains explaining behavior and providing tools to change it, however, in all of these methodologies, the role of the teacher is more supportive and facilitative, and less authoritative and directive. Instruction is designed around the child's interests and the child's motivation is a key component of these methods.

KEY CHARACTERISTICS OF NATURALISTIC TEACHING METHODS

- Embedding instruction toward goals and objectives into routine and child-directed activities.
- Using common and routine antecedents to elicit behaviors.
- Targeting functional and generalizable skills.
- Providing logical and ordinary consequences that are inherently interesting and that are related to the current situation or environment.
- Arranging the environment to increase the likelihood that children will initiate communication.
- Taking advantage of naturally occurring learning contexts to develop responsiveness, turn-taking, mutual engagement, and joint attention.
- Promoting independent and child-initiated behaviors.
- Teaching skills as the situation arises, often spontaneously shaping a behavior immediately within the present environment.
- Gradually shaping behaviors as opportunities arise.

Activity-Based Instruction

In activity-based instruction (ABI), activities are planned to develop high levels of engagement and provide multiple opportunities to apply systematic instruction to achieve educational goals (Bricker & Cripe, 1992). This teaching method embeds learning opportunities in experiences that are potentially of high interest to children. For example, an activity built around playing with playdough might provide an opportunity for the teacher to guide the child toward objectives such as requesting clay of different colors; following directions to roll, pat, or squeeze the clay; imitating attempts to make animals out of clay; and commenting on the finished products. When using ABI, the activity itself rarely is the objective and the focus is on the opportunities for systematic practice of the target objectives throughout the session. The activity is the means through which the teacher creates learning opportunities.

In effective ABI, the teacher plans an activity to target several specific objectives for each child. As the activity unfolds, the teacher watches for opportunities to model, prompt, and shape the targeted behavior. One of the most important teaching skills in using ABI effectively is to keep control of the reinforcing items so that the activity doesn't deteriorate into totally unstructured play.

For example, a playdough activity might be designed around the following targeted objectives.

Objectives for Luke
* To initiate requests for items
* To imitate actions of peers
* To requests turns from peers
* To make comments

Objectives for Samuel
* To imitate actions of the teacher
* To follow directions such as roll, pat, squeeze
* To request by color when prompted

Objectives for Sariyah
* To imitate sounds
* To imitate actions
* To request items by pointing and making a sound

In beginning the activity, it is helpful to have all of the materials outside of the child's grasp, but within easy reach of the teacher. To start, the teacher can signal that the materials are available and then respond to requests from the children.

It might be effective to start the activity by showing the items to Sariyah and waiting to see if she points and makes a sound. If she doesn't, the teacher should prompt her, possibly using a physical prompt to help her point and a verbal model of a word such as playdough or clay. Then, the teacher should provide some clay for Sariyah. If Luke makes a request for playdough, the teacher should respond by asking, "What color?" If he doesn't respond, the teacher should prompt him, possibly with a nonverbal, positional prompt such as holding two colors of clay closer to Luke. When Luke has made a choice of colors, the teacher should provide a small amount of playdough to him. Hopefully, this has allowed time for Samuel to initiate a request spontaneously. If not, the teacher should interact with Sariyah and Luke for a few more minutes. If Samuel still does not initiate the request, it's ideal if there is a second adult to come over and prompt Samuel to request playdough. If there is no second adult, the teacher should try a nonverbal, positional prompt first, going to a higher level of prompting if necessary.

In ABI, the reinforcers for the behaviors are natural. So, when the children make the requests, they are provided the items requested along with attention and social praise. Natural language such as, "Sure, you can have some blue playdough!" and "Yes, and by the way, thanks for saying please!" are better than more artificial comments such as, "Good asking for playdough!"

To help the child increase and improve language, the teacher should use informational feedback and require additional information. For example, if Samuel says, "I want some playdough," the teacher can say, "Thanks for asking, but can you make that sound nice by adding a magic word?" If Samuel needs more explicit feedback, the teacher can say, "Say I want some playdough, please!" Of course, such language should be simplified when necessary, but it should be said in a natural, conversational tone of voice.

The reason small amounts of playdough were provided in the example was to create multiple opportunities for requesting to occur within the session. Effective practitioners of ABI create a need for children to communicate and watch for indicators of what children want. They then require the highest level of language the child is capable of producing before providing what the child wants. In good ABI, there is relatively little teacher talk, especially compared to DTT. However, there is a great deal of teacher action designed to increase talking and interaction among children. The actions might include gesturing, questioning, facial expressions, and moving items around. When the teacher does talk, it more often is to model, prompt, or shape, and less often to direct.

To continue the ABI session, the teacher might model rolling, patting, and squeezing the clay. Attention and praise are used as reinforcers, so comments such as, "Look at Sariyah squeezing the playdough" serve to increase the chance that she will squeeze again. In addition, such comments provide good models for the children whose objectives include commenting. If Sariyah is not rolling, patting, or squeezing, additional prompts should be used.

A skillful teacher continues the session by creating opportunities for Samuel to imitate actions of peers, request turns from peers, and make comments; for Luke to imitate actions of the teacher and to follow directions such as roll, pat, and squeeze; and for Sariyah to imitate sounds and actions and make additional requests.

ABI differs from more controlled presentations in that instead of teaching skills in isolation, skills are presented (Noonan & McCormick, 1993):

- in sequence with other skills as they typically would occur;
- at times when they are needed using natural stimuli and consequences; and
- with strategies that promote independent, child-initiated behaviors.

The advantages of using activity-based programming include the following:

- Activities and actions initiated by children are more likely to maintain a child's attention.
- Initiation develops and is strengthened through activities that are likely to recur.
- Teaching is less stressful and less intimidating to families than more intensive instructional methods.
- Generalization often occurs sooner as instruction takes place in a more natural environment.

Incidental Teaching

Incidental teaching (IT) is a naturalistic strategy for promoting children's communication skills by designing interactions to shape child initiations. First recognized by Hart and Risley (1968, 1978) as a way to teach disadvantaged preschool children, IT is a process that begins when the environment is arranged to attract children to desired materials, objects, or activities. The teacher waits for the child to indicate an interest and initiate communication and then stands by to provide reinforcement and instruction related to the child's interest. When children don't initiate communication, the teacher uses a series of least-to-most prompts to increase interactions.

The most important element of effective IT is that the environment must include items and activities that are of high interest to the child, but under control of the teacher, so that the child must interact with the teacher in order to gain access to the items. The adult uses indications of the child's interest as an opportunity to wait for communication from the child and to model more elaborate language. This procedure can be used any time the child initiates to an adult, but it often is used in low-structured situations in which such initiations are likely.

Research has shown that using IT within the context of typical preschool activities results in greater acquisition of skills and stronger generalization of skills across environments than many other traditional teaching procedures (McGee, Morrier, & Daly, 1999). Also, because so many children with ASD wait for adults to prompt them to interact, this method aims to increase the child's motivation to initiate an interaction without waiting for a prompt.

As described earlier, in DTT the teacher might place colored pieces of paper on the table, point to one, and ask, "What color is this?" A teacher using IT might teach color labels within the context of an activity. In the following example, the teacher placed a number of interactive toys on a table and positioned herself between Hannah and the table. Initially, Hannah showed no interest in the toys. She sat down on the floor and patted the floor repetitively with her hands. The teacher began playing with one of the toys. Hannah stopped patting the floor and watched the teacher place a blue ball on top of the toy. The teacher held up the toy hammer and tapped the ball a few times. Hannah stood up and reached for the hammer. As Hannah was reaching, the teacher said, "Hammer?" Hannah said hammer, took the hammer, and hit the ball hard enough to send it down through the toy's maze. The teacher said, "Wow—you hit that ball and look where it went!" The teacher held up a red ball and Hannah said, "Ball." The teacher gave Hannah the red ball and Hannah put it in place and hit it with the hammer. The teacher said, "You hit another one!" The teacher then waited silently and Hannah said, "Ball." The teacher held up the green and yellow ball and waited. Hannah again said, "Ball." The teacher said, "What color?" Hannah said, "Ball" again and the teacher said, "What color—yellow or green?" Hannah said, "Green" and the teacher handed Hannah the green ball. Hannah hit the green ball and the teacher said, "Woo-hoo, you've done three!" When Hannah looked toward the teacher, the teacher held up the yellow, blue, and green balls and waited. Hannah said, "Ball" and the teacher said, "What color?" Hannah said green and was given the green ball.

A series of interactions such as the one above can be used to shape increasingly complex requests. In future interactions, Hannah's requests could be developed as follows:

- One-word requests such as "Ball."
- Two word requests such as "Green ball" or "Red ball."
- Three word requests such as "Yellow ball, please."
- Requests for two objects at once such as "Green ball and blue ball."
- Requests in complete sentences such as "I want the green one."

In addition, the activity could be restructured so that Hannah requests the teacher to do an action. A series of skills such as this also could be taught with the same toy.

- A request for the teacher to "Hit it!"
- A request for the teacher to hit the green one.
- A request for the teacher to hit the blue and yellow ones.
- A request for the teacher to hit all of them.

This teaching technique includes the same A-B-C chain of events used in Discrete Trial Training or direct instruction. However, in those controlled presentations, the teacher begins each trial and usually selects the task to be taught. The teacher begins each trial with a clear direction or instruction and the task may or may not be of interest to the child.

In IT, the ideal antecedent is the stimulus item itself and it is chosen by the child. In the above example, if Hannah had reached for the ball first, the teacher would have prompted her to say, "Ball." If she had reached for a different toy, for example, a musical pop-up toy, the teacher might have waited, then prompted her, if necessary, to say, "Music." It is important to have multiple objectives in mind so if, for example, the child had chosen a playground ball, the teacher might be ready to shape requests such as throw, bounce, or catch. The key to effective IT is to have realistic objectives in mind for each child for each activity.

Consequences in IT should be natural. In the above example, the primary reinforcer is the activity itself. The action of hitting the ball and seeing it go through the maze was reinforcing enough that Hannah reached for another ball. The teacher's praise hopefully acted as a secondary reinforcer. To keep the praise more natural, the teacher should say something like, "Wow—you really hit that ball!" instead of "Good hitting the ball." The more natural statement also serves as a model for language that Hannah might be prompted to use in subsequent interactions. In later sessions, the teacher might ask, "What happened?" Perhaps, having heard the teacher say, "You hit the ball!" Hannah would be able to say "Hit the ball," or even "I hit the ball!" Of course, if Hannah did not respond appropriately based on the teacher's model, the teacher could provide and gradually fade prompts until Hannah could answer the question independently.

Children who have participated in programs using DTT and di often develop large numbers of skills that they use only in response to the teachers who taught them and sometimes only in the environment in which they were taught. The IT strategy is designed to prevent this. First, in IT, children learn that they do not have to wait for an adult to begin the interaction because they are reinforced for initiating the interaction. Second, children practice skills in many environments with different materials. This increases the chance that they will use these skills with other people, in other settings, and with other materials.

TIPS FOR IMPLEMENTING INCIDENTAL TEACHING

- Be available to children and wait for their initiations.
- When a child initiates an interaction, the adult should:
    - Focus on the child and decide whether to use this initiation as a teaching opportunity, attempting to understand the purpose of the child's initiation.
    - Ask for more elaborate language from the child by saying, "Tell me more," "Use words," "What about _____?" or a similar statement that would be understood by the child.
    - Wait a few seconds for the child to produce a more elaborate or complex statement; while waiting, look expectantly at the child.
    - If the child uses more elaborate language, provide praise and respond to the content of the request (e.g., if the child asked for more materials, help get them; if the child asked for help, provide it).
    - If the child does not produce a more elaborate statement, model a more complex statement and look expectantly for a response, indicating to the child to imitate it. When the child imitates it, respond to the content of the statement.

- When prompting, require language responses from the child that are directly related to the prompt supplied by the adult. This practice allows for the child to gain understanding that language responses result in direct consequences. For example, after the child correctly responds to the prompt, "What do you want?" the child obtains the requested object. This helps the child understand the relationship between his or her language use and its consequences.
- Follow the child's lead. Encourage frequent child initiations by presenting novel or new materials, placing some preferred toys in view but out of reach, providing some materials for which the child may need help, and providing materials with missing parts.
- Identify the communication goals that are relevant for the child and identify the times, activities, and routines in which the procedure will be used. Plan systematic, targeted instruction on these goals during the activities and routines in which the child has shown interest.
- Engage the child in interactions in which natural reinforcers (interesting objects or persons) can be made contingent on certain behaviors.
- Reinforce all communicative attempts. All communicative attempts by a child are valid and should be positively reinforced.
- Place emphasis on turn taking in conversations, making both the adult and the child active, dynamic participants.
- Intervene (prompt, model, or rearrange the environment) to elicit more complex behaviors; provide supports so the child will elaborate in a manner that successively approximates the desired behavior.

Pivotal Response Training

Pivotal response training (PRT) is another naturalistic teaching method based on the principles of ABA. PRT was developed specifically to target language skills, play skills, and social behaviors in children with autism. Pivotal behaviors are those that affect a wide area of functioning, so positive changes in them have significant effects on other behaviors. Koegel and Koegel (1999a) identified two key pivotal behaviors they called motivation and responsivity to multiple cues. PRT aims to increase motivation by implementing instruction through child choice, reinforcing attempts, and interspersing maintenance tasks. PRT also helps children learn to attend to and respond to multiple cues, which serves to help them generalize their skills to new environments (Koegel & Koegel, 1999b). An example of using pivotal response training to increase communication follows.

One of Jack's favorite toys was a red fire engine that makes sounds when he pushes it around on the floor. He usually played with it for about two minutes before losing interest in it. He would imitate the words "fire truck" in response to a verbal model, but would not spontaneously make a request. For many days, his teacher put the fire truck on a shelf just out of Jack's reach. While he was watching, she rolled the truck along the shelf so that it would make a sound and then she waited. For the first 3 days, Jack made no verbalization, but continued to look at the truck. Each time, after giving Jack 10 or 15 seconds to speak, his teacher said "Fire truck?" and waited. When Jack said "Fire truck," she handed him the truck. As soon as Jack lost interest in the truck, the teacher put it back on the shelf. His teacher followed Jack's lead, waited for him to initiate, and offered a verbal model for the things he seemed to look at and reach toward. Periodically, his teacher would remind him about the truck by rolling it a little on the shelf. On the fourth day, when the teacher rolled the truck, Jack made a sound. Although the teacher wasn't sure he said, "Fire truck," she immediately handed him the truck. In several other instances that day, she was certain that Jack was attempting to say, "Fire truck." Near the end of the day, his teacher felt confident that Jack was consistently making a sound and she decided to hold out for a more understandable request. So, this time, instead of handing him the fire truck when he made the sound, she said, "Fire truck?" Jack's much clearer version of the word earned him his time with the toy. Within a few days, his request was much stronger and clearer and by the end of the next week, he was initiating requests for the fire truck even when the teacher wasn't near it.

Here's an example of a teaching activity designed to increase Erin's responsivity to multiple cues.

TIPS FOR PIVOTAL RESPONSE TRAINING

- Implement teaching in the natural environment during ongoing activities (e.g., snack time, free play, transitions, art and fine motor activities) as well as setting up pivotal response training sessions.
- Watch for opportunities to follow the child's interest or lead and use those opportunities to reinforce initiations and to shape the child's responses to multiple cues.
- Work to make each opportunity clear to the child.
- Provide plenty of time for the child to initiate, especially if the child is attending.
- Provide prompts to help the child understand what is expected, especially if the child's attention has wandered.
- Distribute individual teaching interactions over a period of hours and days, interspersing fun and easy tasks with more challenging tasks.
- Gradually shape initiations by creating chances for children to respond to prompted opportunities (e.g., "Do you want music?"), open-ended opportunities (e.g., "What do you want?"), nonverbal opportunities (e.g., facial gestures or body language indicating that a request is expected), and opportunities for spontaneous initiations (where the teacher doesn't necessarily appear to be expecting a request).
- Use the least intrusive prompt that is effective in evoking an initiation and continuously try to fade the use of prompts.
- Provide reinforcement for attempts to communicate and gradually increase the expectations for success.
- Gradually increase the complexity of the child's responses to cues by requiring the child to make more precise discriminations (e.g., first ask the child to select a red cup from a grouping of a red cup and a blue cup and later ask the child to select a red cup from a grouping of a red cup, a blue cup, and a red ball).
- Use natural consequences (objects and events that are related to the situation and are highly desired by the child) that correspond directly to the child's behavior. Use natural consequences:
  - to increase the chance for generalization,
  - to increase daily interactions that will continue even after training has ended, and
  - to increase the likelihood that what is taught will be functional for the child.

After intensive Discrete Trial Training, Erin became proficient at responding to requests to select a designated colored block from a field of five different colored blocks. She was inconsistent in responding to requests such as "Get the red ball" or "Find the blue cup." Her accuracy with colors was limited to the blocks with which she had been taught. To help Erin generalize her skills with colors, her teacher developed a game, much like a lotto game. She provided Erin with a set of objects and a large poster board with 20 spaces. The box of objects included several of each of four different objects (block, bear, chip, and bead) in five colors (red, blue, green, yellow, and orange). In each space on the board, the teacher had written words that Erin could read. In some spaces on the board, there were two-word combinations such as blue bear, red chip, green block, green bead, orange chip, and orange bear. Toward the bottom, there were spaces that included three-word phrases such as two blue bears and multiword phrases such as one green chip and two red beads. Erin's intense desire to complete things helped motivate her to fill the board and she worked hard to select the correct objects to place in each square of the board. Eventually, her teacher developed many boards, often requiring Erin to put together unique combinations of pictures based on many features. For example, later she became skilled at finding pictures based on descriptions, such as "one with wheels" and "two with feathers" or "one that you write with" and "one that you drink from." Erin's games progressed from those with visual supports such as the written words on the board to auditory games she could play with others, more like Bingo games. In these games, the children listened to the description and placed a chip on the picture if it was on their card, winning the game if they were first to fill five spaces in a row.

Erin's progress in attending to these cues did seem to help her follow increasingly complex directions in her classroom and at home. For example, she then was able to follow a sequence of three requests given at once such as "Go to the bathroom, then get your shoes and coat, and then come to the car."

ENVIRONMENTAL ENGINEERING APPROACHES

Environmental engineering approaches (EEA) structure the environment for success by arranging and manipulating the physical environment to assist children in functioning more successfully and independently in the classroom, home, therapy room, or other locations. Visual schedules, social stories, visually cued communication, and other EEAs can help create a sense of predictability for the child in an otherwise chaotic world. Creating an environment with visual supports helps increase the child's understanding of expectations and decreases the potential for interfering, challenging behaviors.

EEAs help set the stage for the appropriate behavior to occur. Considering the A-B-C behavior timeline, the focus of EEAs is on the antecedents or what happens before the behavior occurs. For example, Emily's anxiety is reduced when she knows how many more multiplication flashcards she must answer in order to finish the activity. Her teacher sets up the activity by using two small colored plastic baskets. The flashcards she must answer are in the green basket; once the flashcard is answered it moves to the red basket. When all of the flashcards are in the red basket Emily knows the activity is finished and she may do a more preferred activity. Another example of using EEAs is when Anthony's concern about going to a new school was eased by a social story describing his new school. Reviewing the social story and subsequently visiting the school made what might have been a traumatic situation much more pleasant. EEAs help teachers and parents organize surroundings, activities, and expectations for their children.

In the section below, we will explain one EEA, structured teaching, in detail. In Chapter 6, you will find information on many other EEAs including social stories, the Picture Exchange Communication System, visual schedules, and other visual supports.

KEY CHARACTERISTICS OF ENVIRONMENTAL ENGINEERING APPROACHES

- Using visual strategies to communicate clear expectations to children.
- Providing visual symbols and instruction to assist children with communication and social skills.
- Providing predictable routines and using rehearsal strategies to prepare for unexpected events.
- Teaching the finished concept to assist children in knowing how much work they must complete to be finished with an activity.
- Defining each activity by clearly marking its beginning, middle, and end.
- Arranging and labeling the physical environment to communicate expectations for behavior in each area.
- Providing prompts (errorless learning) to assist children through an entire task.
- Fading prompts systematically to develop independence.

Structured Teaching

Structured teaching (Mesibov, Shea, & Schopler, 2006) refers to an approach to instruction that uses visual and environmental cues, schedules, routines, direct instruction, and environmental or instructional adaptations to facilitate learning and independence. This is the major methodology used by TEACCH (Treatment and Education of Autistic and related Communication-Handicapped Children), a statewide program in North Carolina.

TEACCH classrooms use visual cues and organizers because visual processing is a strength for children with ASD. When using the structured teaching methodology, the physical environment is arranged with boundaries, picture and picture-word schedules outline the activities for the class and each child, and work systems are used to teach independent work skills and take advantage of the child's preferences for routine and predictability.

Mesibov et al. (2006) outlined six major components of structured teaching that should be considered when setting up the classroom environment for children with ASD.

Component 1: Organization of the Physical Environment

The physical layout of the classroom is an important consideration when planning learning experiences for children with autism. A teacher needs to spend time teaching the children the physical layout of the classroom and that specific activities occur within each area in the classroom. The teacher should provide specific instructions on expectations at the workstations, play zones, and break time areas. For example, at the workstations, the teacher should instruct children on how to work independently, locate and use materials needed to complete the activity, return those materials to a designated place, and follow their individualized activity schedules.

When planning for the physical organization of the classroom the following design tips and considerations should be taken into account:

- The arrangement of classroom furniture can help or hinder the children's independent functioning and their recognition and compliance with rules and limits.
- When arranging your classroom remember to consider the location of doorways, windows, sinks, bathrooms, and carpeted areas and how these areas can best be utilized.
- Areas in the classroom for learning specific activities should be visually well defined, marking each activity area with clear boundaries. For example, the carpet could designate an activity area while the bookshelves clearly define another area. Materials needed for each particular activity are kept in that area and are easily accessible by the children or the teacher.
- Every classroom and every child will not need the same amount of structure. Periodically, the physical organization of the classroom should be evaluated for effectiveness and restructured as needed.
- A teacher of younger children will want to structure learning areas for play, individual/independent work, snack, self-help skills (including location of the bathroom for toilet training), and prevocational skills.
- A classroom for older children could have a leisure area, workshop area, domestic skills area, self-help/grooming area, independent work area, and a place for group teaching sessions to occur.

- Many classrooms need a time-out or destimulation area (Fouse & Wheeler, 1997). A destimulation area is an area located in the classroom that anxious, overstimulated children can access to calm down and regain self-control.
- All classrooms should have a designated place for children to put their personal belongings, either in cubbyholes, lockers, or special boxes.
- The teacher's desk also should be another established place in the classroom.
- Remember, no physical space is perfect, but most classrooms can be modified to become meaningful learning environments.
- Teachers should assist parents in the organization of the child's home environment to establish clear, ordered, and safe boundaries.

Component 2: A Predictable Sequence of Activities

Providing a sequence of activities that is predictable (e.g., the arrival routine) helps children understand their environments while reducing the anxiety that can be caused by uncertainty and surprise. Using visual supports to illustrate the sequence of activities will help children remember what to do in situations in which they are not quite sure what is expected. Some suggestions for establishing some sense of predictability are:

- Define each activity with a clearly marked opening event (e.g., checking the picture schedule and gathering the needed materials), the way to participate in the activity (e.g., using the materials), and a closing event (e.g., putting the materials away).
- Use a sequence of steps that is logical and predictable to the children, with clearly marked turn taking that indicates to children when it is their turn.
- Establish a booklet of steps to follow for transition activities from one place in the building to another. For example, the booklet may contain the materials to gather to take to art class, what steps are needed to get ready for recess, how to pack up for home, and directions for walking to therapy sessions within the school.
- Create a booklet of social stories (Gray, 2000) to describe behavioral expectations within different settings in the building. The stories can each have their own color, helping to further organize the system. The teacher can simply say, "It's time for recess. Let's read your blue story."

Component 3: Visual Schedules

Visual schedules for children are necessary to facilitate transitions from one activity to another and/or to enable children to predict when an activity will be occurring. If adults continue to verbally remind children of the events of the day, children may become prompt dependent and unable to transition from one activity to another without verbal direction from the adults. Schedules promote independence and smooth transitions between activities without adults' prompts. Every classroom should post a general classroom schedule for all children to use. Deciding to use an individual daily schedule for a particular child is determined by that child's needs. Does the child have a difficult time transitioning from one activity to another or does she continue to ask when a specific activity is going to occur? If you answered yes to either or both of those questions, then you may want to consider creating an individual schedule for the child.

Individualized and general schedules can take many forms and should be designed to match the functioning levels of the children:

- Objects representing the various activities (e.g., a spoon on the schedule indicates to the child the activity is lunch) may be used for early learners.
- Photographs of the daily activities may be used for children who can discriminate pictures.
- Picture symbols or line drawings that represent the activities may be used for children who can match a line drawing of an object to a photograph of a similar object.
- Lists of activities may be used for more advanced learners.
- All schedules should be presented in a top to bottom or left to right format.
- It is suggested that text be included with all photographs, line drawings, and picture symbols (e.g., a picture of Circle Time should have the words "Circle Time" also included).
- Remember to evaluate the effectiveness of the individualized visual schedule and change the format as the child's abilities improve.

Daily schedules cover chunks of time (e.g., lunch, music class, language, recess). In Chapter 6, we will discuss work/activity schedules that cover what to do during a specific time period. For example, the children's daily schedule may direct them to spelling time. The children may then use an activity schedule or a work system to tell them exactly what they need to do during spelling time. This is similar to adults who use their daily planner to remind them they have to go to the grocery store after work. The activity schedule or work system would be comparable to the list of items to be purchased at the store.

Schopler and Mesibov (1995) provided five reasons to use visually clear schedules:

1. They minimize problems of impaired memory or attention.
2. They reduce problems with time and organization.
3. They compensate for problems with receptive language, which also cause obstacles to following verbal directions.
4. They foster child independence, especially from negative teacher interactions that include the repeated need to know what comes next.
5. They increase self-motivation by readily available visual reminders that students "first work, then play."

TIPS FOR USING SCHEDULES

- Review the general daily schedule frequently, initially prior to each activity and gradually fade how frequently the schedule is checked. Some children may find presenting the entire school day in a schedule format too overwhelming. Presenting a partial daily schedule is suggested for those children.
- Teach children the procedures for checking their individualized schedules. Any prompts used to teach children must be faded until the children check their schedules and transition to the next activities independently.
- Include children when setting up schedules. When appropriate, have them choose which activities are to be done and in what order, or have the children make a choice between two activities or different materials to be used.
- Use schedules to help children anticipate changes in their daily activities. Children are taught to follow their schedules. When a change in their daily activities occurs, it is reflected on their schedule. For example, the child goes to music class on Tuesdays. On one particular Tuesday, music class may be cancelled and the child is to go to the auditorium for a special program. This type of change should be indicated on the schedule. If checking and following the schedule is a routine for a child, he will more readily accept the change indicated on his schedule.
- Consider using the "OOPS!" strategy (Fouse & Wheeler, 1997) when a change occurs in the child's schedule. Place an "OOPS!" card over the activity that is not occurring, while providing a picture of the event that will occur instead. For older children, the international no symbol can be used. This helps children adjust to change in their day.

Component 4: Routines With Flexibility

Establishing routines to assist in the understanding of expectations often will decrease the child's agitation as well as assist in skill development. As teachers we have many routines we follow throughout the school day. There is the arrival routine, departure routine, lining up for lunch routine, putting a heading on your paper routine, clean-up routine, getting homework ready to go home routine, and the list could go on. Teachers need to plan the routines they are going to use in their classrooms and then teach those routines to their children. If a child is not provided and taught the established routine, he often will develop his own routine. However, his routine may not be the desirable response the teacher is looking for! For example, Dalton, a second grader in the general education classroom, waited every day for his teacher to prompt him through the arrival routine. His teacher created a pictorial sequence of the steps Dalton needed to follow upon arrival at school. Using the visual support, Dalton was taught to follow the routine, checking off each step as he completed it. In a very short time Dalton learned the routine and no longer needed the teacher's prompts or the visual support.

Established routines also can help in transitioning from one activity to another. Transitioning throughout the school day often is a challenging time for children with ASD. They have a difficult time stopping one activity and beginning another activity. This problem is compounded when you consider the number of times a teacher and her children transition throughout the average school day. Some tips for assisting in teaching routines and flexibility are:

- Design the physical space and schedule to promote smooth transitions between activities and foster a sense of the school routine.
- Mark the opening and closing of each activity with a ritual (e.g., taking materials out and putting materials away).
- Develop school routines for arrival, morning circle, centers, snacks, lunch, dismissal, and so on. Teach those routines to your children.
- Assist parents in recognizing the importance of routines and help them in developing home routines for getting ready for school, afterschool activities, dinner, and so on.
- Teach children to be more flexible by gently challenging established routines. For example, if children wash their hands before lunch in the sink in the hallway bathroom, have them wash their hands in the classroom sink on a day the class is running late. The routine is the same, and you have just introduced a slight variation. Remember to reinforce the children who follow the modified routine.

Component 5: Work Systems/Activity Schedules

Once the children's physical environment is organized, the school day is predictable, a daily schedule is in place, and routines are considered and taught, the children are ready to "go to work" using a work system. Work systems, sometimes called activity schedules, visually tell children what they need to do before accessing a reinforcer. Work systems/activity schedules may be used for simple activities (e.g., sorting colored bears before playing with the ball) to more complex activities (e.g., completing a math assignment before working on a model car). They also may be used for a single activity (e.g., finishing the five steps in a child's departure routine before the child goes home) or several activities (e.g., a work system that depicts a written list of assignments a child must complete in his English class before he can read his favorite book). Work systems are visually organized systems that provide information to the child. This information answers four related questions:

- What task or activity am I supposed to do?
- How much work is required or how long will the activity last?
- How will I know that progress is being made and I am finished?
- What do I do after I finish the activity?

TIPS FOR CREATING WORK SYSTEMS/ACTIVITY SCHEDULES

- For an early learner, organize 2–5 activities in separate bins. The activities should be those the child can do independently. Label the outside of each bin with a different color (e.g., a red square of color, a blue square of color), a different symbol, or a different picture. Each child is given a work system schedule that has depicted the order in which the child will complete each bin. To determine the order in which the bins are completed, the child matches the color, symbol, or picture to the one on his work system schedule. For example, the child looks at his schedule and sees a red circle. The child will look at the red circle and go get the bin with the red circle on it or take off the red circle on his schedule and match it to the red circle on the bin and then complete the activity in the box.
- For an advanced learner, a work system may be a 3" × 5" card depicting the 2–5 assignments the child needs to complete. Next to each assignment is a check box. As the child finishes each assignment he checks off that assignment. The last item on the schedule is a reinforcing activity. This increases the child's motivation and cooperation.
- Organize tasks in a three-drawer bin that is numbered top to bottom showing what to do "first, next, and last." This should be depicted on the work system schedule.
- Use a work system to help children know how to complete a task independently (e.g., use a blue bin for the parts to be assembled, a yellow bin to present a model or jig as a guide, and a green bin for the assembled product).
- Be sure to teach the method chosen so the child understands the system to complete tasks.
- Take care to deliver minimal verbal prompts that may be difficult to fade.
- Design work schedules to have a place for 2–5 tasks with one additional space indicating a final activity that is generally a reinforcement activity for completing the work activities.
- Display work schedules in either a top-to-bottom order or a left-to-right sequence.

Component 6: Visually Structured Activities

Engaging children with ASD in learning activities can be best accomplished when activities are visually clear and meaningful to the child. Visually structuring activities within a classroom can assist a child with special needs when included in the general education classroom. These supports can help the teacher engage the child's attention to tasks when the tasks are organized efficiently. The structure of the tasks should include aspects of visual information that provide visual instructions, visual organization, and visual clarity.

Structured Teaching Examples

Marco's Work System. Marco was just beginning to respond to directions such as "put in" and "match." His reactions to teacher directions were consistent, but he rarely, if ever, worked independently. His teacher set up a work schedule that eventually would include the following three tasks: putting plastic chips in a container, putting the pieces in a 12-piece puzzle, and matching plastic chips to their corresponding colors.

Marco's motor skill level was such that he often bumped or dropped items, so the materials were created to minimize these accidents. For the first task, a cookie sheet was prepared with 10 pieces of fuzzy Velcro® stuck on the left side of the cookie sheet. A bit of prickly Velcro® was stuck on each plastic chip. Then, all 10 chips were pressed into place so that even if the cookie sheet was held upside down, the chips would not fall off the tray. On the right side, a container with a lid was glued to the tray. An opening on the top of the container was made, just large enough to poke one chip down into the container. For the second task, Velcro® also was attached to the puzzle pieces and the spots in which the pieces were to be placed. Another tray was used to attach a puzzle-piece container (with lid) on the left side and the puzzle frame on the right side. For the third task, a file folder with six colored squares of construction paper (three on each side of the inside of the folder) was laminated. A piece of Velcro® was attached to the center of each colored square and fuzzy Velcro® was attached to each of the corresponding plastic chips.

The three tasks were lined up on a shelf from left to right and the camera was placed at the end of the right side of the shelf. Marco's worktable was placed near the shelf so that he could easily reach the tasks. A large finished container (laundry basket marked "Finished" was placed to the right side of Marco's worktable.

A three-ring binder became Marco's activity schedule. His picture, name, and a visual schedule were on the front. The visual schedule had a small picture

TIPS FOR PROVIDING VISUAL INSTRUCTIONS

- The instructions can be a model of a finished product for the child to copy.
- A jig can be provided to show the child where to place items, such as the outline of a table setting.
- Written directions can be provided for children who are capable of reading.
- Altering the order or sequence of the tasks over time will help the child develop some flexibility while overcoming the need for sameness often experienced by children with autism.
- Changing the pattern of visual instructions also fosters generalization through the use of different materials or different procedures to obtain the same outcome.

TIPS FOR PROVIDING VISUAL ORGANIZATION

- Present materials that are neatly organized and accessed.
- Keep academic tasks for each subject in separate, color-coded folders.
- Stabilize the tasks by using a variety of folders, trays, bins, baskets, and colored tape boundaries.
- Provide separate containers that are visually distinct for tasks such as self-help skills that require a variety of materials.

TIPS FOR PROVIDING VISUAL CLARITY

- Provide highlighting on worksheets denoting exactly which sections need to be finished.
- Underline, highlight, or circle "direction words" on a worksheet to assist in following instructions.
- Streamline the materials needed for a task by beginning with very few necessary items and working up to more items or objects. For example, begin with only two crayons in the bin with the coloring sheet as opposed to an entire box of crayons to choose from.

TIPS FOR VISUALLY STRUCTURED ACTIVITIES

- When using physical and/or verbal prompts, have a plan to fade all prompts to promote complete independence.
- The ultimate goal is for the child to independently walk to his schedule, check for the work to be done, complete the work, and transition to the next activity.
- Assess your children and determine what is reinforcing to them before teaching an activity. Suggestions for reinforcement include: social praise or edibles given intermittently throughout an activity or a picture of a reinforcing activity to be earned.
- Complete a task analysis of the task to be taught and determine if teaching the whole task to the child is appropriate or teaching only one step at a time is appropriate. As each step is mastered the next step is introduced until the whole task is learned. With some tasks it might be appropriate to present the whole task, then teach specific steps of the task, and finish the work session by re-presenting the whole task. This approach (called whole-part-whole) is a good teaching strategy to use when teaching self-help skills.

of each task in a row across the middle of the binder cover. Underneath the three small pictures, the teacher placed a picture of Marco using the classroom Polaroid camera, one of his favorite things to do. Inside the binder there were four transparent protective sheet covers. A large picture of each of the three tasks was printed and each one was placed in one of the first three protective sheet covers. In the last protective sheet cover, his teacher placed a big picture of Marco using the Polaroid camera.

To teach Marco to use the activity schedule, his teacher stood in front of him each day and said, "It's time for you to work." She showed him the activity book and pointed to the visual schedule on the front of the book. She said, "Do these three things and then you can take a picture with the camera!" She put the book back on the shelf. On the first few days, she silently prompted him throughout the entire task. For example, she used physical prompts to assist Marco in getting his activity schedule notebook and putting it on the left side of his table. She pointed to the book and he opened it. She pointed to the picture and guided him to get the first task and put in on the right side of his table. She helped him take off each plastic chip and poke it down into the container. When the chips were gone, she helped him put the whole tray into the finished basket. Marco's teacher then helped him turn the page and touch the second picture. She oriented him toward the shelf and he put the second task on his table. When the puzzle was finished, she pointed to the finished basket and Marco put the task in the finished basket. She helped him turn the page and then, with pointing prompts, Marco completed the third task and put it in the finished basket. His teacher then said, "Hooray! You finished your work! You can take a picture with the camera!" Marco got the camera off the shelf and grinned and laughed as he took a picture. After the first few days, Marco was able to complete the activity schedule independently. His teacher then began varying the tasks so that eventually Marco's activity schedule could include any three of a set of 10 different tasks. It generally took Marco about five minutes to complete his schedule. His teacher then gradually increased the length and complexity of the tasks.

Markesha's Activity Schedules. Markesha's teacher used activity schedules to help Markesha learn to set the table independently. She started with an object visual schedule, created on a large presentation poster board. From left to right she attached items to the poster board in the following order: paper plate; plastic fork, knife, and spoon; paper cup; and paper bowl. Markesha's teacher labeled each object by writing the word underneath it. Although Markesha was using real plates and silverware, she was able to understand that the paper objects represented the real objects she was using. Stacks of plates, cups, and bowls, and piles of silverware were placed on the table by the presentation board.

Markesha's teacher placed a jig at each of the four places at the table Markesha was going to set. The jig was a placemat-sized piece of paper with the outline of a plate, fork, knife, spoon, cup, and bowl on it. The outlines on the jig were labeled with words as well.

Markesha's teacher also made her a visual schedule that included her task and reward. In Markesha's case, the reward was either the opportunity to eat a healthy snack at the table (providing a natural reward for setting her place) or the opportunity to listen to music (first work, then play).

On the first day, Markesha's teacher showed her the activity schedule that included the words "Set the table" under a picture of the finished table and "Eat your snack" under a picture of Markesha sitting at the table eating grapes. The teacher then pointed to the paper plate on the presentation poster board. She also pointed to the stack of plastic plates. Silently, Markesha's teacher provided a combination of physical guidance and pointing prompts to help her place all of the items in the appropriate place on the table. Then, she pointed to the picture of Markesha eating grapes. Markesha immediately went to get her snack and sat down at the table.

Markesha quickly learned to follow the activity schedule and her teacher faded the prompts rapidly. Within a week, Markesha was using only word prompts and by the end of the second week, she did not need the jig or the presentation board to set the table. Markesha's teacher continued to use the activity schedule and now has added several other tasks to the beginning of the schedule. For example, she now unloads the dishwasher, putting all of the items away, wipes the table, sets the table, eats her snack, loads the dishwasher, and then listens to music.

5

CREATING AN EVIDENCE-BASED CLASSROOM

S o far, this book has included information about general characteristics of children with diagnoses of ASD, the requirements of IDEA, the research related to evidence-based practices, the principles of ABA, and ABA methodologies. The goal of Chapter 5 is to provide information related to setting up the school environment to serve children with diagnoses of ASD.

Three steps should be taken to create an evidence-based classroom: (1) develop the Individualized Education Program (IEP), (2) create a supportive classroom team, and (3) set up the school environment.

DEVELOPING IEPS

The first step in creating an evidence-based classroom is to develop an IEP for the child with special needs. Teachers will serve as part of a team of professionals to evaluate and assess the child, set instructional goals, collect data, select activities and methodologies, and create a supportive environment. A detailed outline of the IEP process is included in Figure 4.

The IEP process can help:

+ Assess and write the present level of performance.
+ Define specific measurable goals and objectives.
+ Select appropriate methodologies.
+ Determine the services, setting, and supports.
+ Define the least restrictive environment by considering the continuum of least restrictive to most restrictive placement options.
+ Apply the specific individual needs of the child to the continuum.
+ Establish the supports needed for specific goals.

The following sections address several of these elements in more detail.

Comprehensive Assessment

A comprehensive assessment is required to create an effective Individualized Education Program (IEP) for a child with special needs. A comprehensive assessment:

+ supplements the information from an evaluation that is conducted to determine if the child meets the criteria for a disability category that would qualify the child for special education services;
+ focuses on the child but also includes an assessment of the environment within which the child operates (e.g., communication and learning styles of the staff within the classroom, environmental supports, and the physical arrangement of space);
+ provides a profile of a child's strengths and needs across domains of physical, socioemotional, communicative, language, and cognitive development; and
+ is an ongoing, dynamic process.

The purpose of a comprehensive assessment is to:

+ target goals and objectives,
+ determine appropriate educational placement,
+ monitor a child's progress, and
+ evaluate the effectiveness of the child's educational services.

The information obtained is to be used to develop an individual profile of the child's strengths, needs, and interests. A present level of performance

I.   Complete an evaluation to determine if the child is eligible for IDEA services.
    A1. Review existing records to establish whether any additional testing is required to determine if the child meets the criteria for a disability category. OR
    A2. Conduct an evaluation by
        1.   obtaining:
            a.   parental consent,
            b.   parents' confidential background information,
            c.   teacher observations, and
            d.   prereferral information and/or records; and
        2.   administering standardized testing instruments.
    B.   Determine if the child is eligible for services under IDEA.
        1.   Evaluate the child to determine if the child meets the state criteria for a disability category.
        2.   Decide if the child's needs can (or cannot) be met in the regular program without special education.

II. Conduct a comprehensive assessment.
    A.   Review and compile information about the child's:
        1.   ability and achievement;
        2.   strengths, needs, and interests;
        3.   learning styles; and
        4.   response to previous interventions.
    B.   Conduct additional assessments (if necessary).

III. Use the evaluation and comprehensive assessment information in the IEP Team process to:
    A.   create a child profile (strengths, needs, and interests);
    B.   determine skill levels and write clear present levels of performance;
    C.   develop meaningful goals and objectives that lead to the necessary skills for succeeding in school, home, and community environments;
    D.   select effective methodologies that are research-based and tailored to the individual child's learning style and present needs;
    E.   choose effective strategies and create a behavior plan to manage any challenging, deficient, or excessive behaviors;
    F.   determine the services and supports and decide on the least restrictive placement.

IV. Use the IEP information to:
    A.   select instructional activities that incorporate the goals and objectives,
    B.   designate the methodologies to be used, and
    C.   determine data collection procedures.

V.   Implement the IEP.
    A.   Create individual, classroom, and staff schedules.
    B.   Structure the classroom environment.
        1.   Create visual supports.
        2.   Arrange the physical environment.
            a.   Train the classroom staff.
            b.   Provide parent training.
            c.   Maintain ongoing assessment and evaluation by collecting data for making decisions regarding goals, objectives, methodologies, and strategies.

FIGURE 4. An overview of the IEP process.

is written based on this profile, and IEP goals and objectives are written and prioritized accordingly. Checklists, developmental scales, and questionnaires are included in this document to assist with this process. Any assessment must be tailored to the unique characteristics of each child.

Many children with diagnoses of ASD need a Functional Behavior Assessment (FBA). This assessment can range from taking a very brief look at behaviors that cause mild interference with the child's ability to function successfully to an in-depth study that includes a thorough analysis. An actual analysis of the function of the behavior is implemented by manipulating variables to see what effect each variable has on the behavior. For a sample FBA, see Chapter 7.

The ABLLS-R and the VB-MAPP

In creating educational programs for children with diagnoses of ASD, research supports using a curriculum designed specifically for these children (NYSDOH, 1999). The Assessment of Basic Language and Learning Skills-Revised (ABLLS-R) by Dr. James W. Partington (2006) is an excellent program in that it is an assessment, curriculum guide, and skills tracking system (graph) designed specifically for children with language and social impairments. The ABLLS-R contains a task analysis of the many skills necessary to communicate successfully and to learn from everyday experiences.

The purpose of the ABLLS-R is to identify language skills and other critical skills that a child must have in order to learn and respond in his or her everyday environment. Special features of the ABLLS-R include: assessing a variety of language skills, accounting for the child's motivation to respond, assessing the child's ability to attend to verbal and nonverbal stimuli, focusing on generalization of learned skills, and looking at a child's ability to use learned skills spontaneously.

The ABLLS-R is designed to function as a criterion-referenced skills assessment in which the results provide information helpful in selecting IEP goals and objectives. The skills tracking system makes it possible to observe and document the child's progress in the acquisition of critical skills. The ABLLS-R is not designed as a norm-referenced test and does not compare the child's skills to skills of a defined peer group.

The ABLLS-R includes tracking skills for the following domains: basic learner skills (15 areas assessed), academic skills (4 areas), self-help skills (4 areas), gross motor skills (1 area), and fine motor skills (1 area).

An emphasis is placed on assessing and teaching the 15 basic learner skills. Most typically developing children in kindergarten acquire skills in a group

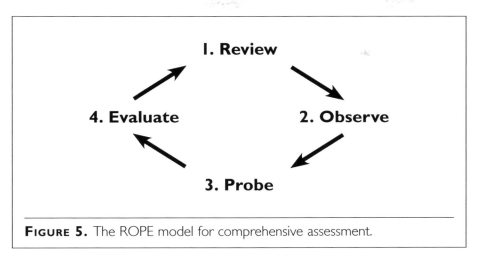

FIGURE 5. The ROPE model for comprehensive assessment.

instructional format and have accomplished these basic learner skills by the end of kindergarten. This domain focuses on skills that are necessary to be able to "learn to learn" from the environment.

Another important tool for teaching children with autism is the Verbal Behavior Milestones Assessment and Placement Program (VB-MAPP; Sundberg, 2008). In addition to being comprehensive assessment tools, both the ABLLS-R and the VB-MAPP serve as curriculum guides and skills tracking systems. However, the VB-MAPP includes normed-referenced information, making it useful for comparing the language, social, and academic performance of the child with ASD to typically developing children.

Comprehensive Assessment Steps: Review,
Observe, Probe, and Evaluate (ROPE)

In the following section, the steps for implementing a comprehensive assessment are outlined. To organize this process, we have suggested a ROPE model with the major tasks being to Review, Observe, Probe, and Evaluate. Figure 5 shows how this is an ongoing process. Comprehensive assessments should be implemented regularly throughout the child's education program.

Review. The first step in a comprehensive assessment is to review information about the child to gain the preliminary knowledge needed for planning a program. To do this, teachers and coordinators will want to (1) read background information and (2) examine data related to observations, trials, performance, and progress.

Reading the background information could include reviewing:

- family structure,
- developmental history,
- educational history including,
  - description of previous interventions, and
  - evaluation of the effectiveness of interventions, and
- medical history.

Examining data could include reviewing information from:
- observations,
- trial presentations,
- performance notes, and
- progress reports.

Observe. The second step in a comprehensive assessment, the observation stage, requires teachers and coordinators to collect additional information to provide baseline data and a present level of performance using the following steps: (1) watch, (2) collect data, and (3) record anecdotal information.

Watching could include informal observations:
- across settings,
- over time, and
- with family members, peers, and school personnel.

Collecting data could include:
- marking checklists and tally sheets, and
- using formal data collection procedures.

Recording anecdotal information could include making notes about the child's:
- performance,
- interactions with others, and
- behavior.

This stage requires observation of multiple facets. While observing, watch, collect data, and record anecdotal information about the:
- child, including his or her:
  - skill levels (strengths and needs),
  - learning characteristics,

- problem-solving strategies, and
- behavioral patterns and characteristics;
- environment, particularly the:
  - physical setting and surroundings,
  - daily routines/activities, and
  - supports for the child; and
- interpersonal relationships, especially the:
  - staff-child interactions,
  - parent-child interactions, and
  - child-child interactions.

Probe. The third step in a comprehensive assessment is to probe, or expand knowledge by exploring further possibilities. Steps for probing can include: (1) use trial presentations, (2) use criterion-referenced instruments, (3) administer standardized tests when appropriate, and (4) explore the functions of behaviors.

Using trial presentations could include:
- presenting discrete trials for specific skills:
  - across settings,
  - over time, and
  - with family members, peers, and school personnel, and
- providing opportunities for child-initiated behaviors during:
  - natural interactions, and
  - contrived situations.

Using criterion-referenced instruments could include administering:
- checklists of state standards or benchmarks,
- curriculum-based measures,
- developmental scales, and
- basic skill inventories.

Administering standardized tests could include administering:
- intelligence tests,
- achievement tests,
- adaptive behavior measures, and
- speech and language tests.

Exploring the functions of behavior (through functional analysis) could include manipulating the:

- antecedents of the behavior, and
- consequences of the behavior.

Functional analysis is a method of testing a hypothesis about specific behavior to find the communicative intent or maintenance variables that support this behavior (Iwata, Dorsey, Slifer, Bauman, & Richman, 1982). It can be used to examine the functions of behavior of children with autism, such as screaming, hitting, or biting. Through the process of implementing a good functional analysis, teachers and parents can learn much about why a behavior is occurring.

Evaluate. The fourth step in a comprehensive assessment, to evaluate, means to monitor, make judgments, and adjust goals, objectives, and strategies by (1) analyzing data, and (2) synthesizing information from reviews, observations, and probes.

Analyzing data could include:

- converting tabulated information into frequencies, percentages, rates, or averages; and
- comparing a child's performance to:
  - criteria set by IEP objectives,
  - peer performance, and
  - grade or age level expectations.

Synthesizing data could include:

- creating a profile of a child's strengths, needs, and interests;
- compiling the information to develop:
  - present levels of performance, and
  - goals and objectives;
- integrating the information to select methodologies and strategies; and
- interpreting the information to determine the supports and setting.

Selecting Methodologies and Services

Just as no two children are alike, we believe no two IEPs should be alike. We believe IEP teams should consider many different strategies and techniques when designing IEPs for children with ASD.

It's our opinion that IEP teams should set the goals and objectives for the child and then review methodologies and strategies, selecting the approaches that have the best chance of helping a particular child accomplish the goals and objectives in the IEP. When choosing a teaching strategy or methodology to employ with children with ASD, we recommend considering the following ideas posed by Guralnick (1997):

- No one strategy or methodology will be effective for every child. Curriculum and teaching approaches should be individualized and customized to meet the needs of each individual child.
- The goal of any strategy and/or methodology should be to allow each child to function at his or her most independent level.

It's our belief that it is imperative to incorporate ABA principles throughout all instruction, regardless of the strategy chosen. For example, even though Structured Teaching usually is not thought of as an ABA methodology, when we include Structured Teaching in a program, we would set a goal and objective for a child to follow a work system and then teach the child by using ABA principles such as prompting and fading. We also would use successive approximations and positive reinforcement to improve the child's ability to follow increasingly complex work systems.

As we mentioned in Chapter 4, there are many varied methodologies based on ABA. Given this, IEP teams must not only review, but also compare and contrast methodologies that are supported by research before determining what is best for each child at each particular time. For example, controlled presentations generally focus on isolated skills, providing repeated practice in drill form. Naturalistic teaching methods may involve multiple skills at one time, providing practice in high-interest, child-friendly activities. Environmental engineering approaches provide accommodations for the characteristics of ASD in addition to providing instruction.

In controlled presentations, adult direction begins immediately. Initial program objectives include getting the child to attend to the teacher ("Look at me"), imitate actions, and follow simple directions. Directions often are given in a firm tone and loud voice. Physical prompting is sometimes used to ensure that the child follows the adult's directions, with food or other rewards being used to reinforce the child's compliance.

When using naturalistic teaching methods, the adult is more supportive and less directive. The role of the adult is to capture or contrive motivation and then to guide or facilitate instruction. The adult uses natural, child-friendly language and the reinforcers are natural consequences to the behaviors.

Environmental engineering approaches have yet another way of addressing the characteristics of children with ASD. They make accommodations for these characteristics, while other methodologies focus directly on changing them.

Once the methodologies and strategies are reviewed, it is up to the IEP team to determine which should be included in a child's IEP. We recommend considering a blend or integration of these methodologies.

For example, there might be times that a child needs to focus on one skill in isolation and other times that a child can learn multiple skills at once. Periodically, the IEP team also must look at whether to focus directly on remediating a deficit behavior or providing supports and accommodations for it. At times, there might be behaviors to change; at other times, it might be more effective to make an accommodation for certain behaviors.

Many children with diagnoses of ASD have difficulty processing and producing speech. IEP teams also must consider whether manual communication, picture systems, and/or voice output communication aids should be included in a child's program.

Many other factors, including parent preference, must be taken into account when choosing methodologies. It is important to note that the teacher and the school system are primarily responsible for choosing the methodology, for implementing instruction with fidelity, and for the child's progress and outcome. However, success is more likely when the teachers and parents work closely together with common goals and agreed-upon methodologies.

Our recommendation is to look closely at the assessment, the goals and objectives, and the learning skills of the child. Once a methodology has been chosen, the child's progress should be monitored closely. If the child is not making significant gains, the IEP team should review the methodology decisions.

Making Placement Decisions

A continuum of placement options should be available and placement decisions should be made individually. The IEP team for each child should develop the goals and objectives and then look for the least restrictive environment (LRE) in which the child could achieve those goals. Care should be taken to thoroughly explore services in the general education classroom for each child. Placement in more restrictive settings should be made only when the goals and objectives can't be met in general education settings.

In general education settings, there will be a need for differentiated instruction. To adapt instruction for all learners, we suggest consulting Tomlinson's (1999) work on differentiating instruction.

Data Collection

Why Should We Collect Data?

We are living in an age of accountability that requires us to look increasingly at the results of what we do. We no longer can rely on subjective measures that might indicate that we are implementing effective programs. We need reliable and valid data for the following reasons:

- to assess the level of each child in order to set appropriate goals and objectives,
- to monitor the progress of each child to determine what to teach next,
- to track the progress of each individual child so that we can determine the effectiveness of the intervention strategy, and
- to communicate the child's progress to his or her parents.

When Should We Collect Data?

Collect data at the beginning of the IEP process. This helps the IEP team get a good understanding of the child's present level of performance before developing the IEP goals and objectives and to get a baseline before implementing a behavior change program.

Collect data during instruction. It's necessary to measure the child's progress periodically and determine the effectiveness of the instruction or other intervention. Do a complete IEP assessment at the end of the IEP period. It is important to evaluate the previous year and set realistic, challenging goals and objectives for the next year.

How Should We Collect Data?

There is no single method for collecting data. Teams must decide the structure of the data collection process together to best analyze the effectiveness of the program and the instruction. The data collected must be reliable enough to answer important questions about the child's progress. Some data-collection procedures include:

- *First response data*: Data are collected only on the initial response given by the child after the instruction is delivered.

- *Percentages of correct responses*: A percentage of correct responses is recorded for a particular skill after a series of trials.
- *Anecdotal notes*: This system uses a written description of an observed behavior in a specific setting. The notes are a complete account of what may have occurred during the particular time frame to assist the team in calculating progress or areas targeted for change.
- *Task analysis performance checklist*: Once a step-by-step procedure for a particular task has been developed, data are collected on each step of the process. This system often is used in the area of self-help skills.
- *Teacher-made tests*: Many general education teachers work with the special educator to adapt tests given to special education children in their classroom. Items for testing will correlate directly to the items on the child's IEP but may not include all areas assessed for the entire class on a given subject.
- *Rubrics*: A rubric is a rating scale with a system of performance criteria to use to assess a particular skill or task. Rubrics provide feedback to the children as to areas of strength and areas that need improvement.

Data also should be collected on the dimensions of behavior (Baer, Wolf, & Risley, 1968), including the:
- *Rate*: The frequency of a behavior expressed in a ratio with time.
- *Frequency*: The number of times a child engages in a behavior.
- *Topography*: The shape of the behavior; what it looks like.
- *Duration*: How long a child engages in a behavior.
- *Locus*: Where a behavior occurs.
- *Force*: The intensity of a behavior.
- *Latency*: The length of time between instructions and the occurrence of the behavior.

TIPS FOR TEACHER-FRIENDLY DATA COLLECTION TECHNIQUES

- Make tally marks on an index card that has sections for each day of the week.
- Place or transfer pennies in your pockets or a container each time a behavior occurs, then count and record totals at the end of the day.
- Place a strip of masking tape on yourself or elsewhere and each time an event occurs, mark the tape.
- Place rubber bands on your wrists for each occurrence of a behavior or action.
- Use a pen to write tally marks on your hand.
- Line up items on your desk or another space to represent frequency tallies.
- Use a commercially made counter to record data collected during the day.

Making an IEP Book

An IEP book is a useful tool for implementing ABA programs. This book has three major parts: (1) an overview page, (2) objective pages, and (3) data collection pages. The overview page lists the goals and objectives from the child's entire IEP in a chart or table. The task analysis pages state the objective, break it down into steps, and describe the teaching procedure. The data collection pages provide guidance on documenting the progress toward the objective. Data collection pages allow different parties to share data and observations on the child (see Figure 6).

FIGURE 6. An autism consultant and home trainer compare data using an IEP book.

The Overview Chart

The overview chart is set up so that the goals and objectives are listed in the left column. Across the top is a line for dates and the rest of the page is a set of boxes for teachers and consultants to mark when they have worked on the task with the student. (See Figure 7 for a sample chart for one student, Leah.)

The Objective Pages

The rest of the book is divided into sections, one for each objective. When a section is opened, the left page (the objective sheet) describes the objective, criterion for mastery, and teaching procedure (see Figure 8).

IEP Overview for Leah

Please mark your initials below each time you work with Leah on the objective listed

Objective	5/5	5/6	5/7	5/8	5/9
Requests	WA	BK	MA	BK	WA
Imitation	MA	WA	WA	MA	MA
One-Step Commands	WA	BK	MA	BK	WA
Body Parts	MA	WA	MA	MA	MA
Toys	WA	BK	MA	MA	BK
Food Items	BK	WA	MA	BK	MA
Activity Schedule	WA	MA	WA	MA	WA
Greetings	MA	BK	MA	BK	BK
Matching Colors	WA	BK	MA	MA	BK
Coloring	MA	BK	MA	BK	BK
Stacking Blocks	BK	WA	MA	BK	MA
Completing Puzzles	WA	BK	MA	MA	BK
Taking Turns	WA	BK	MA	BK	WA
Climbing Stairs	BK	WA	MA	BK	MA
Throwing a Ball	WA	BK	MA	MA	BK
Putting on a Jacket	MA	WA	MA	MA	MA
Eating with a Spoon	WA	BK	MA	MA	BK

FIGURE 7. Overview chart for one student.

We find it helpful to use an electronic copy of the IEP to cut and paste the goals and objectives into the IEP books. Here is a sample objective from Leah's IEP:

> When provided with an appropriate S^D such as "Show me," or "What's this?" Leah will be able to demonstrate knowledge of five body parts
> * receptively by pointing or touching, and
> * expressively by labeling verbally.
>
> Criterion for Mastery: Leah will respond accurately on the first trial of the day for three days in a row.

Remember that the S^D is the discriminative stimulus or the antecedent that sets the occasion for the response (R). The S^D may be in the form of:

Objective: When provided with an appropriate S^D, such as "Show me," Leah will be able to demonstrate knowledge of five body parts
* receptively by pointing or touching, and
* expressively labeling verbally.

Criterion for Mastery: For each step to be mastered, Leah will respond accurately on the first trial of the day for three days in a row.

Teaching Procedure: Get Leah's attention and say, "Show me your nose." In the initial stages, model by touching your own nose, and if necessary, by helping Leah touch her nose. Praise Leah immediately and enthusiastically.

S^D: Show me (body part)

	Introduced	Mastered
Nose	_____	_____
Foot	_____	_____
Foot and Nose	_____	_____
Ears	_____	_____
Ears, Foot, and Nose	_____	_____
Mouth	_____	_____
Mouth, Ears, Foot, and Nose	_____	_____
Head	_____	_____
Head, Mouth, Ears, Foot, and Nose	_____	_____

Notes:

_____

FIGURE 8. Sample objective sheet.

* a command,
* an instruction or direction,
* a question,
* an item, or
* a gesture.

The S^D for a particular response could be an object, sound, motion, facial expression, signal, word, or sentence.

Examples:	**S^D (Discriminative Stimulus)**	**Response**
	Teacher says, "Sit down"	Child sits down
	Teacher says, "Touch red"	Child touches red
	Teacher holds up 3 balls	Child says, " I want red ball"

The Teaching Procedure

This section is very important for consistency in working with the child. The procedure should be described in enough detail so any trained member of the child's IEP team could implement the instruction. The teaching procedure provides descriptions of the strategies or approaches, a task analysis, and/or a teaching sequence.

For example, if the child is in the beginning stage of language acquisition, you might be shaping the response and accepting a close approximation to the sounds requested. If you will accept "ba" for "ball," it's important to indicate it here.

This also is a good place to describe whether the approach is teacher-directed or child-led and what other strategies and materials will be used. For example, a teaching procedure section for teaching colors might be as follows:

> Use Katie's favorite toys to interest her in using her language to request items by color and shape. Get control of the pieces (e.g., colored balls, shapes, puzzle pieces). As she reaches for a piece, hold it and wait for her to initiate a communication. If she doesn't, use the least restrictive prompt necessary to get her to make a request by color or shape.

Instructions concerning the number of items in the field also are important. How many objects or cards to be presented may be indicated here or in the Task Analysis and Teaching Sequence section of the data sheet.

The Task Analysis and Teaching Sequence

The last section to complete on the objective sheet includes the task analysis and teaching sequence. These describe the steps toward meeting the objective and goal. It's important to understand the concept of breaking down goals in manageable parts. Here are some important points to consider:

- A task analysis breaks the target behavior into small, manageable steps. The task analysis should be done before determining the teaching sequence.
- A teaching sequence describes the steps that will be taught first and how the steps will be chained together.

Here's an example of how a teaching sequence using forward chaining might look for reciting a home address.

Objective: Mark will recite his address when asked, "Where do you live?"
Teaching Sequence:
1. Recite the first two digits in his house number.
2. Recite all four digits in his house number.
3. Recite his house number and his street name.
4. Recite his house number, his street name, and his city.

This example outlines a teaching sequence using backward chaining to teach putting on a sock.

Teaching Sequence:
1. Finish pulling up a sock that is pulled on over the heel.
2. From midfoot, pull the sock over the heel, and pull the sock up completely.
3. Pull the sock up from the toes, over the heel, and up completely.
4. Grasp the sock, pull it over the toes, then heel, and up completely.

The Data Collection Pages

The right page of each section is the data collection sheet and provides spaces to collect data (see Figure 9). There are several choices of data sheets that can be tailored to the objective and the teaching methodology. (See previous section for procedures for collecting data.)

WHO'S ON THE TEAM?

Successful education of children with autism requires that teachers build a supportive team in the classroom. Although related service providers such as speech-language pathologists and therapists often take part in helping to improve education, we suggest starting with a team of peers, paraprofessionals, and parents to help the child with autism find success.

Peers

Peer tutoring is a practice in which one child acts as a teacher, providing instruction to a peer (Meyen, Vergason, & Whelan, 1996). Peer tutoring arrangements can be cross-age or same age. Tutors help peers by providing instruction, opportunities for practice and review, and feedback by following a step-by-step, teacher-developed lesson. Peer tutoring is most effective when

Key

+	Accurate and Independent Response
-	Incorrect Response
0	No Response
PP	Physical Prompt Provided
VP	Verbal Prompt Provided
GP	Gestural Prompt Provided
PoP	Positional Prompt Provided

Step	First Response	Notes

FIGURE 9. Data collection sheet.

the teacher introduces a lesson or concept and the tutor provides review. The teacher is solely responsible for the program and should provide:

- step-by-step training for the tutor,
- continual monitoring by periodically observing sessions for effectiveness, and
- daily interaction with each pair to keep them focused and on track.

Positive benefits of peer tutoring include:

- gives one-on-one review,
- increases social interactions between children with disabilities and their peers, and
- allows children with disabilities to be peer tutors to younger children.

Peer guidance helps children recognize and respond to the verbal and nonverbal communicative behaviors of the child with autism (see Figure 10). Three

FIGURE 10. A peer tutor provides a treat upon request. When children work with peers with autism, they can learn to recognize and respond to the unique communication methods of their peers, fostering interaction.

strategies that focus on the peer's understanding of a child's communication attempts, the peer's ability to initiate and respond to the child, and the peer's ability to maintain an interaction with the child are:

1. *Direct instruction*: Teaches peers to be aware of different forms of communication and begin to understand how their friends with autism attempt to communicate. Must be incorporated in activity routines and naturally occurring situations using different strategies to have successful results. First, peers learn through discussion of different forms of communication examples: talking, pictures, objects, written words, facial expressions, gestures, and eye contact. They learn to be good "listeners" by learning to interpret unconventional communication such as throwing and grabbing. Next, peers are instructed how to directly get their friends to talk with them. By using role-playing, peers are taught how to gain a friend's attention and what to say when initiating and maintaining an interaction. They also learn what to do when engaged with a particular child with autism such as where to stand, how to speak clearly, and how to redirect attention. Lastly, peers are shown how to ignore inappropriate behavior, persist if their friend doesn't respond, and how to wait for a response.

2. *Modeling*: Modeling is the most common role taken by an adult to promote interactions among children by observing social situations and then showing a peer what to do or say in that situation. Peers are provided step-by-step support, either verbally or in the form of a

demonstration. Teachers can either serve as the facilitator or a participant in an activity, routine, or social situation.

3. *Environmental supports*: Charts or cue cards remind the peers what they are to do and say and can help fade out teacher modeling. Usually a written script or pictorial reminder of how to talk with a friend with autism helps the peers remember what they should say and do.

The overall goal of peer guidance is for peers to incorporate the techniques that they learned in the classroom and community without adult support.

Characteristics of Peer Tutors

Sometimes programs will involve all children who volunteer to work as peer tutors. Others might choose children who excel in school and still others might select well-behaved children who have some academic difficulties. Sincerity and commitment to the tutoring process are extremely important qualities as well.

All children should have good skills in:

* listening,
* following directions,
* prompting (see Figure 11),
* modeling, and
* reinforcing.

FIGURE 11. A peer tutor provides physical and verbal prompting for handwashing.

Teaching Peers to Interact Appropriately

Peer interaction is an important aspect of a transition to an inclusive setting. Because many children with diagnoses of ASD have trouble with social interaction, it is necessary to help them establish bonds with their peers.

Before starting, provide discussion time with peers about the characteristics of autism, behaviors they might encounter, and the similarities and differences among children. Provide instruction on how to give directions, administer reinforcement (see Figure 12), provide corrective feedback, and respond to inappropriate behavior.

FIGURE 12. A peer provides positive reinforcement.

TIPS FOR ESTABLISHING PEER BONDS

- It is helpful to have a group of children serve as buddies for children with ASD. Some of their responsibilities could include center play and rotation, teaching the classroom routine, and helping the child transition between two classroom settings.
- Prepare the children for their new classmate (and paraprofessional) and answer any questions the children have.
- Have a positive attitude. The children will follow your lead.
- Break down activities so a child who cannot fully participate can take part in as much as possible.
- Use mixed-age grouping to provide a range of developmental levels among learners.
- Ask typical peers to model appropriate behavior and initiate interaction.
- Coach typical peers on interaction strategies.
- Teach scripts for the child with ASD to learn and use during routine classroom activities.

Paraprofessionals

We believe it is best when the role of a paraprofessional in the general education classroom is viewed as an assistant to all children and their teachers. This helps the general education teacher take an active role in the child's progress toward the IEP goals and objectives. The most effective way to get children with diagnoses of ASD to talk to other children and adults directly, not through the paraprofessional, is to set up the paraprofessional as an assistant to the entire classroom.

As an integral part of the inclusion team, the paraprofessional is the strongest link between the special education and regular education classroom. Just as in the special education classroom, the paraprofessional is a team member in the regular classroom. However, the paraprofessional must be present to help the child be included in the program without taking the place of the teacher. The child must be taught to listen to and follow directions from the regular classroom teacher.

TIPS FOR A SUCCESSFUL TEACHER/ PARAPROFESSIONAL RELATIONSHIP

* The paraprofessional can assist best by helping the entire classroom, not just one child.
* The paraprofessional and regular classroom teacher need to have open communication. Everyday courtesies are especially important and should be extended to each other.
* Duties and expectations should be clearly defined before the paraprofessional and child enter the regular classroom.
* The paraprofessional will need explicit instruction when responsible for collecting data based on the child's IEP for the regular classroom.

Parents

Parents play an important role in the educational process. Communication between school and home often is critical to the academic and social success of the child. One important part of this communication is the IEP meeting. At this meeting information can be exchanged and both parties can share ideas and goals for the child's education program. It is vital for parents to attend the meetings and be prepared to ask questions. Teachers also must be prepared to ask and answer questions. It is critical to explain educational jargon and provide examples so parents can make informed decisions. Keeping the lines of communication open is essential. It is important to send home a periodic journal or communicate regularly by phone or e-mail.

It is valuable to provide parents with skills they need to teach their children. Families are the most enduring resource a child can have. Families need intervention and evaluation strategies for the home that are family friendly, flexible, and meet their needs.

Asking parents to volunteer during special events or scheduling a time that they may come observe and ask questions gives them a chance to see their child's performance at school. By communication and observation, parents and teachers will be able to discuss and try new ideas or teaching strategies, reject strategies that are not working, and modify techniques where needed.

TIPS FOR PARENTS

- Communicate openly with classroom teachers.
- When corresponding with general education teachers, be patient when waiting for a detailed response to a note or question. It may take a little longer to respond due to a larger class size.
- Think about volunteering in your child's classrooms. Volunteering provides opportunities to establish rapport with your child's teachers and peers and to see what is involved in the classroom program.

TIPS FOR TEACHERS

- Include parents as much as possible.
- Communicate daily or weekly with parents to keep them informed of behaviors and/ or performance.
- Respect parents' knowledge. Use the information they have, combine it with your knowledge, and provide a truly individualized program.
- Create a positive atmosphere to build an effective team that focuses on the needs of the child.

SETTING UP THE ENVIRONMENT

This section includes information on setting up the environment in order to maximize comfort for both the children and the adults in the classroom. The physical settings should be both attractive and functional. Interactions with children should be supportive and caring. Instruction should be provided so that children experience a high degree of success. Action should be taken to make activities predictable and plans should be made to help children manage unpredictable situations in the least distressful way. Setting up the environment involves more than just arranging the classroom, but also includes creating a meaningful learning community. When setting up the classroom, remember to arrange, attend, and adjust.

Arrange the Physical Environment

- Consider the layout and organization of the classroom. Set up areas with clear boundaries and labels for the different activities in the classroom. For example, designate areas for one-on-one or small-group instruction, large-group instruction, and independent work.
- Consider the layout and organization of the students' workspaces and materials. Design work systems to go from left to right or top to bottom.
- Use visual adaptations to aid organization. For example, use colored folders for different objectives or subjects or use markers to designate portions of work to be completed.
- Use concrete ways to demonstrate time. For example, use timers and provide calendars or planners for organizing and understanding sequences and first-then concepts.

Attend to the Emotional Needs of the Children

- State positively what children should do, rather than what they should not do.
- Provide accurate information about change and expectations.
- Watch, listen, wait for, and encourage children to initiate communication.
- Let children know when to respond and prepare them for it, rather than putting them on the spot.
- Respond positively to children's attempts to interact.
- Provide adequate time for children to respond to social and instructional opportunities.
- Take time to gradually desensitize children to specific fears or frustrations.
- Model correct language rather than correcting communicative attempts.
- Provide redirection when something isn't possible instead of just saying "no."
- Use individualized social stories, schedules, and rehearsals to reduce anxiety and worry.
- Narrate or label what is occurring in language that is slightly above the child's level.

Adjust Instruction for Success

- Specifically engage a child's attention before initiating communication or giving instructions.
- Adjust the pace of communication and instruction for each individual child.

- Provide alternative input to the child. For example, provide a visual demonstration to visual learners, added explanations for auditory learners, and opportunities for hands-on practice to tactile learners.
- Use vague terms and abstract language (e.g., later, maybe) sparingly.
- Use visual supports (e.g., pictures, gestures, models, demonstrations) when providing extensive verbal information.
- Give directions in small and clear steps and use ordered, sequential lessons.
- Provide instruction in steps that are just manageable for the student.
- Provide needed prompts and cues and repeated opportunities to practice, then fade the prompts gradually.
- Provide consistent use of words, expectations, and strategies.
- Teach outlining and organization strategies.
- Use specific teaching, rehearsal, and practice in natural settings of identified skills such as imitating, sharing, and turn taking.
- Teach rules of politeness and manners in specific settings.
- Teach social problem-solving skills and recognizing other people's perspectives using visual supports.
- Provide specific materials for accommodations of sensory, behavioral, or other needs.
- Modify difficulty and/or shorten assignments as needed.
- Allow alternative output modes. For example, allow a child to draw a picture instead of writing a paragraph or do a project instead of a paper.
- Use one-on-one instruction and small- and large-group instruction as needed.
- Specifically preteach vocabulary, materials, or structures.
- Apply learning to real situations.

In this chapter, we have discussed aspects of creating evidence-based classrooms. Next, we will complete the book with explicit examples of methodologies and strategies based on principles of ABA. Some of the strategy descriptions are brief and simple and others are more complex. It is only possible to provide introductions to these strategies. Many are intricate and require ongoing training and practice. Please think of these descriptions as just the very basic information you need to get started and then seek out support and training from other professionals and parents.

6

STRATEGIES FOR ADDRESSING THE MAJOR CHARACTERISTICS OF ASD IN THE CLASSROOM

This chapter will provide teachers and parents strategies to help children with ASD succeed at school, at home, and in the community setting. These strategies are based on the principles of applied behavior analysis and are known to be effective for children with ASD. We have implemented many of these strategies in our own programs and have provided photos to aid you in using these techniques.

We have chosen to organize the chapter by providing suggested strategies for each characteristic of autism (see Table 1 for a refresher of the 10 characteristics of autism). Keep in mind that many of the strategies could be used to address multiple characteristics. For example, we'll provide a way to use direct instruction to teach conversation (language skills), but it also could be used to teach appropriate ways to respond in group situations (social skills) and relaxation procedures for times of stress (behavior).

The examples included with each characteristic are meant to help explain the strategies and are not provided to limit the use of a strategy to the situation in the example. So, although we might describe the use of DTT with young children to teach a basic skill such as labeling toys, remember that DTT could

TABLE I

Review of the 10 Characteristics of Autism

Characteristic Number	Features of the Characteristic
Characteristic 1	Individuals With ASD Often Have Difficulty Communicating With Others, Both in Understanding What Others Say and in Conveying Their Needs and Desires
Characteristic 2	Individuals With ASD Frequently Have Deficits in the Area of Social Skills, Making It Challenging to Develop and Maintain Meaningful Relationships
Characteristic 3	Individuals With ASD Usually Display Stereotypic Motor Movements and/or Have Ritualistic, Odd, or Inappropriate Behaviors Generally Considered Socially Unacceptable
Characteristic 4	Individuals With ASD Typically Like Routines and May Have Significant Anxiety About Changes in Their Environment
Characteristic 5	Individuals With ASD May Focus on Specific, Sometimes Irrelevant Details, Possibly to a Degree That May Result in Undergeneralizing, and/or Overgeneralizing and/or Even Prevent Complete Understanding of a Concept or Situation
Characteristic 6	Individuals With ASD Might Experience Difficulty With Auditory Processing and Thus Learn Best When Visual Supports Supplement Verbal Instruction
Characteristic 7	Individuals With ASD May Be Hypersensitive or Hyposensitive and Thus React Atypically to Input From the Five Traditional Senses (Sight, Hearing, Touch, Smell, and Taste) as Well as the Vestibular and Kinesthetic Senses
Characteristic 8	Individuals With ASD Often Struggle to Understand the Perspectives of Others, May Have an Impaired Ability to Read and Interpret the Emotions of Others, and Might Have Difficulty Understanding Social Cues
Characteristic 9	Individuals With ASD Might Demonstrate Predominantly Concrete Thinking and Thus Make Literal Interpretations of Statements and Situations
Characteristic 10	Individuals With ASD Could Have Executive Functioning Challenges Such as an Impaired Ability to Initiate Tasks, Difficulty Stopping One Task and Starting Another, and an Inability to Organize Complex Tasks Independently

be used with older children to teach word associations, analogies, and answers to "who, what, where, when, and why" questions. We hope readers will consider the examples and apply these strategies in many situations to teach many objectives, perhaps to many children.

There are various factors to consider when choosing strategies. For some children, teachers may use the more controlled and teacher-directed approaches. For other children, a more naturalistic, child-directed methodology may be effective. Sometimes the objective will help determine the strategy, as it may be more effective for some skills to isolate them and provide repetitive drills. For others, embedding practice in a less structured, less focused activity will lead to greater success.

In addition, for an individual child, it may be useful to address some objectives with teacher-directed instruction and others with more naturalistic instruction. In all cases, environmental engineering approaches, particularly the use of visual supports, can enhance the effectiveness of most strategies.

In Chapter 7, we'll provide an example of blending a number of methodologies and strategies to provide a complete and effective program. Please remember that the ongoing process of assessment is extremely important to ensure that children are succeeding and that the strategies implemented are effective.

CHARACTERISTIC 1: DIFFICULTY COMMUNICATING WITH OTHERS

The tools discussed in this section will address the first characteristic of ASD, difficulty in communicating with others. We'll provide examples for teaching basic understanding of what others say. We include the following strategies for addressing this characteristic:

- Discrete Trial Training,
- Verbal Behavior,
- Picture Exchange Communication Systems, and
- direct instruction.

Discrete Trial Training

One of the easiest ways to get started teaching communication skills is to use Discrete Trial Training. (DTT). It is helpful to practice implementing A-B-C (antecedent-behavior-consequence) chains in the focused, systematic way that DTT is designed as these chains are used in all ABA instruction. Once skilled in DTT, it is easier to see how to embed such teaching chains in other less structured instruction.

To get started addressing language with DTT, an assessment of language skills should be implemented. Many effective publications outline assessment procedures and provide good sequences of skills for using DTT (see Leaf & McEachin, 1999; Maurice, Green, & Luce, 1996).

Many DTT programs begin by setting language objectives for the child to imitate actions, follow one-step commands, match, label objects and actions (expressively and receptively), and request. Examples are listed below for teaching imitation and receptive labeling.

Use the following steps to teach imitation with DTT:

Step 1: Make a list of 8 to 10 actions you want the child to imitate, such as banging a stick on a drum, clapping, shaking a rattle, touching his head, patting his thighs, stomping his feet, waving, and knocking on the table.

Step 2: Prepare a chart such as the one below.

Objective	Date Introduced:	Date Mastered:	First Attempt Date:	First Attempt Date:	First Attempt Date:	First Attempt Date:	First Attempt Date:	First Attempt Date:
Banging drum								
Clapping								
Shaking rattle								
Touching head								
Patting thighs								
Stomping feet								
Waving								
Knocking								

Step 3: Develop a key to record the child's response on the first trial of the day such as the following:

+	Correct response, performed accurately and independently
−	Incorrect response
NR	No response
A	Approximation
PP	Physical prompt
VP	Verbal prompt
GP	Gestural prompt (e.g., point, eye gaze, nod)
PoP	Positional prompt

Step 4: Set up the materials and potential reinforcers in a way that makes it easy to work with the students and manipulate the items. It often is effective to keep data sheets in a notebook with the holes punched on the left side of the paper (see Figure 13). A sheet describing the objective and teaching procedure should be developed and holes should be punched on the right side of the paper. When the notebook is opened flat, both the objective sheet and data sheet can easily be seen.

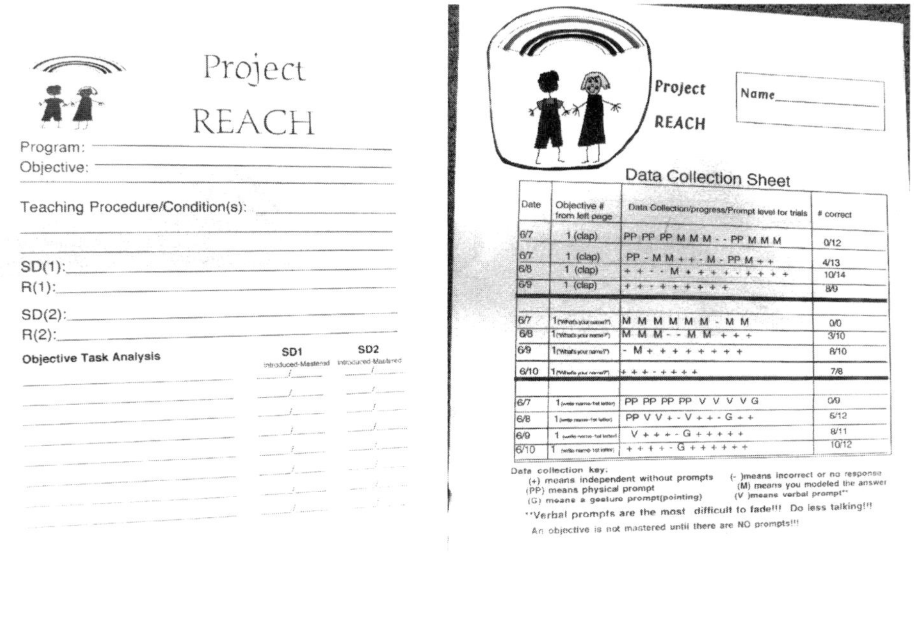

FIGURE 13. The left side describes the objective and defines the S^D and the right side provides a place to collect data.

Step 5: To begin teaching imitation with DTT, sit across from the child with a table to the side. Put the materials you'll need on the side of the table, making sure that you have in mind items and activities the child enjoys. These highly motivating rewards will hopefully act as reinforcers and increase the chances that the child will respond correctly. Then, implement instruction using a sequence such as the one below:

* Get the child's attention and say, "Do this," while modeling the action.
* Wait 3–5 seconds to see if the child responds.

- If the child responds correctly, provide a reinforcer (e.g., a sip of juice, a cracker) along with enthusiastic praise and a high five. On the data sheet, mark the first response as correct.
- If the child responds incorrectly or has no response, gently say, "No" or "Try again," and put the appropriate code for the first attempt on the data sheet.
- Repeat your S^D ("Do this" and model the action) and provide a physical prompt to assist the child in making a correct response. Provide a reinforcer immediately. In most cases, no further information needs to be recorded on the data sheet.
- Provide several repetitions of the trial (S^D, prompt if needed, response, feedback, intertrial break).
- Intersperse the trials with breaks and other tasks to distribute practice. As children gain more skills, S^{D}s for mastered skills should be given frequently to build positive behavior momentum and keep the child's success rate high. However, don't introduce any other imitation objectives until the child has achieved a first-response success for three sessions in a row. A child's program might include imitation drills in the morning, afternoon, and evening. Or, the instruction might be just one time per day. If the first responses are separated by at least several hours and the child responds correctly on the first attempt, there is a good chance the child has truly mastered that particular skill, meaning that the child can reliably and consistently perform the skill in the presence of the S^D.

Add another step (action to be imitated) to the child's imitation program when the child consistently imitates the first action accurately (i.e., a correct response on the first attempt of three separate sessions, each session separated by several hours). Work on the second action until it is mastered.

Follow the sequence below for introducing new target objectives as the child progresses:
- Introduce "banging a stick on a drum" and work on this target alone.
- Once banging the drum is mastered, introduce "clapping" and work on this target alone.
- When "clapping" is mastered, put the stick on the table and continue to work on "clapping."
- Once "clapping" (with the stick in sight) is mastered, alternate "banging" and "clapping." (Remember, this is an imitation drill, so the S^D is

always "Do this" accompanied by the model. The S^D does not include a verbal direction to bang or clap.)

- When the child is successful in imitating both actions in response to the appropriate S^D, introduce "shaking a rattle."
- Add additional actions, reviewing previously mastered ones until the child can accurately, quickly, and fluently imitate the whole series of actions in response to the appropriate S^D.

The following steps can be used to teach labeling with Discrete Trial Training:

Step 1: Make a list of 8 to 10 objects (toys) you want the child to identify, such as cup, ball, car, spoon, shoe, dog, top, and rainstick.

Step 2: Prepare a chart such as the following:

Objective	Date Introduced:	Date Mastered:	First Attempt Date:	First Attempt Date:	First Attempt Date:	First Attempt Date:	First Attempt Date:	First Attempt Date:
Cup								
Ball								
Car								
Spoon								
Shoe								
Dog								
Top								
Rainstick								

Step 3: Develop a key to record the child's response on the first trial of the day. (See Step 3 in the previous section.)

Step 4: Set up the materials and potential reinforcers in a way that makes it easy to work with the child and manipulate the items. Use a notebook as described in Step 4 of the previous section.

Step 5: Sit across from the child with a table to the side. Put the materials you'll need on the side of the table, making sure you have in mind items and activities the child enjoys. Then, implement instruction with a sequence such as the one below:

- Put the cup on the table, get the child's attention, and say, "Give me the cup," while holding out your hand.
- Wait 3–5 seconds to see if the child responds (called the R).
- If the child responds correctly, provide a reinforcer (S^{R+}; e.g., cracker, marshmallow, small candy), along with enthusiastic praise and a high five. It is ideal if the reinforcer can be more natural (e.g., you pour a sip of juice into the cup for the child). On the data sheet, mark the first response as correct.
- If the child responds incorrectly or has no response, gently say, "No" or "Try again," and put the appropriate code for the first response on the data sheet.
- Clear the table, pause, repeat your S^D ("Give me the cup" and hold out your hand), and provide a physical prompt to assist the child in making a correct response. Provide a reinforcer immediately. In most cases, no further information needs to be recorded on the data sheet.
- Provide several repetitions of the trial (S^D, prompt if needed, response, feedback, intertrial break).
- Intersperse the trials with breaks as described above.

Figures 14–16 show the steps of DTT for a receptive labeling program.

FIGURE 14. Introduce the S^D: "Point to 4."

FIGURE 15. Response: Child points to 4.

FIGURE 16. Consequence: "Great! High five!"

Add another step to the child's program when the child consistently responds to the first step accurately (i.e., three correct responses on the first attempt of a session). Work on this second step until it is mastered. Follow the sequence below for introducing new target objectives as the child progresses:

◆ Introduce "cup" and work on this target alone.

◆ Once "cup" is mastered, introduce a distracter object. This object should not be on the list to be taught. When the child consistently picks the cup from the field of two objects, add another distracter object. When the child masters "cup" from a field of three objects, move onto the next step. The distracter object should be changed frequently.

- Introduce "ball" and work on this target alone.
- Once "ball" is mastered, introduce a distracter object. When the child consistently picks the "ball" from the field of two objects, add another distracter object. When the child masters "ball" from a field of three objects, move onto the next step.
- When "ball" is mastered in a field of three, put the ball on the table along with the cup, and continue to work on "ball."
- Once "ball" (with the cup in sight) is mastered, intermix your requests for "ball" and "cup." Make sure you are not creating a pattern by just alternating the S^Ds.
- When the child is successful in selecting both objects from a field of three in response to randomly delivered S^Ds, introduce "car."
- Add additional objects, reviewing previously mastered ones until the child can accurately, quickly, and fluently identify a whole series of objects in response to the appropriate S^D.

Teachers and parents should arrange for success by introducing distracters gradually. However, when children make mistakes, provide a gentle "No" or "Try again" to make your feedback clear. Pause and/or rearrange the materials and then give the S^D again to make sure each trial is discrete. Do not let the child practice the incorrect response by making several mistakes in a row. Instead, after the first or second mistake, provide a prompt to show the child the correct response.

The example below is a sample sequence for teaching colors, but the sequence can be adapted to any content. For example, this sequence is good for teaching pictures representing objects, actions, prepositions (e.g., in, under, on), emotions (e.g., happy, sad, mad; see Figure 17), or attributes (e.g., empty, full, wet, dry). It also is appropriate to use a similar sequence for teaching sight words.

1. Introduce the target alone. Provide as many trials as needed, until the child responds quickly and accurately on the first trial of the day for 3 days.

Introduce red	S^D	"Point to red."
(target alone)	R	The child points to red.
	S^{R+}	"Great job finding red!"

FIGURE 17. The use of DTT to teach matching emotion words to pictures of people demonstrating the emotion.

2. Ask for the target color with one distracter available. Provide as many trials as needed, prompting and fading as necessary, until the child responds quickly and accurately on the first trial of the day for 3 days.

Practice red	S^D	"Point to red."
(with one	R	The child points to red.
distracter)	S^{R+}	"Hooray, that's red!"

3. Ask for the target color with two distracters available. Provide as many trials as needed, prompting and fading as necessary, until the child responds quickly and accurately on the first trial of the day for 3 days.

Practice red	S^D	"Point to red."
(with two	R	The child points to red.
distracters)	S^{R+}	"You got red!"

4. Introduce a second target (blue) alone. Provide as many trials as needed, prompting and fading as necessary, until the child responds quickly and accurately on the first trial of the day for 3 days.

Introduce blue	S^D	"Point to blue."
(target alone)	R	The child points to blue.
	S^{R+}	"Terrific, you found blue!"

5. Ask for the second color, with one distracter available. This distracter should not be the first color learned. Provide as many trials as needed, prompting and fading as necessary, until the child responds quickly and accurately on the first trial of the day for 3 days.

Practice blue	S^D	"Point to blue."
(with one	R	The child points to blue.
distracter)	S^{R+}	"Hooray—it's blue!"

6. Ask for the second color, with two distracters available. Provide as many trials as needed, prompting and fading as necessary, until the child responds quickly and accurately on the first trial of the day for 3 days.

Practice blue	S^D	"Point to blue."
(with two	R	The child points to blue.
distracters)	S^{R+}	"Good job finding blue!"

7. Ask for the second color, with first color used as the distracter: Provide as many trials as needed, prompting and fading as necessary, until the child responds quickly and accurately on the first trial of the day for 3 days.

Practice blue	S^D	"Point to blue."
(with red as the	R	The child points to blue.
distracter)	S^{R+}	"Woo-hoo, you found blue!"

8. Ask for the first color, with second color as distracter: Provide as many trials as needed, prompting and fading as necessary, until the child responds quickly and accurately on the first trial of the day for 3 days.

Practice red	S^D	"Point to red."
(with blue as	R	The child points to red.
the distracter)	S^{R+}	"Super, that's red!"

9. Practice both colors, with the color not requested serving as distracter: Provide as many trials as needed, prompting and fading as necessary,

until the child responds quickly and accurately on the first trial of the day for 3 days.

Practice red	S^D	"Point to red."
and blue	R	The child points to red.
(with red or blue	S^R+	"You found red!"
as the distracter)		

Working on steps repetitively, as in the sequence above, often is called providing continuous practice or mass trials. However, students can become accustomed to responding repetitively without attending to the S^D. For example, they sometimes guess randomly at the expected response or get into habits such as always picking the item on the left, alternating responses left and right, or in fields of more than two, working in sequence from left to right.

To guard against such guessing behaviors, effective DTT includes analyses of such response patterns and should involve strategies such as rearranging the field after each trial and distributing practice. Rearranging the field can make DTT fun and interesting as teachers can move items all over the table, almost as if hiding the correct item from the student. Distributed practice involves practicing skills at different times and on different days. Sometimes, however, students will forget the correct responses when asked a day, or even an hour later. In these cases, teachers can distribute practice on newly acquired skills by alternating the target skill with previously mastered skills. A good way to lengthen the time between target skills gradually is to increase the number of mastered skills inserted between the targets. A sample sequence is described below.

Previously mastered skills: Following directions to wave, stand up, jump, stomp, and sit down
Target skill: Turn around
Sequence of S^Ds:
Turn around
Wave
Stomp
Turn around
Jump
Wave
Turn around

Verbal Behavior

Although traditional DTT is a useful teaching methodology, it is adult-directed. A criticism of DTT has been that some children develop a large vocabulary of words they never use without prompting from an adult. The verbal behavior approach (VB) was designed to teach children the power of language by first teaching children to make requests. Targeting skills that teach the child to use language to get what the child wants can produce significant increases in the use of language.

Skinner (1957) described taking a behavioral approach to understanding the development of verbal behavior (i.e., communication). To analyze verbal behavior, Skinner broke down communication into units of language, with each unit serving a different function. The primary verbal operants (i.e., behaviors) taught to children with ASD are mands, echoics, tacts, and intraverbals:

- A *mand* is a request. The child sees the ball (antecedent) and says, "Ball" (behavior), and the teacher gives the child the ball (consequence).
- *Echoic* is defined as vocal imitation. The listener repeats what the speaker said. For example, the teacher says, "Ball" and the child repeats the word "Ball."
- A *tact* is labeling or naming anything found in the environment. A tact teaches the child to comment. For example, the child (who does not want the ball at this time) sees the ball and says, "I see the red ball."
- An *intraverbal* is a verbal exchange with responses such as answering questions, filling in a missing word, or engaging in other reciprocal language interactions. For example, the teacher asks, "What bounces?" and the child answers, "A ball." Intraverbals are crucial for the development of conversation.

The goal of the VB approach is for the child to use a word across various operants (i.e., a mand, tact, echoic, or intraverbal). Practitioners of the VB approach believe that pointing to a picture of a ball on command does not indicate a true understanding of the word. It is only when a child is able to mand (request), tact (label), engage in intraverbals (answer questions about the ball), and read and/or write the word that the child truly comprehends the concept and can communicate effectively.

Because a full introduction to VB is beyond the scope of this book, we will focus on the first step: manding. VB programs begin by setting language objectives for the child to mand (request an item, action, attention, or information). Manding is the first verbal behavior learned by all children. The baby cries (a mand) and gets food. Eventually the child learns to say words to ask for different things that are reinforcing.

For children with ASD, we cannot assume that learning to imitate or to identify items receptively and expressively will result in manding (requesting) skills. Some children must be taught how to mand as mands do not necessarily emerge by training on other verbal operants. In fact, for some children, the development of a strong manding repertoire may be necessary for the development of other types of verbal behavior such as tacting and intraverbals.

Teaching a mand repertoire can help replace problem behaviors related to an inability of the child to make his or her needs known verbally. The child's behavior, of course, can serve as a communication system, however, this is not as effective and efficient for the child as communicating verbally. Steps for teaching manding are:

Step 1: Identify the motivation. Mands should be taught when the motivation is the greatest for an item or activity. Remember, the motivation will change from day to day, even moment to moment.

Step 2: Pair the adult (and eventually the child's work area) with the child's reinforcers. Provide enough fun items and activities so the child wants to come to the adult because the adult has the items or activities the child desires. Pairing is successful when the child excitedly approaches the adult before any demands have been placed on the child.

Step 3: In the beginning, provide immediate reinforcement to as many mands as possible to teach the child that a mand produces immediate benefit. When the child is reinforced, the verbal behavior of manding is strengthened.

Step 4: Arrange for instruction to begin when motivation for an item or activity is strong. For example, the following antecedent variables must be present when teaching a child to mand to eat: the child must be hungry and a favorite food item must be present. (Later, the food need not be present, but in the early stages of teaching manding, it is more effective when the child sees the food.)

Step 5: Hold the food so the child notices it. When you have the child's attention ask, "What do you want?" (*a verbal prompt*) and/or provide an *echoic prompt* (name the item). (Remember, each child is unique and a variation of this format may be more appropriate for your child.)

Step 6: Provide feedback as follows:
- *Correct response:* Deliver praise and the item.
- *Incorrect response:* Repeat the original trial. If the child continues to fail, consider using another item, approaching the child at a different time of day, or modifying other conditions that may have an impact.

Note. Many VB practitioners recommend delivering the reinforcer if, after several trials, the child doesn't attempt to say the word. This reduces escape responses and such thoughts such as "This is too difficult," "I don't want to be here," or "Let me act inappropriately and 'escape' from the situation."

Step 7: Use a transfer procedure to fade the echoic prompt. This involves using a time-delay prompt (wait 0–5 seconds before prompting the name of the item), a partial verbal prompt ("ba" when the desired item is a ball), or a combination of the two prompts. (*Note.* At this point, the adult may still be providing the verbal prompt, "What do you want?")

Step 8: Introduce a second mand, following the same procedures as outlined above.

Step 9: While training a second mand, the new mand should be interspersed with the ongoing training of the first mand, as well as continued echoic training, imitation training, and receptive training trials.

Step 10: Once the child is manding for 2–3 items, the adult should attempt to fade out the presence of the desired item as a source of control. (*Note.* A pure mand is requesting things not present.) Once the child has manded successfully for a desired item several times, place the item behind the adult's back or place the item in a box or bag.
- *Correct response:* Reinforce immediately with the item!
- *Incorrect response:* Repeat trial using a time delay prompt and/or a partial visual prompt. For example, if the adult is attempting to get the child to request a cookie, partially cover the cookie.

Note. It is important to work on Step 10 so the child will not become prompt dependent (when the item must always be present in order for the child to mand for it).

Step 11: Fade out the verbal prompt of "What do you want?" For example, the question "What do you want?" becomes "What?" paired with a gesture indicating "What?" The verbal prompt can be faded and then the gesture faded. A time-delay prompting procedure also could be used to fade the verbal prompt. For example, the adult might indicate the presence of the item with a gesture and wait 5 seconds to see if the child mands without the prompt. If the child does, the item is provided immediately; if the child doesn't, the prompt is provided. In a series of interactions, the wait time in a time-delay procedure gradually increases. So, for example, if the child didn't respond to a 5-second delay, in subsequent opportunities, the time would be gradually increased by a few seconds.

Mands do not have to be vocal to communicate requests (see Figure 18). In the picture, a model is being provided for a child who uses sign language to mand. This is comparable to the echoic prompt mentioned in Step 5 and, in most cases, the adult prompts by saying the word along with the sign.

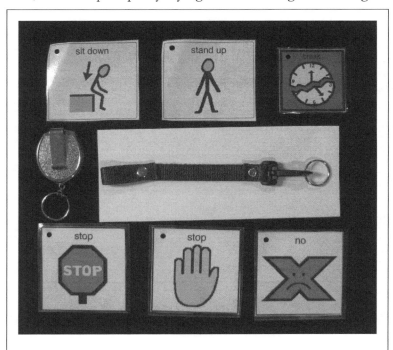

FIGURE 18. Visual symbols for teaching a child to mand for a break, an opportunity to sit or stand, to stop an activity, or to say no.

Additional points to consider when teaching a child to mand include:

- Typical children mand hundreds of times throughout their day. Teachers and parents need to create many, varied opportunities for the child to mand throughout the day. For example, give only a very small portion of a child's snack to her and then provide the child with many more opportunities to mand for the rest of her snack. Add a drink and the number of opportunities to mand increase greatly.

- It is important to watch children and look for language opportunities throughout the day. Often these opportunities are missed because the adult is anticipating and meeting the needs of children before they ask. If language opportunities do not occur, create them. For example, give a child a cup without any liquid in it or give a child scissors but no paper to cut (or paper, but no crayons).

- The adult needs to keep data on the mands a child performs throughout the day, recording the number of mands and the prompt levels on a data collection sheet.

- Start by making it easy for the child to mand for desired items and then gradually increase the difficulty. The goal is to get the best quality mand with the least amount of prompting.

Selecting First Mands

When determining what words or signs to teach as mands to a child, the following points should be considered (Sundberg & Partington, 1998):

- Select words that represent items or activities that are known reinforcers to the child: those that are consumable, last a short time (e.g., bubbles, tickles), easily removed, easy to deliver, able to deliver on multiple occasions (e.g., sips of juice), and always seem strong.

- Select words familiar to the child (i.e., the child looks toward the place where cereal is kept when he or she hears the word cereal).

- Consider words that are easy to say (e.g., eat vs. shoe), words a child is already echoing (e.g., "eee" can be shaped into "eat"), or signs that are iconic (e.g., the open hands that represents the sign "book" look like a book).

- The words selected should be functional, meaningful, and found in the child's everyday environment.

- Be sure to select a variety of words from different areas (i.e., not all edibles).

- Avoid selecting words that rhyme (e.g., cat/hat), or words that look alike when signed (e.g., eat/drink).
- Words that have a negative connotation for the child should be avoided.
- To avoid overgeneralization, work on 3–5 mands at a time.
- Avoid words that represent an abstract concept, like "more" or "please."
- Mand for an actual item in sight, then eventually fade it out of sight. For example, the child might learn to mand for ice cream, but eventually the ice cream is out of sight (in the freezer).

Mand Training: Moving From Beginning to Advanced Mands

Carbone (2002) described the following general scope and sequence of mand training:

First level: Teach the child how to mand, using one word, for desired items, activities, and actions. The items should be present. (This step consists of part mand/part labeling.)

Second level: Teach the child how to mand for desired items when the items are not present.

Third level: Teach the child how to mand for others to perform an action (e.g., "Turn it on" or "Move.").

Fourth level: Introduce using a carrier phrase (e.g., "I want _____ .") when manding.

Fifth level: Teach the child how to mand for others to stop an activity or to provide help.

Sixth level: Teach the child how to mand for another person's attention.

Seventh level: Teach the child how to mand for information.

Eighth level: Teach the child how to mand for future events.

Ninth level: Teach the child how to mand using adjectives, prepositions, adverbs, and pronouns.

Tenth level: The child acquires mands without intensive teaching.

Picture Exchange Communication System (PECS)

The Picture Exchange Communication System (PECS) is a way to teach children with limited speech abilities to communicate (Bondy & Frost, 2001). It was designed for children who are nonverbal or who have ineffective speech-language communication skills.

PECS instruction begins by teaching the child to present a visual symbol for a desired item or activity to a communication partner. The visual symbol actually is given (not just shown) to the partner in exchange for the item or activity. An adult or capable peer uses physical prompting, shaping, and fading procedures to ensure that the child approaches the partner and presents the picture. It is important for the helper to be behind the child so as not to interfere with the communication between the child and the communication partner. The helper should not use verbal prompting to decrease the chances of developing prompt dependence. Verbal prompts are harder to fade and can cause the child to wait for the verbal prompt instead of initiating communication. Upon receiving the picture, the communication partner should respond immediately to the request. Once this step is mastered, the child advances to the next phases of the system, which includes learning to discriminate among symbols and then putting symbols together in simple sentences such as "I want bouncing." In the advanced stages of PECS, the child responds to questions. The final phase of the six phases teaches the individual to respond to a question and to make a comment.

Some parents worry that the introduction of a communication system other than speech will interfere with the child's development of speech. However, research demonstrates that implementation of PECS enhances the child's language development by, in some cases, increasing vocabulary and spontaneous communications (Ganz & Simpson, 2004; Schwartz, Garfinkle, & Bauer, 1998).

The following steps describe the process of using PECS:

Step 1: Find motivating items and activities and create visual symbols or pictures for several. Arrange the environment so that one adult (Adult 1) has control of these reinforcing items. Initially, the other adult (Adult 2) has control of the visual symbol, but as soon as possible, the visual symbol should be made available to the child at all times that communication is possible. To begin instruction, let Adult 2 stand behind the child. Adult 1 should attempt to interest the child in an item or activity. As soon as the child reaches toward the item, Adult 2 should silently and physically guide the child to hand the visual symbol to Adult 1 who immediately takes the card and provides the item or activity, saying, "You want _____." As soon as possible, Adult 2 should fade out so that the child initiates communication independently. It is important to make sure that the adults do not initiate the interaction with questions such as, "What do you want?" or directions such as, "Tell me what you want." The goal is for the child to initiate the interaction.

Step 2: Move the items and activities further away from the child so that the child must come over to the adult to exchange the card. Expand the child's vocabulary and provide training in different places and with different people. At this point, keep just one symbol at a time available to the child.

Step 3: Start requiring the child to discriminate among multiple symbols when requesting an item. In the beginning, it is OK to ask, "What do you want?" and direct the child to an array of symbols. However, as soon as possible, the question should be faded so the child is responsible for initiating the communication (see Figure 19).

FIGURE 19. A speech-language pathologist waits for a student to initiate a picture exchange.

Step 4: Teach the child to put several symbols together, starting with an "I want" symbol. This symbol should be combined with an item and they should be put on a sentence strip. This often is a plastic or laminated cardboard rectangle with Velcro® (the picture cards have the corresponding Velcro® piece). The child places the symbols on the strip and hands the entire strip to the communication partner.

Step 5: Add vocabulary words and teach the child to use the sentence strips to make longer requests. For example, the child might create a sentence strip that says, "I want the red ball." To create a need for longer sentences, it is a good idea to play games that need several colored balls or puzzles pieces, requiring the child to request one ball or piece at a time.

Step 6: Teach the child to comment by responding to questions such as, "What do you hear?" or "What do you see?" Teach children to use their expanding vocabulary to point out interesting information to adults. It's a good idea to place new and noticeable items in the room, enticing the child to communicate about them with others.

Using Direct Instruction for More Advanced Language

Direct instruction also can be used to teach more advanced language skills. Gather the material for your lesson and arrange for a group of children to be seated in a circle or around a table (see Figure 20). Prepare to provide social praise and/or tokens for food, activities, or privileges. The following examples show how direct instruction can be used to teach more advanced language concepts:

Using Past Tense

> **Teacher:** Watch me! (Teacher starts to drink from a cup.) I'm about to drink from a cup. What am I about to do?
> **Students:** Drink from a cup.
> **Teacher:** Super! Now watch! (Teacher takes a drink.) What did I just do?
> **Students:** You drinked from the cup.
> **Teacher:** I drank from the cup. What did I just do?
> **Students:** You drank from the cup.
> **Teacher:** You're right! I drank from the cup!

Identifying Emotions

> **Teacher:** Look at this picture of a person who's sad. How is this person feeling?
> **Students:** Sad
> **Teacher:** Right! Here's a person who's feeling happy. How is this person feeling?
> **Students:** Happy
> **Teacher:** Correct! How is this person feeling?
> **Students:** Sad
> **Teacher:** Perfect! How is this person feeling?
> **Students:** Happy

Teacher: Excellent! Look at the picture of the person who's sad. Josh, how do you know the person is feeling sad?

Josh: She looks sad.

Teacher: Right, she looks sad because she's crying. How do you know the person is feeling sad? Because she's crying. Josh, how do you know she's sad?

Josh: Because she's crying.

Teacher: Great, Josh! James, how do you know she's sad?

James: Because she's crying.

Teacher: Good answer! We know she's sad because she's crying. James, why do you think she's crying?

James: Because she's crying.

Teacher: Look at the picture. Her toy is broken. She's sad because her toy is broken. And, we can see that she's sad because she's crying. Why is she crying?

James: Her toy is broken.

Teacher: That's right, James! She's crying because her toy is broken.

FIGURE 20. A direct instruction lesson with a circle of students.

In the above examples, the teacher teaches specific answers to specific questions. In each case, the teacher should remain on one or two questions until the students can answer the questions correctly and independently. A good time to add new questions is when a student can independently answer a question correctly the first time it is asked that day, for 3 days in a row. Correct answers that are prompted, or that follow another student's correct answer, should not count toward mastery.

When a skill is mastered, new targets can be added. In the first case, the teacher might aim to teach a set of 10 irregular past tense verbs. In the second case, the teacher might teach a set of 5 emotions, asking the students to identify the emotion depicted in the picture and answer questions such as, "How do you know she's _____?" and "Why is he _____?"

Once students learn the correct responses to a given set of questions or instructions, they should be given opportunities to apply their knowledge in new, untaught situations, adding to their mastery of concepts (see Figure 21). So, for example, after learning responses to 10 pairs of opposites, the teacher should probe with a question such as, "What's the opposite of night?" In a direct instruction approach, we teach by example and we hope that in teaching the multiple exemplars, students will be able to generalize this information to new situations. In working with students with autism, it is possible that some will need more examples than other students as they might have a tendency to undergeneralize. However, it is possible they might overgeneralize as well. One reason for teaching irregular past tense verbs is to prevent the overgeneralization that often occurs when children add "ed" to all verbs, saying things like "swimmed" and "runned."

Figure 21. With direct instruction, an advanced learner can add several new targets to a set of mastered cards.

All of the above examples should be conducted at a brisk pace. Students should have the opportunity to respond very frequently, perhaps as many as 10 to 15 times a minute. Unison or choral responding makes it realistic to have a response rate this high and clear signals (that provide a cue for individual or group responses) prevent lengthy teacher explanations from slowing down the pace. Teaching to mastery (ensuring correct responding over time) and brief error corrections also help keep the pace quick.

CHARACTERISTIC 2: DEFICITS IN THE AREA OF SOCIAL SKILLS AND CHALLENGES MAKING AND MAINTAINING MEANINGFUL RELATIONSHIPS

The tools discussed in this section will address the second characteristic of ASD, the deficits in social skills that lead to challenges in developing and maintaining relationships. We'll look at the following methods for addressing this characteristic in the classroom:

- script fading,
- joint action routines,
- Skillstreaming, and
- interactive instruction.

Script Fading

Krantz and McClannahan (1993, 1998) developed a procedure called script fading to help children with diagnoses of ASD to communicate more effectively. A script is an audiotaped or written word, phrase, or sentence used to prompt children to interact with one another. Children who were provided specific instruction in learning to use scripts to interact continued to use their scripts and even improved their interactions, increasing their verbalizations and generalizing their skills to different activities and different people (Krantz & McClannahan, 1998).

Using Script Fading With Younger Children

Use the following steps to fade scripts with younger children with autism in your classroom:

Step 1: For early learners, pair scripts with desired objects or activities. An adult or capable peer provides physical prompting to help the child use the script. This might include orienting the child toward the communication partner and then helping the child run a card through a card reader or push a button with a prerecorded message. Or, it might be a prompt to help the child pick up the picture or word and say it. The script might be "I like popcorn" or "My favorite puppet is Elmo."

Step 2: The communication partner responds with a response that acknowledges and supports the conversation, such as, "Popcorn tastes great!" or "Elmo's friend, Dorothy, is a fish!" It is important to make sure the responses are related to the topic, but are not praise specific as in other behavioral interventions. Examples of phrases that don't encourage conversation are responses such as, "Good talking" or "That's a good sentence." To encourage conversation, it is more effective to rely on more natural responses that the child might experience with typical peers.

Step 3: After the child is able to use several scripts, a gradual script-fading process begins. To start, the last word of the script is removed and the child using the script supplies the last word independently. Once the child is able to complete the script without the last word, the next to the last word is removed. This process continues until the script is entirely faded. After scripts have been introduced and faded, many children learn to spontaneously initiate social interaction.

Step 4: Once the child is communicating with a partner sitting near the preferred objects, scripts should be developed for some favorite activities. For example, scripts could be prepared for a few favorite activities such as, "I like puzzles," or "I'm going to swing." The scripts can be placed near the activities. To start instruction, the helping adult or peer provides minimal physical prompting for the child to read the script, orient toward the communication partner, and make the comment. Once again, it is important for the communication partner to respond with appropriate comments in a natural, conversational tone. Perhaps comments such as, "You're very good at doing puzzles" or "I love to watch you swing" would be appropriate. Scripts also can include questions such as, "What else do you like?" or "Are you going to swing fast or slow?"

Using Script Fading With Older Children

The following steps show how to use script fading to teach social interaction between two or more older children who are participating in a fun activity.

Step 1: Plan an activity for two students such as decorating cookies. Write the scripts on paper, punch holes in the left side of the paper, and put the pages in a notebook. Make two notebooks, one for each child.

Step 2: Set out the materials for the activity and seat participants so they are facing each other. Arrange the materials so that each child has all the materials necessary for one half of the task. For example, give one child all of the cookies and two plastic knives and give the other child icing of different colors and decorations.

Step 3: Prompt the children through reading the scripts and completing the activity in a sequence such as this:

> **Child 1:** Let's decorate cookies!
> **Child 2:** That will be fun.
> **Child 1:** May I have two cookies, please?
> **Child 2:** Sure—here are two cookies. I have two cookies, too!
> **Child 1:** Thanks! I'll start with blue icing. What color do you want?
> **Child 2:** I want yellow icing, please.
> **Child 1:** Here's your yellow icing.
> **Child 2:** Thanks.
> **Child 1:** May I have a knife, please?
> **Child 2:** Sure. I have a knife, too.
> **Child 1:** Look—I'm spreading on blue icing.
> **Child 2:** Cool! Look at mine—I'm spreading on yellow icing.
> **Child 1:** Awesome! I'm putting on sprinkles.
> **Child 2:** Awesome! I'm putting on sprinkles, too.
> **Child 1:** Let's eat our cookies.
> **Child 2:** OK!
> **Child 1:** Mine tastes great!
> **Child 2:** Mine is delicious, too!

Step 4: Use as few physical prompts as possible and provide no verbal prompts. Make sure all adults stay behind the children so as not to interfere with the social exchanges.

Joint Action Routines

Joint action routines (JARs; Snyder-McLean, Solomonson, McLean, & Sack, 1984) are predictable, logical sequences involving two or more people. The goal is to encourage communication skills, particularly spontaneous conversation related to the routines. To use JARs, set up a routine to be followed repeatedly over time. Provide frequent repetition of language related to the routine and prompt children to use the language themselves. To increase the probability that children will initiate communication, disrupt (or gently sabotage) the routine once it is well established.

When using Joint Action Routines to create social interaction, you may follow these steps:

Step 1: Decide on a meaningful, purposeful routine or activity that requires a shared experience between the children and the teacher and has well-defined, exchangeable roles. Determine the key vocabulary words and/or phrases related to the selected routine. For example, establish a routine for snacks that involves letting a child give each child a napkin, straw, cup, and cookie.

Step 2: Teach the routine. Practice the routine or activity regularly, focusing on the targeted vocabulary. Exchange roles in the routine, letting different children hand out the items. Teach all of the children to say "thank you" when receiving an item. Repetition of the routine will assist children in learning the predictable sequence of the routine.

Step 3: Narrate the routine while the actions are happening. Say things such as, "Adam is giving out the napkins" or "Jenny is giving each person a straw." Provide natural language, but include as much repetition as possible. For example, it is possible to repeat essentially the same phrase at three different points in the activity. "Shelley is going to give each person a cookie," then "Shelley is giving each person a cookie," and last, "Thanks, Shelley, for giving each person a cookie."

Step 4: Once the routine is learned, vary it by leaving out necessary materials, using new materials, or using the materials in a different way. If necessary, prompt communication until spontaneous language develops. Some examples include:
* Announcing that Isaiah will be giving out straws, but give him an empty container.

- Ask Chad to hand out cookies, but give him a bag of carrots instead.
- Pour juice in cups, leaving out two children.

Step 5: React positively to the communication attempts of the children. Wait for words if possible, however, provide minimal prompting if a child doesn't initiate communication. Respond immediately to their requests, admitting a mistake in an entertaining way. For example, say something like, "Oh, my goodness, how could I have forgotten you?" or "Oh no! Those aren't cookies—those are carrots! Where did I put those cookies?"

Step 6: Build routines around art projects, Circle Time activities, and daily routines. Once the routines are well established, gently sabotage the routines (see Figure 22). For example,
- Demonstrate a cut and paste activity and forget to hand out glue.
- Empty the silverware container in the lunch line.
- Give directions to line up for going outside when it's time for lunch.

FIGURE 22. Joint Action Routine sets the stage for language when the children are directed to clean up the table. Because there is only one jar, the children have to decide who will hold the jar and who will pick up the toys.

Skillstreaming

Skillstreaming (McGinnis & Goldstein, 1997) teaches children strategies to develop meaningful relationships with their peers, ways to solve problems that occur in their daily lives, and how to be proactive in dealing with situations that can cause them stress. To really make an impact, social skills lessons should be addressed three to five times weekly for 25 to 40 minutes per lesson. Younger children often need shorter lessons and older children benefit from longer lessons.

McGinnis and Goldstein (1997) recommended the program be taught in the child's natural setting whenever possible. This encourages children to provide feedback to each other and assist each other in applying newly learned skills. It cannot be assumed that what a child learns in one environment will automatically transfer to another environment. Teaching the skill where it will be used helps eliminate this problem.

It is recommended that teachers observe the child in a variety of settings to determine what social skills to work on and consult parents to find out their child's needs. Parents may not see the same behaviors as teachers (or vice-versa) and the children may see their own skills differently as compared to the views of the adults.

The Skillstreaming curriculum (McGinnis & Goldstein, 1997) utilizes four core teaching procedures to teach each social skill: modeling, role-playing, performance feedback, and transfer/generalization training. Each Skillstreaming lesson is presented in a nine-step format. The four core teaching procedures are incorporated into the nine steps listed below.

1. *Define the skill.* A brief definition of the skill to be taught is discussed with the group. Also introduced at this time are the behavioral steps that are applicable to this skill (i.e., for the skill of listening the behavioral steps are: look at the person who is talking, sit quietly, think about what is being said, say yes or nod your head, and ask a question about the topic to find out more).

2. *Model the skill.* The adults model the skill that was introduced. As the skill is being modeled, the teacher guides the children in a discussion to identify when each behavioral step is being modeled. The behavioral steps are listed on the chalkboard.

3. *Establish trainee skill need.* The children identify situations that relate to the current skill being taught.

4. *Select a role-play.* From the situations suggested by the children the teacher selects one to role-play.

5. *Set up the role-play.* The teacher sets up the role-play, assigning the children to their role. The remaining children in the group are assigned the task of determining if each of the behavioral steps was followed in the role-play. The teacher introduces the role-play by setting the "stage" (i.e., give a description of the physical setting, describing the events immediately preceding the role-play, the role of the coactor, and any

other pertinent information that would help make the role-play more realistic).

6. *Conduct the role-play.* The children conduct the role-play. As the role-play is unfolding, the teacher is guiding the child who is the main actor to apply the appropriate behavioral step. Children should think aloud about the behavioral steps being applied.

7. *Provide performance feedback.* Review the role-play by discussing each behavioral step for that skill and determining if the child did each step.

8. *Assign skill homework.* Individual homework assignments are made. For each child it is determined how the role-played skill will be acted out in a real-life setting.

9. *Select the next role-player.* The group moves on to the next role-play, still working on the same skill. Each skill is role-played until the group is successfully performing the skill in the group and out of the group.

Parent involvement is another reason the Skillstreaming intervention program is successful with children with ASD. Parents complete an assessment to help determine what skills will be addressed during the program. Parents also assist the children with transferring and generalizing the targeted skills learned in class through the homework component of the program. The homework forms, provided with the Skillstreaming curriculum (McGinnis & Goldstein, 1997) and filled out by the teacher, explain the targeted skill and the behavioral steps learned by the child to address that skill. The parents observe and prompt, as needed, the targeted skill being used in the home and community setting. The homework form is then signed and returned to school.

Interactive Instruction

Today's focus on inclusion provides many opportunities for children with ASD to interact with their peers who do not have disabilities. In general education classrooms, much of the instruction is interactive. Children work together, collaborating on projects in many subjects. Interactive instruction often is very motivating for children, yet can be a challenge for some children with ASD. This broadens educational experiences beyond the limitations of individual instruction and the knowledge, skills, and abilities of one individual teacher. However, the noise, confusion, and unpredictability of interactive classrooms can be overwhelming for children with ASD. Some children may need specific instruction to learn to cope in such situations.

Preparing children for interactive instruction includes preteaching brainstorming skills and rehearsing experiments or projects. It also is effective to use layered grouping to teach early learners to participate in group sessions and to make group instruction effective for everyone in the group.

Teach Brainstorming

Teach children to brainstorm individually (see Figure 23) and then with one or two other children. Choose topics that are of interest to the children and show them how to put their ideas in lists or graphic organizers (see Figure 24). Help them make appropriate comments to others and gradually increase the number of children in the group until the child can participate in the general education class.

FIGURE 23. A one-on-one session is ideal for practicing brainstorming individually before working in a small group or large class.

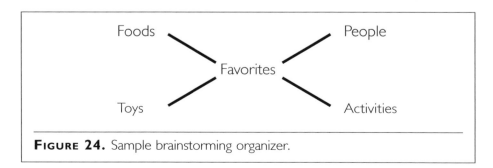

FIGURE 24. Sample brainstorming organizer.

Rehearse Experiments or Projects

Rehearse experiments or preteach specific skills before working in cooperative learning groups. Use lists of steps (pictures or words) to help children understand the routine and use social stories or cue cards (see the suggested techniques for Characteristic 8 later in this chapter) to help children understand some of the many irregular things that might happen. Introduce cooperative learning groups by starting with simple, structured activities and appropriate child role models before requiring high-level problem solving. Practice debating issues in groups of two or three before participating in full-class discussions.

Use Layered Grouping

Children who are not ready for interactive instruction may need explicit instruction in learning how to be a part of a group. Frequently, young children with autism experience their first group instruction in Circle Time activities in preschool. Circle Time activities usually include greetings, discussions of the day, and instruction in basic academic skills such as colors, shapes, numbers, letters, weather, days of the week, and months of the year. Music often is used to enhance instruction in these areas. Through such Circle Time activities, children have the opportunity to listen to and watch others, take turns and share, and answer questions.

Circle Time can be an opportunity to provide explicit teaching in social skills. However, sometimes the group activity is not appropriate for all of the children. The goal of the layered grouping strategy is to adjust the members of the group so developmentally appropriate instruction can be provided for each person in the group at the same time.

Start with basic activities that are appropriate for everyone in the group (e.g., doing motions to lively music, identifying the children's names). After this initial period, dismiss children for whom the upcoming activities are no longer appropriate (see Figure 25). Consider using a timer to indicate when it is time for the children to leave.

When this second activity is completed, dismiss more children and keep the last group for the most challenging or focused activities. Arrange for individual or small-group instruction for the children leaving the group. As children develop new skills, gradually lengthen their group instruction time. Teach children to do independent activities when they leave the group instruction.

FIGURE 25. A teacher uses layered grouping to differentiate instruction.

CHARACTERISTIC 3: DISPLAY OF STEREOTYPIC MOTOR MOVEMENTS AND/OR RITUALISTIC, ODD, OR INAPPROPRIATE BEHAVIORS

The tools discussed in this section will address the third characteristic of ASD, the presence of stereotypic movements and socially unacceptable behaviors. We'll look at the following methods for addressing this characteristic in the classroom:

- functional behavioral assessment,
- sensory activities,
- cue cards,
- quiet strategies, and
- wait programs.

Functional Behavior Assessment

A functional behavioral assessment (FBA) is a process for gathering information about the causes and possible interventions for problem behaviors (O'Neill et al., 1997). Direct assessment consists of actually observing the problem behavior and describing the conditions that surround the behavior (its context). This context includes events that are antecedent (i.e., that occur before the behavior) and consequent (i.e., that occur after the behavior) to the behaviors of interest. Multiple measures of behavior and its social and environmental contexts usually produce more accurate information than a single measure. This especially is true if the problem behavior serves several functions or purposes that may vary according to circumstance.

It is important to pay as much attention to the function (purpose) of the behavior as to the form of the behavior. Once the function of a behavior is determined, socially acceptable behaviors can be taught that are functionally equivalent and more efficient for the child than the challenging behavior.

Chapter 7 includes an example of an FBA, along with an example of a positive behavior support plan based on information gathered during the FBA process.

Conducting a Functional Behavior Assessment

The following steps should be used when conducting an FBA:

Step 1: To investigate the "function" (purpose) of behaviors, consider the following question (Durand, 1990; Paul, 1967): "Why is this person engaging in this behavior at this time, in this setting, with these people?"

Step 2: Collect information about the behavior such as:
* What is the behavior? What does it look or sound like?
* When does the behavior happen?
* What happens before the behavior?
* What happens after the behavior?
* Where does the behavior happen?
* Consider collecting data in one or more of the following ways:
    * Determine the rate at which the behavior occurs. For example, does it occur one time per day, six times per hour, or 30 times per week?
    * Measure the duration of the behavior. For example, does the behavior last a few seconds, 2 minutes, or 20 minutes?
    * Judge the intensity of the behavior, perhaps on a scale of 1 to 5. For example, how loud is the behavior, how upset is the child, or how hard is the child hitting?
    * Assess the latency of the behavior. For example, how long does it take for the child to respond to a command, instruction, direction, or question?

Step 3: Determine whether the answers to the questions in Step 2 indicate that the behavior is occurring to:
* gain attention,
* obtain something,
* obtain desired sensory input,
* avoid attention,
* avoid something, or
* avoid unwanted sensory input.

Step 4: Write down a hypothesis regarding the function and summarize the data collected. Then, create a baseline, documenting the behavior in terms of its rate, duration, latency, and/or intensity (see Step 2).

Step 5: Conduct a functional analysis (if necessary) to check the validity of the hypothesis. A functional analysis is the part of the functional assessment process that involves manipulating variables to see if the hypothesis is correct. For example, if the hypothesis was that the child is avoiding work because it is too difficult, provide easier work to see if the child stops engaging in avoidance behaviors.

Step 6: Once the function is identified, use the many strategies in this book to aim for more appropriate replacement behaviors that achieve the same function. These strategies can be incorporated into a positive behavior support plan to help teach children to:

- gain attention in an appropriate way,
- obtain something by asking for an object or activity,
- avoid something by protesting politely or requesting a break, and
- request sensory activities or communicate discomfort or pain.

Sensory Activities

As behaviorists, we can observe the relationship of sensory activities and the behavior of children. For some children, it is effective for them to engage in several sensory activities (e.g., running, bouncing, swinging) before starting on work that requires concentration and focus. For some of these children, their energy level is raised from lethargic to more focused. For others, their energy level is decreased from overstimulated to focused. When children can increase their productivity by such activities, it makes sense to schedule them before challenging instructional sessions as antecedents to working.

At other times, and for other children, such activities seem to create too much energy and decrease focus. For these children, such exciting, fun activities might better be used as positive consequences. It makes sense to use these activities as reinforcers if it motivates children in challenging sessions.

Multisensory instruction teaching uses sight, sound, touch, and movement to help children learn. Combining kinesthetic experiences with activities that involve listening, watching, and doing often help children remember things they would otherwise forget.

Some examples of using multisensory instruction include using:

* games to teach children to imitate, follow directions, and take turns;
* dramatic skits or plays to teach using manners or solving problems appropriately;
* dancing to teach following directions or taking turns (see Figure 26);
* marching or skipping to teach counting sequences or math facts;
* obstacle courses with signs to learn the concepts of left and right, over and under, up and down;
* hands-on demonstrations or science experiments to help children grasp, internalize, and maintain abstract information; and
* actions and objects (rather than pictures), to help children learn language. For example, rather than using pictures, teach open and close with a door or box and teach prepositions (e.g., over, under, through) with an obstacle course.

FIGURE 26. The use of kinesthetic teaching in a classroom.

Cue Cards

Cue cards are words and pictures that provide visual supports to help children understand and remember things about social situations (see Figure 27). These "cues" are usually easier for the learner to remember than auditory information. They are less intrusive than verbal assistance or prompts.

FIGURE 27. An example of cue cards.

Some children cannot process verbal messages well when they are upset. When stress is high, cue cards can provide a simple message that clarifies a solution to a problem. A visual reminder, especially one with a picture or symbol, often can communicate more than many spoken words.

Cue cards can help children:

- remember what to do and not do for a particular task or activity (see Figure 28)
- see what an expected behavior looks like and sounds like,
- see the relationship of ideas or variations of meaning,
- see the relationship of behaviors to consequences (see Figure 29),
- recall a word or phrase to use in social interactions,

FIGURE 28. Cue card showing dos and don'ts of a situation.

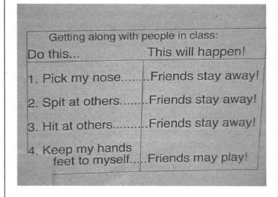

FIGURE 29. Cue card showing how behaviors relate to consequences.

- recall a new or difficult step or skill to complete a routine or solve a problem,
- support choice and decision making, and
- transition from one location to another.

Steps for using cue cards include the following:

Step 1: Identify a situation. For example, consider the case of a child who has difficulty making transitions from the classroom setting to other locations.

Step 2: Create a cue card notebook of 3" by 5" index cards describing what each setting would look and sound like. Here's an example:

Going to the Cafeteria for Lunch

Cafeteria looks like:
Many children sitting at tables
Adults walking around
People eating their lunch

Cafeteria sounds like:
Many people talking
Adults giving directions
People laughing and joking

Step 3: Review the cue card and rehearse the transition, perhaps providing reinforcers for making the transitions smoothly and calmly.

Step 4: Add additional cue cards for transitions to music, art, PE, and other activities.

Step 5: Develop cards for the family such as "Being Safe in the Car," "Sitting at the Table for Dinner," and "Getting Ready for Bed."

Quiet Programs

Once children with ASD learn to talk, it can be a challenge for them to learn when it is appropriate to talk and when to be quiet. Also, for some children, it is difficult to learn to use a voice volume that is appropriate for the situation.

Quiet programs use visual supports such as charts, scales, quiet tokens, and timers to teach children either to refrain from talking or to use a quiet voice in certain situations. Steps for using a quiet program include:

Step 1: Make a simple chart on paper with three boxes and a place for a reinforcer symbol. A more permanent quiet chart can be easily made by attaching Velcro® spots to a laminated card. The tokens are smaller laminated cards with happy faces or quiet symbols (see Figure 30).

FIGURE 30. A visual example of a quiet program with the token for completing the program.

Step 2: Set up a practice session by bringing the chart, reinforcers, and a digital timer to the table. Start with a small amount of food as a reinforcer in order to provide several trials at a time.

Step 3: Fill in two of the three spaces with a token. Ask the child to sit and show the child the chart and the reinforcer.

Step 4: Set the timer for 3 seconds, hold up your hand and say, "Quiet." As soon as the timer goes off, put in the last token and provide the reinforcer if the child was quiet. If the child wasn't quiet, say, "Try again, quiet."

Step 5: Provide several trials in many short sessions throughout the day. When the child is consistently remaining quiet, gradually lengthen the time.

Step 6: Begin starting sessions with only one token in place, requiring the child to stay quiet for two periods before getting the reinforcer. For example, set the timer for 6 seconds and put a token down after 3 seconds. When the timer beeps, put down the last token and provide the reinforcer. Be sure to say, "Quiet" only once when trying to extend the time.

Step 7: Start providing three tokens as the wait time lengthens. This gives the child encouragement along the way. Once the child is able to stay quiet for 15 seconds (with a token every 5 seconds), start practicing the quiet program in other settings and situations.

Another example of a quiet program, to teach children to use an appropriate voice volume, uses a chart and a visual volume scale to demonstrate "too loud," "too soft," and "just right" (see Figure 31). Teachers should rehearse "too loud," "too soft," and "just right" with the child, providing tokens when the child reaches the appropriate quiet voice.

FIGURE 31. An autism consultant teaching a quiet program using a visual volume chart.

In both sample quiet programs, teachers will want to do the following:
* allow the child to exchange the tokens for meaningful rewards;
* slowly increase the time the child is required to remain quiet;
* provide practice in a variety of situations, and
* gradually fade the chart, using only a sign, gesture, quiet symbol, or cue card.

Wait Strategies
Children with autism may have difficulty responding appropriately to directions such as, "Wait a minute," or "It's not time yet." These children might need a specific, systematic instructional program in learning to wait. Because

time is an abstract concept, it is useful to provide visual supports to clarify our expectations.

When provided with systematic instruction, children can learn to wait for several minutes, even during situations where the need to wait wasn't anticipated. Look for opportunities to teach waiting during activities such as walking down the hall, sitting in class, ordering in a restaurant, preparing for lunch, or taking turns with a toy. Use the following steps to teach children the skill of waiting:

Step 1: Hand the child a visual symbol of "Wait" when the command is given (see Figure 32).

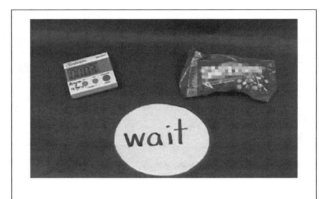

FIGURE 32. A wait symbol.

Step 2: Wait for a short period, perhaps 3 seconds in the beginning.

Step 3: Take the "Wait" card back, saying, "nice waiting" and simultaneously provide the reinforcing item or activity.

Step 4: Gradually increase the time the child is required to wait.

Step 5: Practice the waiting program in many environments with many people.

For activities that require waiting, teachers can use simple charts to provide visual and verbal feedback during the wait period. Figure 33 shows a chart to help a child sit during the morning announcements. After waiting for the required period, the child is given a reinforcer, perhaps a healthy food along with social praise. Eventually, the schedule of reinforcement can be thinned and the reinforcer can become social praise.

FIGURE 33. A waiting chart.

Use another wait strategy for children who process language slowly. Instruct children to think about their answers (or even write them down) before responding to questions. This wait time improves the quality of the answers of all children. Rowe (1972) discovered that short periods of silence following a teacher's question improved student responses. The use of even a 3-second period of wait time during instruction was found to increase the length and complexity of responses and decrease the number of "I don't know" responses. To use this strategy with children who have ASD, practice counting to 3 or 5 after giving an instruction or asking a question. In some cases, wait even longer, especially if the child shows signs of thinking or concentrating.

CHARACTERISTIC 4: PREFERENCE FOR ROUTINE AND ANXIETY ABOUT CHANGE

The tools discussed in this section will address the fourth characteristic of ASD, the need for routine and the anxiety many children experience when routines are changed. We'll look at the following methods for addressing this characteristic in the classroom:

- schedules,
- "OOPS!" strategies,

- choices, and
- yes management.

Schedules

Schedules make the day predictable, help with transitions, and assist in helping children understand upcoming, otherwise surprising events. Even regular, everyday events can seem surprising to some children with ASD and seeing a schedule can help them see patterns and organize their thinking. Schedules also increase independence by allowing children to use schedules on their own to accomplish tasks and make transitions. Schedules should be thought of as lifelong supports for children with ASD.

The best schedules for children with ASD are ones that are created to serve as clear, visual representations of the activities for a certain time period. For some children, a written list of words describing activities can be provided. For others, objects, photographs, line drawings, or symbols might be needed.

To create a schedule:

Step 1: Consider the purpose of the schedule and whether it is for a class or an individual. It might be:
- a monthly calendar,
- a daily class schedule (see Figure 34),
- an individual child schedule (see Figure 35),
- a mini-schedule for parts of the day (see Figure 36), or
- an activity schedule for sequencing tasks.

FIGURE 34. Daily class schedule.

Step 2: Determine the format for the schedule. It might be:
- created with objects, photographs, line drawings symbols, and/or printed words (see Figure 37 for an object schedule);
- arranged horizontally or vertically; and

Sam's Schedule:
☐ Earlybird
☐ Math
☐ English
☐ Break
☐ Computer Lab
☐ Lunch

FIGURE 35. Individual student schedule.

FIGURE 36. Mini-schedule for part of the day.

displayed, using a blackboard or poster on the wall, card taped to a desk or tucked in a wallet, or file folder or notebook with the schedule attached.

Step 3: Rehearse the schedule with the child. If necessary, follow the steps below to teach an early learner to use a schedule (see Figure 38).

* Place pictures on the actual object, activity, or location addressed in the schedule.
* Put identical pictures on the child's schedule, arranging them vertically or horizontally.
* Guide the child to pull the first picture off the schedule and take it to the matching picture. Spend a short amount of time in that activity.
* Direct the child to pull off the next picture and find that activity by locating the corresponding picture.

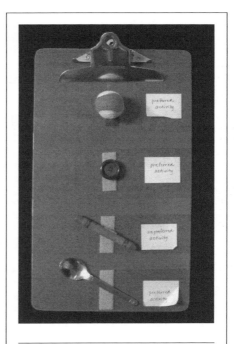

FIGURE 37. An object schedule.

FIGURE 38. A picture schedule.

- Rehearse small segments of the schedule and gradually fade the prompts. Be sure to stand behind the child, using physical prompts as necessary. It is easier to fade out physical prompts than verbal prompts.

"OOPS!" Strategies

Children with ASD often have difficulty accepting changes in their established routines. The schedules we mentioned above actually can contribute to that difficulty in that it creates an even greater expectation that things will happen as they are written.

"OOPS!" strategies offer children a predictable way to deal with uncertainty by providing visual support to help explain change. It can be used to develop a routine for accepting change. Steps for using "OOPS!" strategies in the classroom include:

Step 1: Develop routines for the children by regularly using visuals to make the day organized and predictable.

Step 2: Review the routines frequently and teach children to check their schedules often throughout the day.

Step 3: Vary the activities daily so children rely on their schedules to tell them what comes next.

Step 4: Begin to introduce unexpected events by putting "OOPS!" next to the activity and substituting an alternate activity. When scheduled events or activities need to be changed, put "OOPS!" next to the activity and write down what will happen instead (see Figure 39). Depending on the needs of the child, it might be possible to cross out a word or draw a "no" sign over the activity.

FIGURE 39. An example of the "OOPS!" strategy.

Another way to use the "OOPS!" strategy is to use it to help children deal with making mistakes. Some children with ASD get extremely upset when they make errors and do not handle correction well. Use the "OOPS!" strategy by saying or writing "OOPS!" when a child says, does, or writes something wrong. Then, provide suggestions for something better to say, do, or write and, in some cases, explain why. Casual, but consistent, use of this strategy can help children accept their mistakes and become accustomed to accepting constructive feedback.

Choices

In our work, we have noticed that children with ASD who experience little control over their lives can have challenging behaviors. In an analysis of 13 studies, Shogren, Faggella-Luby, Bae, and Wehmeyer (2004) found that the opportunity to make choices has been shown to decrease problem behaviors.

Children with ASD, particularly those who participate in programs characterized by DTT and direct instruction, may have few opportunities to make choices. In some cases, these children may act out their frustrations with lethargic responses. In other cases, children may respond with noncompliant or defiant behaviors.

Also, when children are suddenly presented with too many choices, they seem overwhelmed and unable to choose. This may develop from a lack of experience making choices.

It is important to begin providing choices early. Teaching young children to make choices can help children feel a sense of control over their lives. Helping them make good choices at a young age can set the stage for them to make good decisions about more important choices as they grow older.

A choice board or choice display can provide a visual representation of the choice possibilities. These displays can offer two, three, or more choices and can be presented with objects, photographs, line drawings, symbols, or words. As with other visual supports, choice boards are nontransient and can be effective in giving the child with autism an extended opportunity to respond. When presented with words, the message is over in a few seconds. Providing the visual stimulus allows children to consider their choices for longer periods of time.

Once children are accustomed to making choices, they may be able to make decisions without visual supports. However, some children with ASD will always need to see their options and have extended time to make their decisions.

Yes Management

Because many children with ASD have anxiety about changes to their routines, it is a good idea to use ideas from yes management strategies. These strategies start with the idea of keeping the classroom atmosphere as positive as possible by saying "yes" as often as you can. This in itself can reduce anxiety.

Children with challenging behaviors may hear negative words such as "no" and "don't" quite often. Even though it might be for their safety, their day can be filled with "Don't do that!", "Stop that!", or "No climbing!" They also are often told "no" in response to requests such as, "Can I have a cookie?" or "Can I go outside?" It's not surprising that some children with ASD then say "no" when they are asked to participate in an activity of our choice.

Of course, it's not possible to say "yes" to everything. And children do need to learn to accept no answers. But, to keep a high rate of positive interactions, teachers should frequently take the opportunity to try a qualified yes answer instead of a no. For example, try the yes answer below, instead of the no answer, when presented with the question, "Can we have lunch?"

No answer: "No, we can't have lunch until we've finished."

Yes answer: "Yes, we can go to lunch as soon as we've completed our work."

When it's not possible to say yes, try to find a way to make a positive statement. For example:

Question: "Can we cross the street to go to the playground?"
Negative answer: "No, it's not safe."
Positive answer: "We can if we walk to the end of the block and cross at the light."

Saying "no" doesn't tell children what to do. It's more effective to state rules or give directions positively, for example:

* "Walk down the halls." (Rather than "Don't run.")
* "Sit down so we can work." (Rather than "Stop jumping around.")

We so often get in the habit of thinking no. Before saying no, we should ask ourselves, "why not?" If there's a good reason to say no, then of course, we must.

CHARACTERISTIC 5: FOCUS ON SPECIFIC, SOMETIMES IRRELEVANT DETAILS, LEADING TO UNDERGENERALIZATION, OVERGENERALIZATION, AND/OR LACK OF UNDERSTANDING

The tools discussed in this section will address the fifth characteristic of ASD, overgeneralizing and undergeneralizing of information. We'll look at the following methods for addressing this characteristic in the classroom:

* activity-based instruction,
* incidental teaching,
* pivotal response training, and
* direct instruction.

Naturalistic teaching methods can be useful in teaching children to use their skills in a variety of situations as they often start instruction with varied materials, settings, and people. This is referred to as training loosely because these methods begin by providing instruction on multiple skills in the context of many different high-interest activities. When children are successful in learning with these strategies, it usually is because they have learned (or are learning) to respond appropriately to multiple cues and they can attend to several components of a complex stimulus. For some children, it's best to begin their instruction this way and for naturalistic teaching methods to be their primary intervention.

Controlled presentations also can be used to help children generalize. These methods start by training tightly—teaching one skill in one set of circumstances. Then, through a series of systematically introducing variations in materials, settings, or people, the child eventually generalizes the skill to other situations. This is especially useful for children who are confused by multiple cues and complex stimuli. Controlled presentations can be particularly helpful in teaching children who overgeneralize. These methods specialize in discrimination training, that is, teaching a child to act a certain way in one set of circumstances, but not in another. Specific discrimination training can help children identify situations where it is not appropriate to use a skill they have been taught.

Remember, when planning for generalization:

*   To train loosely, teach in different situations, with different materials, with different people, and varied instructions. With this strategy, children are like to be able to generalize more easily.
*   To train tightly, teach in one situation, with consistency in materials, instructions, and people. With this approach, the skills are acquired more quickly yet generalization may take longer.

Activity-Based Instruction

Bricker and Cripe (1992) described activity-based instruction (ABI) as the process of embedding training and intervention in routine, planned, and child-directed activities. ABI assumes that the adult *must* be an active participant in the learning process and that the children do not learn just by playing. Many children with autism may require more instructional support during traditional child-directed activities (Schwartz, Billingsley, & McBride, 1998).

ABI's systematic use of appropriate antecedents and consequences helps children learn to respond to multiple and complex stimuli. Materials, teaching strategies, and prompts are presented to children in naturally occurring contexts. Usually these are very busy environments. Consequences are the logical and natural, rather than contrived or artificial, outcome of the activities. Thus, children who learn effectively with ABI often develop good abilities to generalize their skills to other environments. Steps for using ABI include:

Step 1: Choose activities that:

- can address several objectives for several children. For example, an art project could address the following objectives: answering questions, identifying pictures and actions, requesting materials, sequencing events, and identifying colors.
- can address different goals for the same child. For example, a snack time activity could address fine motor objectives (opening containers), language objectives (requesting, commenting) cognitive skills (empty/full, first/next/last), and self-help objectives (taking one bite at a time).
- can be adapted for various ages and skill levels. For example, a Mr. Potato Head® activity can be used with some children to identify body parts and for other children to put the pieces in place.
- involve minimal adult direction and assistance. For example, an activity involving bathing dolls may require lots of props but minimal direction after the activity begins.
- provide many opportunities for children to initiate. For example, an activity of singing "Up, up, and away" could be arranged for the child to say the name of a peer and then pass a balloon to that peer, thus providing multiple opportunities for children to initiate interactions.
- are motivating and interesting. Children will become more actively engaged in activities that are fun.

Step 2: Develop routines for the activities and use them regularly. For example, a morning might be set up in the following order:

- Singing session with the balloon
- Play time with the dolls or Mr. Potato Head®
- Story time
- Art activity
- Snack time

Provide enough practice in these activities so that children become familiar with them and make significant improvements in their skills.

Step 3: Introduce variations to keep interest and motivation high. For example, add a second song that involves calling a child's name and passing a different object.

Step 4: Create opportunities for children to use the skills from their play sessions in other environments at school and at home. Provide notes on the child's objectives for other teachers and parents to read. These notes can help other adults provide opportunities for the child to demonstrate these newly mastered skills.

Incidental Teaching

Incidental teaching (IT) is a naturalistic strategy for promoting children's communication skills through interactions that are designed to shape child initiations. Incidental teaching uses naturally occurring opportunities for instruction throughout the student's day (Cavallaro, 1983). Similar to ABI, IT often is implemented in busy environments, requiring children to respond to many complex cues. However, in the early stages of learning, IT can be used to work with individual children who are provided with a limited number of high-interest materials. In our experiences, IT can be used effectively to help children generalize their requesting or manding skills. Steps for using IT include:

Step 1: Arrange the environment to encourage frequent child initiations by presenting novel or new materials, placing some preferred toys in view but out of reach, providing some materials for which the child may need help, and providing materials with missing parts.

Step 2: Engage the child in interactions in which natural reinforcers (interesting objects or persons) are contingent on certain behaviors.

Step 3: Be available to children and wait for their initiations. When the child reaches for something, gently block the attempt to take the object and wait for the child to verbalize. If child does not verbalize, use the following procedures developed by McGee, Daly, and Jacobs (1994) to shape initiations:
- Wait for child to initiate.
- If the child does not initiate, ask the generic question, "What do you want?" If the child still does not initiate, tell the child what is expected.
- If the child still does not initiate, make a gesture to show the child that an initiation is expected.
- If the child still does not initiate, prompt the child to complete interaction.

Step 4: Intervene (prompt, model, or rearrange the environment) to elicit more complex behaviors; provide supports so the child will elaborate in a manner that successively approximates the desired behavior.

Step 5: When a child initiates an interaction, the adult should:

- respond immediately to the child's initiation and then wait a few seconds for the child to produce a more elaborate or complex statement;
- consider asking for more elaborate language from the child by saying, "Tell me more," or "What about _____?" or a similar statement that would be understood by the child;
- if the child uses more elaborate language, praise him, expand his statement, and respond to the content of what he has asked; and
- if the child does not produce a more elaborate statement, provide a model of a more complex statement and look expectantly at him, indicating to him to imitate it. When he imitates it, respond to the content of the statement.

Step 6: Follow the child's lead (see Figure 40). Teaching occurs only when the child sustains interest in or communicates intentionally about an object that is related to the activity of the child's choice. The child needs to have varied objects and activities from which to choose.

FIGURE 40. An autism consultant following the child's lead.

Step 7: Provide several opportunities to teach language within the natural environment, using natural, logical consequences. This provides a way to promote generalization of skills to other settings because teaching occurs in contexts similar to typical communicative encounters (i.e., teaching a child to request food at snack times).

Step 8: Use reinforcers that are a direct link to the child's targeted behavior or language form. Acquisition of a behavior or a language form is more rapid when a child begins to understand the relationship between his or her language use and its consequences.

Step 9: Emphasize that communication requires active participants. This practice places emphasis on turn taking in conversations and on the idea that both the adult and the child are responsible for successful and meaningful communication. Both the adult and the child are active, dynamic participants.

Pivotal Response Training

Pivotal response training (PRT) helps children generalize because it focuses on skills central to functioning (Koegel & Koegel, 1999a). In PRT, the pivotal skills include responsivity to multiple cues, motivation to initiate, and self-direction of behavior. Koegel and Koegel (1999b) noted that improvements in pivotal behaviors led to improvements in other areas. They reported signs of improved motivation such as increases in the number of responses a child makes, decreases in delayed responding, and increases in interest, enthusiasm, or happiness.

The following steps will aid you in implementing and using PRT:

Step 1: Create opportunities for choice of activities. Design interventions around materials or topics for which the child expresses a preference. For example, use different-colored pieces of candy or colored goldfish-shaped crackers to teach color recognition rather than colored pieces of paper. To increase motivation, whenever possible, include choices in daily activities such as allowing the child to choose clothes by color. This, of course, also contributes to the child's ability to generalize skills to other materials and other settings.

Step 2: Use natural reinforcers. In PRT, the reward should flow naturally from the child's actions or verbalization. Koegel and Williams (1980) demonstrated that children acquired skills more rapidly when the task was directly related to the reinforcer. They compared the rate of skill acquisition between groups of children who opened a clear jar. When candy was inside the jar, children acquired the skill of opening the jar more quickly than those who received candy after opening an empty jar. Maintain control of the reinforcers. Hold onto the materials, place yourself between the child and the materials, or put the materials on a high shelf or in a box.

Step 3: Reinforce attempts. In PRT, approximations of the behavior and even vague attempts are rewarded. Other models of ABA clearly define expected behaviors that are reinforced. In these models, behaviors that do not meet the criteria are not rewarded because this can create dependence on adults and even learned helplessness (failure to respond unless prompted by an adult). The looser shaping process used in PRT increases the number of attempts the child makes, leading to more rapid learning.

Step 4: Wait for child initiations. Often, it is difficult for teachers and parents to wait for children to initiate communication attempts. It is tempting to prompt the child who has low levels of interaction with others. In the early stages, teachers and parents teach children to orient their bodies toward an adult or look at the adult to begin an interaction. In Figures 41–43, the teacher bounces a child on her lap and waits for him to look at her. Immediately after he looks, she bounces him vigorously on her lap and he laughs and smiles. After another waiting period, he looks in her direction and is bounced again. It is extremely important to wait for the child to initiate the interaction. Teachers and parents should refrain from saying "Look at me," or "Do you want more bouncing?" These kinds of directions and comments decrease the chances of getting independent initiations.

Step 5: In later stages, teach children to ask questions, make comments, and ask for help. For example, to increase question asking, create activities that stimulate curiosity such as shaking a closed box (with a treat or toy inside) in front of the child. If the child doesn't ask about it, reinforce the child for looking at the box by opening it and letting the child eat the treat or play with the toy. Narrate the activity with simple phrases like, "I wonder what's in the box." In future opportunities, use modeling and shaping to reward closer approximations to the skill of asking questions. To increase the chances of eliciting questions, add peer modeling as well. Create opportunities for children to ask questions such as, "What's that?" and "Where is it?"

PRT uses the same behavioral chain (Motivation-Antecedent-Behavior-Consequence) as DTT. However, in PRT, it is critical to follow the child's lead by building teaching sessions around activities that are of high interest to the child. Teachers and parents should provide opportunities for children to respond, however, the role of the adult is more to guide and facilitate than to direct.

FIGURE 41. An autism consultant waiting for eye contact.

FIGURE 42. Eye contact producing an immediate response.

FIGURE 43. The child's response immediately after being bounced, his reinforcer.

In PRT, it is important to create opportunities for the child to respond that:

- are related to the child's interest or choice of activity;
- are clear, uninterrupted and appropriate to the tasks;
- are interspersed with maintenance tasks; and
- include multiple components when appropriate.

PRT uses reinforcement directly related to the task, so reinforcers should be contingent upon behavior, administered following any reasonable attempt to respond, and related to the desired behavior in a direct way.

Direct Instruction

Direct instruction (di) can be used to help children learn to perform behaviors in some settings, but not in others. For example, Shannon laughs loudly whenever something funny happens on the playground. However, she laughs just as loudly in the classroom and this is disruptive to the instructional program. To help children determine whether or not their behaviors are appropriate for the setting, set up a program such as this:

Step 1: Identify the behavior and the circumstances in which the behavior would be appropriate and those in which it wouldn't.

Step 2: Take or find pictures of different environments, taking care to select several environments in which the behavior would be appropriate and several in which it wouldn't.

Step 3: Sit down with the child and describe the behavior. For example, it might be appropriate to say things such as, "On the playground, we can laugh loudly."

Step 4: Introduce environments where the behavior is not considered to be appropriate. Then, say things such as, "In class, we laugh softly."

Step 5: Teach the correct responses. For example, present such situations as a funny movie, a party, a sports activity, a library, a store, and a hospital. Introduce each situation in a procedure such as this:

> **Teacher:** At a funny movie, we can laugh loudly. How can we laugh at a funny movie?
> **Child:** We can laugh loudly!

Teacher: That's right! We can laugh loudly at funny movies! But, in a library, we have to laugh quietly. How do we laugh at a library?

Child: We have to laugh quietly!

Step 6: Continue practicing the above responses and gradually introduce more examples. Teach enough examples so that the child will be able to give a correct response to an untaught example.

CHARACTERISTIC 6: DIFFICULTY WITH AUDITORY PROCESSING AND NEED FOR VISUAL SUPPORTS TO SUPPLEMENT VERBAL INSTRUCTION

The tools discussed in this section will address the sixth characteristic of ASD, difficulties with auditory processing and the need for visual supports. We'll look at the following methods for addressing this characteristic in the classroom:

* visual supports and
* videotaped self-modeling.

Visual Supports

Visual supports are things we see that help us communicate with others, organize our lives, make choices, and accomplish tasks (Hodgdon, 1995). Visual supports often are thought of as objects, photographs, drawings, or words. Body language and the arrangement of the environment also can be visual supports (Hodgdon, 1995).

Some visual supports are static and can be used to communicate with children who need time to process information. Verbal messages, however, are transient; they are gone as soon as the words are said. Manual signs often are transient as well, but can be held in place to provide good visually supported communication.

Visual supports can:

* be used to strengthen a verbal message or make it more clear. For example, gesturing toward the object of discussion or pointing to a picture of it can provide clarification.
* add to the message. Body language such as facial expressions, eye contact, and gestures can emphasize the meaning of the message. For example, adding a frowning face to the words, "I'm disappointed in that behavior" can add to the intensity of the message.

- be used in place of verbal communication. For example, environmental cues such as furniture arrangement, directions on boxes, and menus can eventually communicate messages without the accompanying words.
- be used to provide and organize information and make it more concrete. For example, calendars and telephone books can help children understand a structure and abstract concepts such as time.

To use visual supports:

Step 1: Arrange the environment to communicate things such as places for certain activities; symbols for reminding children of the rules; schedules to help make the day predictable; guides for places to stand in line or sit; and calendars, clocks, and timers to make time more understandable.

Step 2: Provide supports for individuals such as individual schedules and work systems, cue cards as reminders of expected behaviors, comic strip conversations or picture rehearsals for social interactions, wait cards or "I need a break" cards, and transition objects such as a book to go to the library.

Step 3: Implement visual support strategies regularly, such as:
- using gestures, body language, objects, pictures, and symbols to support verbal messages;
- providing ongoing positive feedback with token economies, checklists, and finished procedures;
- preparing students for transitions by reviewing their visual schedules and assisting them with transition objects;
- organizing work tasks for children by highlighting sections to be done, setting up worktables with clear finished procedures, providing "how to" pictorial sequences, or helping children make checklists of tasks to be done;
- exchanging notes or photographs to help parents, other adults, peers, and siblings discuss events and activities with the child;
- creating simple visual supports that record the activities the children have participated in at school and have the children use those supports to initiate communication with their family about their school day; and
- organizing classroom materials so that children can access things they need for independent work and play and so that adults can easily obtain the materials necessary for a teaching session.

Videotaped Self-Modeling

Videotaped self-modeling (VSM) involves making a video of the child performing well (Buggey, 1999). Essential characteristics of the effective use of VSM include developing short, 3- to 5-minute videos, focusing on positive (editing out any negative) behaviors, and providing exposure to the video for short periods of time. Steps for using VSM include:

Step 1: Define a need. For example, Zack needed a relaxation protocol to help him get calm when he was agitated. The steps for this protocol involved taking 3 deep breaths, counting to 10 slowly, and waiting for an adult.

Step 2: Make a videotape of the child that will eventually show the child performing the behaviors fluently and correctly. For example, Zack was filmed following the protocol when he was actually calm and responsive to direction.

Step 3: Edit the video, if necessary. In Zack's case, a movie title, transition slides with written directions, and applause and credits were included to make an interesting movie.

Step 4: Provide opportunities for the child to watch the video several times. For example, Zack watched the video himself and then several more times when he showed it to his friends and parents.

Step 5: Provide reinforcement for the child when the skills are demonstrated in the natural environment. For example, after watching himself on the video, Zack improved his ability to follow the steps in times of stress, and he was praised for his efforts.

CHARACTERISTIC 7: HYPERSENSITIVITY, HYPOSENSITIVITY, AND ATYPICAL REACTIONS TO THE FIVE SENSES

The tools discussed in this section will address the seventh characteristic of ASD, hypersensitivity and hyposensitivity. We'll look at the following methods for addressing this characteristic in the classroom:

- creating a safe area,
- relaxation training,

- ◆ stress thermometers, and
- ◆ crisis management.

Creating a Safe Area

Creating a safe area has big benefits! Children experiencing an overload of anxiety or sensory stimulation (often displayed as tapping, pacing, moaning, screaming, aggression, or self-abusive behavior) may go to the safe area and spend some time regaining control as the incoming stimulation is reduced. Overstimulation can be caused by task demands placed on the child, unfamiliar people (or too many people) in the child's environment, and environmental or physiological factors (e.g., noise, certain smells, bright lights).

The safe area must have well-defined visual boundaries and minimal stimulation. For hypersensitive children, reducing stimulation often helps them regain control. It is not necessary to remove the stimuli that ultimately caused the maladaptive behavior, but it is important to reduce overall stimulation.

Children can learn to use a safe area as a self-control strategy. Ultimately it is hoped that children would learn to recognize the signs of agitation or arousal within themselves and independently go to the safe area before they have lost control. Prior to this children may require prompting from others as a reminder to access the safe area. It is suggested that a complete program be developed to properly address this issue of self-control. Children who are nonverbal can learn to use a visual symbol signifying that they need a break.

Safe areas should not be used as punishment. The purpose is to reduce stimulation and give the child a time to relax, not to provide punitive consequences for out-of-control behavior. Some teachers refer to this area as a "quiet place," "cooling off zone," or "chill out space." Some teachers are hesitant to create such a relaxing place within their classroom because of the worry that the child will not want to come out of the area, creating a situation for another battle. When the classroom itself is reinforcing, and the reward system includes the child's desired consequences, the child will want get back into the classroom as soon as possible. Figure 44 shows a safe area in one teacher's classroom.

Relaxation Training

Relaxation training helps children learn to calm down by using a breathing/relaxation program before they have a total meltdown. This program should be modified to fit the specific needs of a child. When introducing this program, it is important to have practice or rehearsal sessions when the child is calm. The strategy can be taught using DTT or di. Continual practice will allow the

FIGURE 44. Safe area for relaxation.

process to become a routine for the child. Cue cards may be helpful as prompts for relaxation training (see Figure 45). Assess the need for practice when the child uses the protocol functionally during times of heightened stress or anger. Set up a procedure for relaxation training like the following:

> **Cue the child,** "It's time to relax. What do we do first?"
>
> **The child responds by saying,** "Three deep breaths." Monitor the child by counting with or for the child, if needed.
>
> **The adult says,** "What's next?"
>
> "Count to 10 slowly." As the child counts to 10, monitor the speed, volume, and intonation of the child's voice.
>
> **The adult says,** "Then?"
>
> **The child responds by saying, "Sit quietly for 10 seconds."** Watch the clock or listen for the timer. Start with a smaller amount of time to sit quietly and work up to longer times if needed. Using a timer or bell for the younger or more challenged child helps "cue" the child that he or she is finished.
>
> **Ask the child,** "Are you calm?" Determine whether the child is ready to go on or needs to repeat the protocol.
>
> **Use a chart to collect data.** This data collection helps to remind everyone to use the procedure, assesses the usefulness of the procedure, and assists in determining the child's anger triggers.

FIGURE 45. Cue cards to help with relaxation training.

Stress Thermometer

Children with ASD often experience difficulty handling stressful situations. Using the concept of a stress thermometer, McAfee and Attwood (2002) provided a visual strategy to assist children in identifying their stress signals and taking actions to gain self-control. The thermometer has the stress signals on one side of the scale and the child's relaxation techniques on the other. Children should be taught to request alternative behaviors such as asking for a break, going for a walk, listening to music, sitting in a bean bag, or engaging in other sensory activities rather than immediately engaging in inappropriate behaviors. Practice sessions can be implemented using DTT, allowing the alternative behaviors to become more routine when the child is faced with a stressful situation.

Jake's teachers and parents developed a stress thermometer with levels of high, medium, and low stressors and relaxation alternatives (see Figure 46). A poster with this thermometer was made for both school and home.

Stress thermometers also can be colored coded or use pictures to help children who need visual prompts follow the stress chart. An example of a color-coded chart can be found in Figure 46.

Crisis Management

In some cases, in spite of diligent work to decrease undesirable behaviors, a child experiences a period in which behavior deteriorates and crisis management strategies are needed. Teachers and parents must have a plan of action for

"Hot"—Signals for High Levels of Stress	Coping Strategies
Tight fists	Shake hands in the air
Voice loud enough to hear outside	Breathe slowly
Muscles tense	Count to 10
Fast movements	Walk slowly
Angry face—frowning eyebrows/yelling mouth	Open and close mouth

"Warm"—Signals for Medium Levels of Stress	Coping Strategies
Pacing	Shrug shoulders
Walking fast	Walk slowly
Voice loud enough to hear in the hall	Breathe slowly
Mad face—frowning eyebrows/ pouting mouth	Talk about favorite activities

"Cool"—Signals for Low Levels of Stress	Coping Strategies
Relaxed hands	Think about fun things
Voice loud enough to hear in the room, but soft enough not to hear in the hall	Talk quietly about your favorite things.
Arms and legs still	Work on something easy
Face relaxed and calm	Say nice things to people

FIGURE 46. Jake's stress thermometer.

these situations. The plan starts, of course, with prevention, and efforts should be provided to help children learn to cope with stress in appropriate ways. When children become anxious, it is important to take measures to de-escalate their behaviors. All of the strategies in this book are useful for prevention and de-escalation procedures.

Teachers and parents who work with children with ASD should take crisis management courses such as the ones offered by the Crisis Prevention Institute (http://www.crisisprevention.com) or the Professional Crisis Management Association (http://www.pcma.com).

For preventative and proactive measures, the team should consider:

- Consistent communication between home and school so parents can alert teachers if conditions exist that make the child more likely to lose control such as lack of sleep, medication changes, illness, or family dynamics.
- Creating a system of positive reinforcement delivered throughout the school day to keep positive behavior momentum and decrease the likelihood of aggression.
- A data collection system and analysis of the patterns that may exist will help identify triggers that may be antecedents to inappropriate behaviors. These patterns should be included in a Functional Behavior Assessment to assist the team in determining the function of the behavior and antecedents likely to evoke a crisis situation.
- Parents and teachers should work together to develop a strong, positive behavior support plan with strategies outlined to assist the team in keeping the child in control.
- Everyone involved with the child should receive training in crisis management strategies. These strategies provide a foundation for adults to use in supporting each other through a crisis.
- Adults should take care of themselves (e.g. get enough rest, eat right, and take breaks) so they will be better able to be a solution to the problem and not part of the problem themselves.

When intervening in the early stages of a crisis, teachers and parents should consider:

- Is the task too difficult? Can I reduce the demands of the task and avert escalation?
- Is the reinforcement chosen for the child effective? Does the child care about the reward? Is the reinforcement schedule appropriate?
- Have I asked the child to work too long without breaks? Can I deliver an easier instruction and call for a break to interrupt the pattern of escalation?
- Should redirection be used to allow the child time to perform mastered tasks while more positive behavior momentum can be created and compliant behavior is reestablished?
- Is the child being reinforced with too much attention during this phase? Is there an audience that needs to be removed to bring the child back into control?

Oftentimes, even with the best intentions and interventions, children continue to become agitated, engaging in verbal escalation. At this time, teachers and parents should intervene appropriately to establish control. Some suggestions for this stage of intervention are:

- Deliver specific directions in a firm voice such as, "It's time to get calm." Directions given at this time might include a choice the child can make with a positive outcome such as, "Sit and begin your work and you can start to earn your points for play time. Or you can take some time to calm down and come back when you're ready."
- Step back and give the child some space and time to make a choice.
- Recognize any attempts by the child to regain control. This is not the time to deliver lavish verbal praise so closely connected to the inappropriate behavior, but statements such as "You are working," or "You are working for your break," or "You are getting calm" can communicate to the child that attempts he is making to gain control are noticed.
- Avoid lengthy conversations at this time. Keep the instructions short and precise.
- Support a child with limited language with visuals outlining what is to be completed first followed by a more preferred activity such as a pictorial representation of "first color, then puzzles." Refer to the two-step sequence often, making sure the second step is motivating to the child.
- Avoid threatening statements as they often stop the behavior for the moment but are not considered a long-term solution to the difficult behavior. Threats can escalate a situation rather than serve to calm everyone involved.

Teachers and parents should make every possible effort to stop the downward spiral of aggressive behaviors. When behaviors escalate in spite of preventive and de-escalation strategies, trained adults should only use therapeutic crisis management procedures as a last resort when safety issues exist. A protocol for intervening should be developed by an IEP team that includes the teacher and classroom staff, related service personnel, parents, and administrators.

CHARACTERISTIC 8: DIFFICULTY UNDERSTANDING THE PERSPECTIVES AND EMOTIONS OF OTHERS AND SOCIAL CUES

The tools discussed in this section will address the eighth characteristic of ASD, understanding others' perspectives and emotions. We'll look at the following methods for addressing this characteristic in the classroom:

- ◆ social stories,
- ◆ picture rehearsals,
- ◆ comic strip conversations, and
- ◆ power cards.

Social Stories

Carol Gray (1993) described social stories as descriptions of social situations in terms of the relevant social cues and the common responses that people usually have to these situations. Social stories are short stories written to provide children with accurate and specific information regarding what occurs in a situation and why. Communicating within our social framework is difficult for children with diagnoses of ASD and some children display inappropriate behavior due to the misunderstanding of the nonverbal cues. The purpose of a social story is to describe and rehearse a given social situation or event that deviates from the normal routine to teach appropriate language and social skills. It provides visual and written supports to assist the child in following the social rules that often are unclear or difficult to imitate. Social stories can help to reduce the misunderstanding of social cues within interactions, explain the sequence of new routines, and address many behavioral challenges.

When writing social stories, first consider the child's interests, learning styles, and abilities and plan the story accordingly. Compose the social story primarily of descriptive and perspective sentences. Descriptive sentences tell where situations occur, who is involved, what they are doing, and why (e.g., "In our classroom, children sit at their desks and follow directions from the teacher."). Perspective sentences describe the reactions and feelings of the child and of other people (e.g., "When I ask silly questions, it makes the other children laugh, but it makes the teacher mad.").

Then add, at most, one directive or control sentence for every two to five descriptive and perspective sentences. Directive sentences tell children what to do (e.g., "When I want to ask a question, I will try not to be silly. I will try not to giggle and laugh when I talk."). Control sentences include information to help the child remember the information from the social story. These sentences are sometimes considered optional.

When writing social stories, avoid words like "always" and "never," because they may lead to inaccurate information. Include potential variations in the social story so that the child is not set up to believe that everything will always happen just the way it occurs in the story.

Affirm something that the child does well. Gray (1993) noted that the goal of a social story should not aim to change the child's behavior, rather, that a child's increased understanding of events and expectations may help the child cope more effectively in social situations.

Whenever possible, define ambiguous and abstract concepts as concretely as possible. For example, instead of putting "I will talk quietly" in the story, write "I will try to talk so that no one in the hall can hear me."

When appropriate, include illustrations to help the child understand the social story and/or to gain the child's interest. The illustrated social story in Figure 47 captured Abbie's attention. She was interested in reviewing it many times and ended up with a highly successful camp experience in spite of the anxiety of her teachers and parents. However, for some children, illustrations may be distracting or create the idea that the situation must always be as the pictures depict.

The steps for writing a social story are as follows:

Step 1: Identify and describe the current situation, including what the child does well.

Step 2: Describe the expected behaviors and explain the impact of the behaviors on others.

Step 3: Translate the above descriptions into descriptive and perspective sentences using language the child is likely to understand.

Step 4: Use one or two directive and control sentences, starting with, "I'll try."

Step 5: Select a title for the story that describes the goal of the story.

FIGURE 47. Illustrated social story.

Here are two examples of social stories. The first example more directly reflects what can be given to an individual child. The second example includes the type of sentences in parentheses used to write a social story.

Finding My Place in the Gym

My name is Wesley and I am a great athlete. At our school, our class lines up to walk to the gym. This can be very exciting because gym is fun. Sometimes it's hard to go into the gym and sit down. When I run around the gym instead of going to my seat, it takes longer to get the games started. It is important to follow the teacher's instructions to sit in our places on the gym floor because the sooner we get in our places, the faster we will get to start the games. I will try to go to my place right away.

Congratulating the Winners

Lots of times we play games in the gym (descriptive). Sometimes people win games and sometimes people lose games (descriptive). My friends are playing hard and they like to win (perspective). It can make them sad when I get mad about losing and it can make them happy when I say nice things to them (descriptive/perspective). I will try to say nice things, like "Congratulations!" to my friends when they win (directive).

Examples in which a social story might be a useful strategy include:

- Anthony growls at the staff when given a directive involving a task that he perceives as difficult. The staff wrote a story about how to ask for help when work is difficult. A section of the story also included the way people talk and how some animals make other noises to communicate.
- Abigail displays anxiety when separating from her mom in the car line. The team has developed a story that shows what Abigail will be doing when she arrives in the classroom (a preferred activity). The story also includes a picture of her mother coming back later to pick her up.
- Michael has difficulty understanding the protocol for the loud morning announcements while he is in his third-grade classroom. The teacher has written a social story explaining the steps of the morning announcements, the duration of the loud voices and music, and the reward to be given when he remains calm.

Picture Rehearsals

For those children unable to read the words in a social story, picture rehearsals (Baron, Groden, Groden, & Lipsitt, 2006) often are helpful. These rehearsals use the support of pictures to signify the appropriate social responses used to aid the child as he or she encounters difficult situations. The adults read the captions under the pictures to the children as they rehearse what might happen in the given social situation. Practice sessions are implemented regularly as the child learns to interact more appropriately.

Comic Strip Conversations

Developed by Carol Gray (1995), comic strip conversations are simple drawings representing interactions between two or more people. The comic strips (or cartoons) are written to help a child understand and comprehend social situations. The words describe the situation and provide good models for the way children should converse with others. Simple illustrations such as stick figures, line drawings of objects, or symbols are used to help the child visualize the situation. Comic strip bubbles are used to represent the thoughts or words of the character.

Some social situations that might warrant the use of cartooning are:

- realizing how people feel when someone invades their personal space;
- understanding what peers think when people talk on and on about their favorite subjects;
- communicating how people feel when someone bursts into the restroom, opening each stall door; or
- learning what people might be thinking when people talk with food in their mouth and have poor table manners.

Organizing these stories, pictures, and cartoons into one child-specific notebook often is helpful. Using a story or picture to preteach what might happen in a given situation can be easier to implement on the spot if all of the specifics are housed together. A good organizational system can be just the right tool for turning a potentially escalating situation into a teachable moment.

Power Cards

Power cards (Gagnon, 2001) are created to teach and reinforce behavioral, social, or academic skills using the child's special interests to tell a story. The story is written about a character or person of interest who encounters situations similar to the ones that are challenging for the child. The story is used to capture the child's attention by focusing the child's special interest.

For example, for a child who doesn't stop to go to the bathroom, Gagnon (2001) provides a story by Kitty Flinn about Superman's need to use the bathroom periodically. In the story, Superman provides suggestions such as going to the bathroom at home when you need to go, rather than waiting to ask someone to go to the bathroom (Gagnon, 2001).

Power cards should be used when an individual lacks the understanding of his or her expectations, to clarify choices, to teach cause and effect between a specific behavior and its consequence, to teach another's perspective, to aid in generalization, or as a visual reminder of appropriate behavioral expectations of a situation.

The following steps will help with the creation of power cards:

Step 1: Identify and describe a challenging situation for the child. For example, Mary rarely joins in with children at recess or lunch.

Step 2: Identify characters of interest to the child. For example, Mary loves the *High School Musical* movies.

Step 3: Write a brief story about the characters encountering the situation the child faces. Write it in language that the child will understand. For example, in *High School Musical* Gabriella moves to a new school. Sometimes, she doesn't feel comfortable joining in with group activities. When she sits and watches, she sees that other children are having fun together. When girls from Gabriella's school ask her to join them at lunch, Gabriella sits with her new friends and she had fun. Gabriella thinks it is a good idea to eat lunch and play at recess with friends. Gabriella says, "Just give it a try."

Step 4: Read the story regularly until the child knows the story well.

Step 5: Put a picture of the character on an index card and briefly summarize the solution to the challenging situation. For example, write the last sentence of the above story on Mary's power card.

CHARACTERISTIC 9: DEMONSTRATION OF PREDOMINANTLY CONCRETE THINKING AND LITERAL INTERPRETATIONS OF STATEMENTS AND SITUATIONS

The tools discussed in this section will address the ninth characteristic of ASD, concrete thinking and the literal interpretations of statements and situations. We'll look at the following methods for addressing this characteristic in the classroom:

- effective instructions,
- teaching negation, and
- social thinking.

Effective Instructions

Children with diagnoses of ASD sometimes have difficulty following instructions due to concrete thinking and literal interpretations of language. When we give instructions correctly, the chances that children will respond appropriately are high. When giving instructions:

- Get the children's attention by calling their names and/or going closer. Before speaking, look for a response that indicates they are ready to listen. These signs might include looking at you, stopping whatever activity they might be engaged in, or orienting toward you. Remember that some children may be uncomfortable looking at you and for them it may not be effective to require eye contact.
- Break down the task and provide instructions one step at a time. Wait for success in following one instruction at a time before giving instructions with multiple steps.
- Deliver instructions in a quiet and calm, yet firm manner. However, be polite and set a good model for the way you want children to speak to others.
- Use direct and specific language, presenting the instruction as a directive and not as a question. Rather than saying, "Would you like to work now?" give the direction, "Please start your work now." Remember that many children with ASD take things very literally. Say what you mean and mean what you say. If you say, "Let's clean up now," some children with ASD will expect you to be actively cleaning up with them.
- Give directions positively by telling children what to do, rather than what not to do. Directions such as "Don't do that!", "Stop it!", and "No!" not only create a negative atmosphere, they don't teach children what to do. It is more effective to tell children to do things that are incompatible with the negative behavior. For example, instead of saying, "Don't run," say, "Please walk in our classroom."
- Refrain from repeating instructions before getting a response. If children do not respond, move closer and use gestures, signs, pictures, or physical prompts to increase the chance of compliance rather than nagging.
- Ask children to repeat instructions to ensure they understand and to correct any misconceptions or misinterpretations they might have.
- Give instructions from a few feet away to reduce the distractions between you and the children. Then stand back a bit and let them have time and space to comply.

- Check often to see that directions are being followed and provide specific, positive feedback for compliance. Rather than provide vague feedback such as "Good!" say things like, "Thanks for cleaning up so quickly!" or "Good work following directions!"

Teaching Negation

Imagine the excitement that a child feels hearing the word "cookies." Then, think about how confused the child feels when there are no cookies because the teacher actually said, "We don't have any cookies today." Some children with ASD may not hear (or process) the negation in sentences. For them, "No cookies!" might be heard as "cookies!" The following steps can be helpful in teaching children to recognize negation:

Step 1: At first, whenever possible, tell children what *to do* rather than what *not* to do. These types of directions stop inappropriate behaviors by redirecting children toward appropriate behaviors instead of saying "no." Even when children do hear the word, "no," it doesn't teach them what to do.

Step 2: To help children learn the concept of negation, teach them to protest appropriately. For example, gently offer children items or activities they don't like and prompt saying, "No, thanks."

Step 3: Teach children to use and understand negation with a sequence such as this:
- Teach Negation With Nouns
   I have toys in my box.
   I have no toys in my box.

- Teach Negation With Verbs
   Step A: Teach a set of actions such as:
      Play with the car.
      Do not play with the car.

   Step B: Teach a set of actions that are preceded by be verbs:
      They are running.
      They are not running.

Step C: Teach a set of actions that are preceded by should or should not:
> We should go outside.
>
> We should not go outside.

* Teach Negation With Adjectives
> The elephant is big.
>
> The bug is not big.

* Teach Opposites Related to Negation
> Some vs. None
>
> Always vs. Never
>
> Somebody vs. Nobody

In teaching negation, it helps greatly to support instruction with visual aids. Objects and pictures can help children understand the concepts. For example, draw two boxes on a piece of paper, labeling one "fish" and the other "no fish." Draw lots of fish in the first box and leave the second box empty. Multiple visual exemplars such as this help children generalize this thinking to other examples.

Social Thinking

Social thinking is a program designed to teach children to read social cues such as body actions, facial expressions, tone of voice, eye movements, and physical proximity (Winner, 2005). Winner (2005) explained that social thinking is necessary for social skills and noted that successful social thinkers consider the thoughts and intentions of others. This often is called perspective-taking and includes thinking about others' points of view, prior knowledge, emotions, and beliefs.

These are the four steps Winner (2002) described for understanding the thoughts of others during the process of sharing space.

1. When we share a space, I am thinking about you and you are thinking about me.
2. I wonder why we are sharing the same space and whether you are going to talk to me or hurt me.
3. Because I know you are thinking about me, I wonder what your thoughts are.
4. I monitor what I am doing so you will think about me the way I want you to think about me.

When teaching children about social thinking, Winner (2005) advised to refrain from thinking about behaviors as appropriate or inappropriate and describe behaviors as expected or unexpected. Teachers should show pictures of unexpected and expected behaviors and explain that when we perform unexpected behaviors, we make other people feel uncomfortable and they might think that we are different or weird. Helping children understand the thoughts and perspectives of others often helps them manage their own behavior.

CHARACTERISTIC 10: EXECUTIVE FUNCTIONING CHALLENGES

The tools discussed in this section will address the final characteristic of ASD, executive functioning challenges. We'll look at the following methods for addressing this characteristic in the classroom:

* task analysis,
* task organization and timing,
* finished procedures,
* activity schedules
* token economies,
* positive behavior momentum, and
* motivation.

Task Analysis

To help children get started, it often is useful to create a task analysis and work on small segments or steps of a larger task. At first, adults can create task analyses for children and later, with instruction and support, children can learn to develop task analyses themselves. It's helpful to first perform the task yourself and write down the steps used in the process to make sure all of the steps are included in the sequence.

A task analysis involves breaking a task into steps or segments. For instruction, these segments can be taught or practiced in isolation. Each step is taught to mastery before moving on to the next step in the task analysis. When several segments are mastered, they can be chained together so that the child can demonstrate the whole task.

Forward chaining begins by teaching the first step in the chain and progresses systematically to the last step. When the child masters the first step, move to the second step. Sometimes it's helpful to practice steps one and two together to help the child make the connection that each step moves in the direction of task completion. The third step should be taught with the first two steps to help continue the learning process. Any steps that have not been introduced in the chain are to be completed with assistance from the teacher. Reinforcement is given after the completion of all of the steps currently implemented.

In backward chaining procedures, the steps are acquired in reverse order. The last step in the task is taught first. For example, to teach shoe tying, the child first learns to pull the bow tight. Then, for each shoe tying opportunity, the child is guided or prompted through the sequence and then pulls the bow tight. Over time, instruction is implemented from the end of the task to the beginning steps, allowing the child to complete all of the tasks involved in the chain. The natural consequence of finishing the task often can serve as a reinforcer.

Task analyses are useful for academic skills as well. For example, steps for learning to "borrow" and "carry" in a mathematics class can be developed to help a child learn the procedures involved. Writing a paragraph can be broken into steps such as choosing a topic, developing a web or list of subtopics, writing an opening sentence, developing two or three supporting sentences, and writing a concluding sentence.

Because children with ASD may have difficulty getting started on a project, having a written task analysis, perhaps in the form of a checklist, can help a child get focused on a small, manageable segment of the task. The checklist for the task analysis can be presented in pictures, words, or sentences. We also have experienced success when children follow directions played on a CD player or videotape.

The following steps are helpful for developing and using task analyses:

Step 1: Identify the task and perform it yourself as you are writing down the steps. For example, a shoe tying task analysis might look like this:

Lay the laces straight.
Cross the left lace over the right lace.
Use the left hand to pinch the two laces at the cross and lift it slightly off the shoe to create an opening.
Use the right hand to pick up the end of the top lace and poke it back through the opening.
Pull the laces tight.
Use the left hand to pick up the right lace in the middle of the lace.

Use the right hand to pinch the two parts of the lace to make the right loop.

Use the left hand to cross the left lace over the right loop.

Use the left hand to pinch the laces at the cross and lift them slightly to create an opening.

Use the right hand to pinch the straight lace in the middle to create another loop.

Use the right hand to poke the loop back through the opening.

Use two hands to grasp the loops and pull them tight.

Step 2: Teach the steps in a logical order. Note that the task analysis doesn't define the language, nor the procedure used to teach the child. Some task analyses might work better as a series of pictures, rather than instructions (see Figure 48). Or, in the case above, modeling accompanied by simple directions is necessary. It also might be helpful to use prompts such as colored laces to avoid labeling the laces left and right and adding halfway marks on the laces to help determine where to pick up the lace to make a loop. In this case, it may be helpful to use backward chaining to teach the last step first. Once that step is mastered, it may be helpful to practice the next to the last step in isolation and then to chain the last two steps together.

FIGURE 48. A visual task analysis for making a turkey sandwich. The steps are presented visually, rather than only in written directions.

Step 3: Use a chart to mark off each step as it is mastered and continue teaching the steps until the child has mastered the entire task.

Task Organization and Timing

Help children get started by organizing their tasks for them. Figure 49 shows how organizing a task can be as simple as highlighting portions of a worksheet with colors. Yellow highlighting includes the directions and blue indicates the section that should be done first. The other side of Figure 49 shows how materials can be organized by securing them to a cookie sheet with Velcro®. The chips have less chance to fall on the floor during work and the container won't move as the child puts the chips in it. The rows allow the child to practice working from left to right, top row first and then bottom row. These types of organization are simple, yet effective for children who struggle to complete tasks on time.

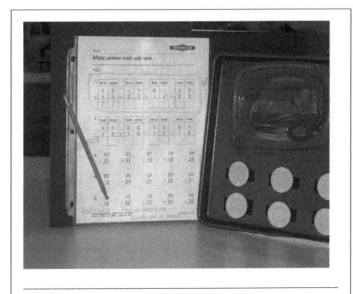

Figure 49. Simple ways of organizing tasks.

Figure 50 shows another method for organizing daily work. The teacher can provide a child working math problems with a laminated folder with Velcro® spots for the answers to the problems. Answers will be on separate cards. A child can work the problem on a calculator, select the correct answer, and put the answer in the correct spot. This is another opportunity to practice working systematically down the page.

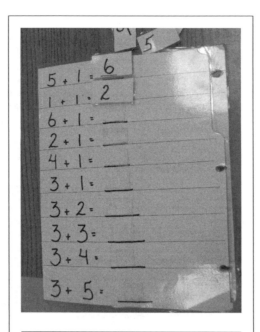

FIGURE 50. An organization system for helping a child practice working problems down a page.

With children with autism, it is important to help them remember to keep working until the task is complete. A checklist that explains a rule for completing a task, along with places where the child can mark off the various subtasks he or she has completed can aid students in remembering to finish their work (see Figure 51).

Help children learn to judge time with visual supports. Many teachers like to use red timers, such as the one in Figure 52, for visual representations of how much time is left to complete a task. This red timer and others can be found at http://www.timetimer.com.

Children with autism also need help remembering what materials they need to complete their classroom assignments. Help children learn to use and make lists such as the one in Figure 53.

Finished Procedures

Clearly specifying what counts as finished work helps children start working in an organized way. Seeing what needs to be done and understanding the potential payoff for working increases children's motivation and cooperation.

FIGURE 51. A checklist to aid a student in remembering to complete all of the work in a task.

FIGURE 52. An example of a red timer.

FIGURE 53. A materials checklist.

Finished procedures communicate important information to children about how much work they need to do and what happens when they are finished working. We use visual representations, rather than verbal directions to clarify the goal and to provide feedback along the way. When children see what needs to be done and how they are progressing, they not only know exactly what work they must do to collect the reinforcer, they also see themselves gradually making progress toward their goal. The following are examples of finished procedures:

- Create a poster that can be used over and over to represent finished procedures. In Figure 54, the child is able to fill the pockets with a card showing that he has completed each step of the activity. When all of the pockets are filled, the child can see that he is done with the task.

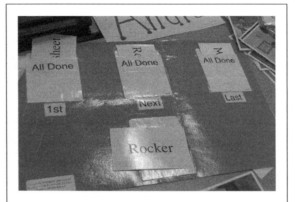

FIGURE 54. A simple, but effective finished process allows the activities and reinforcers to change, but the structure remains consistent.

- Use a token box such as the one in Figure 55. The tokens provide a visual representation of how many tasks need to be done. For example, if a child is identifying pictures, a token can be placed in the box each time the child correctly identifies a picture. As the child develops an understanding of the process, several responses can be required before the token is placed in the box. In both cases, a reinforcer must be provided.
- Set up a work area with three sections on the table. The section on the left will hold the work to be done (e.g., three puzzles, a math game, and a drawing task). The middle section will be the work area and space on the right will be for the finished work. The child takes the

FIGURE 55. A token box for showing progress on activities.

first puzzle, completes it, and puts it in the finished place to the right of the workspace. The child continues until all of the work is placed in the finished place. Then, a reinforcer is provided.

◆ Set up two baskets with flashcards in one of the baskets. Label the other basket "finished" or " all done" and put it on top of a picture of the child's favorite activity. After the child reads each flashcard, move it to the "finished" basket. When all of the cards have been read correctly and moved, the child is finished and can enjoy time in the favorite activity (see Figure 56).

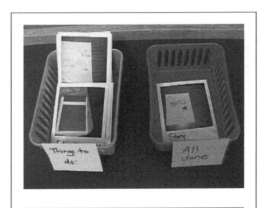

FIGURE 56. Using baskets to aid in completion of activities.

◆ Make a list of assignments on an index card. Put "swing" at the bottom of the list. Instruct the children to put a check beside each assignment as it is completed. When all of the assignments are finished, provide 5 minutes of swinging.

- Write the numbers 10 to 1 on a picture of a rocket (see Figure 57). For correct responses or tasks, mark off a number. When the child is finished, let the child "blast off" to the reinforcing activity.

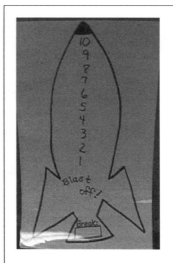

FIGURE 57. Rocketship diagram to aid students in completing a list of 10 tasks.

When using finished procedures in the classroom, remember the following tips:

- It is important to provide effective reinforcement for finishing. This might include enthusiastic social praise or access to food, toys, or favorite activities.
- To assist in developing independence, use the fewest verbal prompts possible when assisting children in learning finished procedures.

Activity Schedules

An activity schedule is a set of pictures or words that cues a child to engage in a sequence of activities (McClannahan & Krantz, 1999). These schedules teach independent work skills and should be individualized for each child. For some children, activities will need to be broken down and depicted step-by-step in order for the child to complete the activity independently. For other children a more general, single cue can help the child to perform an entire task or activity.

An activity schedule can take many forms, but initially it usually is a three-ring binder with pictures or words on each page that cue children to perform tasks, engage in activities, and then enjoy rewards. Any type of photo album, spiral notebook, or notepad can be used to develop a child's activity schedule book. Even simple written lists may suffice for the child who is able to read. However it's designed, the activity schedule should contain the various tasks/activities (and steps if needed) depicted in whatever visual representation system the child best comprehends (e.g., photos, line drawings).

Upon completion, a social reinforcer can be "built in" as the last page in the activity schedule book. Steps for creating an activity schedule include:

Step 1: On the first page of a photo album put a picture such as the one in Figure 58, representing the first task.

FIGURE 58. First task in an activity schedule.

Step 2: On the second page, put another picture, such as the one in Figure 59 that shows a set of cards to sequence.

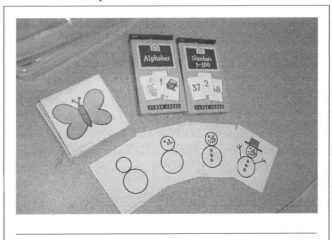

FIGURE 59. Second picture in the activity schedule.

Step 3: On the third page, put another picture, such as the one in Figure 60 that depicts going to a listening center to complete a following directions task.

Step 4: On the last page, put a picture of the child and the child's choice of reward. This might be free time to play with a set of favorite toys.

FIGURE 60. Third task in
an activity schedule.

Step 5: Organize the materials so the child has easy access to them. For example, in Figure 61, the child can first take the basket of beads and complete that task. When finished, the child returns the materials to the "finished shelf." Next, the child carries the tray for sorting to the worktable. This is possible because the cups and sorting container are attached to the cookie sheet with heavy-duty Velcro®. Last, the child can bring the pennies and the Snoopy bank to the worktable to complete the final task.

FIGURE 61. Organization of
materials for an activity schedule.

Step 6: Use graduated guidance to teach children to open their activity books, turn to the first page, perform the task, and then turn to the next page for cues to the next tasks. Teaching children with ASD to use an activity schedule enables them to perform tasks and activities without direct prompting and guidance by parents or teachers. Be sure to use physical prompts (least to most) rather than verbal prompts as physical prompts are easier to fade.

Token Economies

A token economy is a strategy used to reinforce a child by delivering a point or symbol that can be exchanged for a desired object, privilege, or activity. Token economies can be used to increase desirable behavior and decrease undesirable behavior. To increase behavior, a token is provided after the target behavior. To decrease behavior, a token is provided for a period of time during which the behavior does not occur. Tokens may be happy faces, points, plastic chips, stickers, or play money. Figures 62, 63, and 64 provide several examples of token systems that can be used in the classroom.

FIGURE 62. Token system using chips.

FIGURE 63. Token system using letters of a child's name.

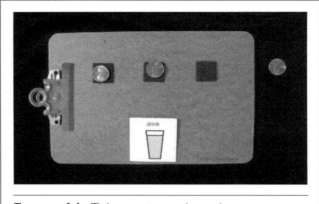

FIGURE 64. Token system using coins.

A token economy system of reinforcement has proven beneficial for many children. Alberto and Troutman (2009) stated that it is important to ensure that tokens are portable, durable, and easy to handle. This will make implementation more likely to occur. If the system is complicated or cumbersome, the team might decide that the system is ineffective.

This system of reinforcement requires two components:

1. the tokens themselves (e.g., objects, poker chips, puzzle pieces, stickers, play money, coupons, check marks, happy faces), and
2. the backup reinforcers (e.g., items/activities identified as reinforcing to the children).

Initially, tokens (secondary reinforcers) have no value, but gain worth when exchanged for meaningful objects, privileges, or activities (primary reinforcers). To increase desired behavior, use continuous reinforcement by providing tokens immediately after the desirable behavior. Allow children to make an immediate exchange for a primary reinforcer. As tokens take on value, thin the schedule of primary reinforcers by increasing the number of tokens required for reinforcement. As the demands increase, increase the amount of the reinforcer. Gradually increase the time and work between earning the token and the exchange, thus teaching delayed gratification.

In some systems, children lose tokens (response cost) for undesirable behavior. However, to decrease undesirable behavior, it is more effective to provide the token for a period of time that the behavior does not occur.

It is recommended that teachers proceed carefully when implementing a response cost system in which tokens are taken away after they are earned. If tokens are taken away often, children will begin to distrust the system and the

- Especially in cases of challenging behaviors, the system should travel with children throughout the school day.
- Clearly define the areas where the tokens will be placed so children can visualize how many more tokens they have to earn before receiving a reward. Use boxes, lines, or Velcro® pieces to define the areas (see Figure 65 for an example of how to define areas in token systems).

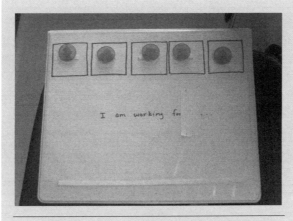

FIGURE 65. Using boxes to define the areas for students to collect tokens.

- The type of token used should be based on the skills and needs of the child. Some children might require a pictorial representation of the item to be earned.
- Once a child understands the system of earning and cashing in tokens, the time between reinforcement can be lengthened as well as the amount of work required before receiving a token.
- Adults can manipulate the time between tokens to create behavior momentum during difficult times. If walking down the hall is a difficult task, the adults can deliver tokens at a faster rate with the reward given as soon as the child reaches his or her final destination.
- When first teaching a token system to a child, the teacher may decide to require only one token before a reward is delivered.
- A variety of tokens can be used. Consider using happy faces, checks, play money, coins, cubes, poker chips, or magnets as items to use for earning rewards.

effectiveness of the plan will be minimal. If you are contemplating the use of response cost, consider reserving the removal of tokens for violations of safety rules such as acts of verbal or physical aggression, rather than for less socially significant behavior.

Positive Behavior Momentum

Children with ASD often need a jump start to get moving on a task. Even in the middle of instructional sessions, children might begin to exhibit behaviors that are undesirable, signaling a need for quick intervention. Teachers can use behavior momentum strategies to create an upward spiral movement toward more acceptable attention to the task. Once behaviors start to occur, they may continue with momentum, whether the behaviors are appropriate or inappropriate. When children experience a series of successes, momentum builds in a positive direction.

To create positive behavior momentum, ask the children to perform simple and/or favorite tasks that require little effort. Once establishing a high rate of quick and successful responses, gradually introduce more difficult questions or tasks. To maintain positive behavior momentum while increasing demands, sandwich some challenging tasks between easy, preferred activities.

Behavior momentum also includes the negative force that builds from a series of inappropriate behaviors. When unacceptable behaviors occur, use the momentum driving the behavior to redirect the energy and efforts toward more appropriate actions. For example, to change the course of negative momentum:

- When a child gets out of his seat without permission, direct him to an easy task such as putting a book on a shelf.
- When a child grabs inappropriately, hand her a puzzle piece and direct her to complete a puzzle.

An effective teacher is flexible during the lesson and able to adapt to situations requiring a needed change. When a teaching session seems to be headed in a downward spiral, this type of teacher can recoup and reorganize on the spot to bring the children back into focus by redirecting the children's energy in a positive direction (Fouse & Wheeler, 1997). This often is accomplished with either a change of pace or a change of the level of difficulty of the task.

Continuing a lesson that is headed in an undesirable direction is not helpful to children. There must be a change implemented on the spot to prevent a crash. Using these tools, teachers can increase behavioral compliance simply by changing the way a request is delivered, the sequence of preferred and nonpreferred tasks, or the timing of reinforcement. Supporting children's learning by changing the direction of the momentum at hand can help a teacher survive the moment while shaping the behavior for lasting change.

Motivation

We have discussed motivation in many of the strategies throughout the book. This most critical component seems like an ideal way to close out the section on strategies, as it is important to note that no strategy will be effective unless the child is motivated.

Motivation is affected by wants or desires. But, the motivation to behave in certain ways is not just related to potential consequences (Michael, 2007). It is important to know the motivating operations (environmental events that influence the effects of consequences) affecting the child. To put it another way, the effectiveness of the consequence depends on the child's state of deprivation or satiation related to that particular consequence. Michael (2007) explained that deprivation increases and satiation decreases the frequency of behavior that has been reinforced with the particular reinforcer.

Motivating operations indicate:

- what the child wants, and
- how much he or she wants it.

Motivation to perform is affected by knowledge and skills as well. It is important to know whether or not a child knows how to do something. We sometimes ask children to do things they do not know how to do and when the child doesn't perform, we sometimes think the child isn't motivated to act. In this case, the task needs to be presented so that the child can just manage completion. Create objectives that are difficult and challenging, but also manageable and ultimately rewarding when accomplished.

When the child does know how to do something, it still may be a challenge to get the child to want to do it. Consider doing the following when attempting to increase a child's motivation:

- Identify potential motivators with a reinforcement survey. Present a variety of reinforcers and observe which items or activities draw the attention of the child.
- Limit access to the reinforcers. There may be a temporary decrease in effectiveness when children are satiated.
- Pair other children with reinforcers to motivate the child to interact with others.

7

PUTTING IT ALL TOGETHER

Each child with ASD is unique and some require specialized instruction to achieve success. For each child who presents instructional or behavioral challenges, teachers and parents must do a complete assessment, develop goals and objectives, and develop a set of strategies to meet that child's needs.

Effective teachers consider the child's learning and behavioral characteristics and educational needs and then select sound educational strategies to meet the child's needs. It is not enough to work with our teaching instincts, we must stay continuously abreast of new research. To achieve the most success, to satisfy our ethical and legal responsibilities, and to justify our choices to parents and administrators, we must constantly review the research and document the results of our instruction.

FUNCTIONAL BEHAVIORAL ASSESSMENT

Sometimes, even when good instructional strategies are in place, children continue to have significant challenges. In these cases, teachers and parents should implement a thorough functional behavior assessment (FBA). For information on FBAs, see Chapter 6. A sample FBA is included below. With this process, teachers and parents can get an idea of why the behavior is occurring and can develop a positive behavior support plan (PBSP) to assist in reducing interfering behaviors and increasing productive behaviors. A sample PBSP is included in the next section

Functional Behavior Assessment

Child: Joe Smith   **Date:** 08/13/09
Date of Birth: 12-7-02   **School:** Berry Elementary

Joe is a 7-year-old boy with autism. His records indicate he also has a diagnosis of ADHD. Joe spends about half of his day in general education. The remaining classes are completed in a special education resource classroom. Joe does not take any medications, but is on a special diet.

Joe was referred for an FBA due to noncompliant, defiant, and aggressive behaviors. His noncompliant behaviors include refusing to follow instructions by sitting and doing nothing or by saying no. His defiant behaviors include screaming phrases such as, "I won't!" or "You can't make me!" His aggressive behaviors include pushing with enough force to knock people down and hitting and kicking hard enough to make a bruise.

Strengths: Joe is able to operate a computer effectively to search and retrieve information appropriately. His ability to create documents using the editing tools of the word processor is improving. His rote memory skills are evident in his ability to recite math facts, vocabulary words, and spelling sequences. Joe often is friendly to familiar peers and adults.

Data Collection: The information in this report was obtained from a review of Joe's IEPs, observations, interviews with Joe's parents and school personnel, and data collection. Periodic data has been collected on Joe's behaviors and has been summarized and reported to Joe's parents along with each report card.

In reviewing Joe's IEP, it was determined that he is meeting, and in some cases exceeding, the expected progress rate toward his annual goals. Of the 22 objectives targeted for December, Joe is making the expected progress toward 7 objectives, exceeding the expected rate on 11 objectives, and is behind the expected rate on 4 objectives.

Joe's teachers and parents report that Joe's behavior does interfere with his ability to perform acceptably in school. They list the interfering behaviors as noncompliance with instructions and hitting and kicking people and property. Joe's aggression toward property has sometimes put him and others at risk and has damaged the property. For example, in kicking shelves, items have fallen and the shelves themselves have almost fallen. Kicking the desk has resulted in large dents to the drawer. His hitting and kicking has caused bruises to school personnel and Joe's parents.

Data collected on Joe's aggression (hitting and kicking) is presented below. (Incidents counted are separated by at least 1 minute between hits or kicks)

Date	Duration	Incident Frequency
8/23–8/25	3 days	25
8/28–9/1	5 days	21
9/5 –9/8	4 days	19
9/11–9/15	5 days	23
9/18–9/21	4 days	13
9/25–9/26	2 days	10

Joe's hitting and kicking behaviors average between four and five per day. The fewest number of incidents on any day was three and the largest number was nine.

After analyzing data collected on antecedents, the following antecedents to noncompliance or aggression have been identified:

- change in schedule, routine, personnel, or activity;
- demand or command, particularly to new or unpreferred tasks; and
- transition to a different task.

In analyzing the consequences Joe experiences for his behavior, the following hypotheses regarding the function of Joe's behavior have been offered:

- His behavior often results in escape from task or work.
- He often gets the items and activities at his choice of time.
- He often gets attention from others.

Meaningful and motivating consequences for Joe include:

* treats such as chewy candies,
* praise and attention from adults,
* computer time, and
* specific videotapes of cartoon characters.

During the observations, the following interventions were noted to appear to increase or escalate Joe's aggressive behavior:

* planned ignoring, and
* physical prompts for him to move away from the computer.

The following interventions did not appear to affect his behavior, neither increasing nor decreasing it:

* discussions or explanations involving lots of language.

POSITIVE BEHAVIOR SUPPORT PLAN

The following strategies are recommended to decrease Joe's interfering behaviors and increase his productive behaviors.

Ongoing Positive Reinforcement

Joe should be provided with a heavy schedule of reinforcement for working appropriately, remaining calm, and making good choices. Both primary and secondary reinforcement should be used, including social praise, edible treats, favorite activities, and praise. Frequent praise and intermittent treats should be provided throughout the day for appropriate behavior. To make reinforcement effective, care should be taken to provide it immediately, frequently, with anticipation and variety, and enthusiastically with eye contact and to describe the positive behavior (Rhode, Jenson, & Reavis, 1992).

Visual Supports for Transitions

When possible, predictable routines should be followed and Joe should be given a visual representation of the next activity he is expected to do. Short segments of a schedule should be presented and explained to Joe periodically throughout the day. Changes to the day's schedule, routine, or personnel should be explained to Joe using visual strategies and the "OOPS!" program, using pictures or symbols to show Joe what will not occur and what will happen instead.

Environmental Engineering

The physical environment should be structured for Joe so he knows what behaviors are expected in each area. Designated work and play areas should be defined for him. Keep a table or small child-sized desk between Joe and the adult working with him. Take care to ensure that if Joe gets up, he must pass an adult before exhibiting any misbehavior.

Token Economy

Joe should earn computer time for staying calm in times of stress. This usually is delivered at the end of the period and visually represented by a chart of the checks he has earned. Points to remember:

- The check chart should travel with Joe wherever he goes.
- More time between tokens can be implemented once Joe trusts the system and understands the "payoff."
- Use the check chart as a data collection system showing how often the rewards were earned, the time between checks, and the preferred reinforcers.
- Proceed carefully when implementing a response cost system with Joe—save the "taking away" of tokens for the safety issues. Joe must trust and understand the system of delivery of rewards. Constant loss of rewards might jeopardize the success of the intervention.

Provision of Choices

Joe should be provided with opportunities to choose his activities when possible, using pictures or symbols to show him his choices. This appears to assist Joe in obtaining some sense of control over his day.

Visual Representations of the Concept of Finished

Joe should be provided with visual representations of the task he needs to do, the amount of work he needs to do, and what he needs to do when he is finished. As work is finished, he needs opportunities to put (or see the work put) in the designated spot for finished work.

Presentation of Tasks with Just-Manageable Difficulty

Preferred, familiar, or mastered tasks should be interspersed with nonpreferred, nonfamiliar, or nonmastered activities. When tasks are new, errorless learning principles should be employed. Tasks should be analyzed and presented so that Joe can succeed. Prompts should be faded gradually, ensuring a high degree of success, even to the degree of providing hand-over-hand assistance. Care should be taken to provide and maintain good behavior momentum.

PRESENTATION OF INSTRUCTIONS AND DIRECTIONS

Effective commands should be used with Joe, ensuring that directions are presented clearly and precisely. Language should be tailored to meet Joe's needs. For example, instructions should be given in sentences of three or four words with a short pause between sentences. The rate of language in giving instructions should be slightly slower than the average rate of speech.

Destimulation Area

Joe should be provided with a destimulation area. He currently calls this a "chill-out room." His steps for using the chill-out room should be posted in both his general education and special education classrooms. Steps include: relax, ask for a break, and go chill.

Relaxation Protocol

Joe still needs cues to start his relaxation protocol. This is the procedure Joe has learned for relaxing:

Verbal cue: "It's time to relax. What do we do first?"
Joe responds by saying, "Three deep breaths." Model the three deep breaths.
Verbal cue, "What's next?"
Joe will respond, "Count to 10 slowly." As he counts to 10, monitor the speed, volume, and intonation of his voice.
Verbal cue, "Then?"
Joe responds by saying, "Sit quietly for 10 seconds." Watch the clock or listen for the timer. Start with a smaller amount of time to sit quietly and work up to longer times if needed.
Verbal cue, "Are you calm?" Determine whether he is ready to go on or needs to repeat the protocol.

Strategies for Teaching Social Skills

All of the strategies listed below have been used with Joe over the course of the last 2 years to assist Joe in understanding social cues. The team should consider use of these strategies as they pertain to Joe at the present time. The suggestions are listed below:

1. *Role-plays*: Joe enjoys acting and has shown an ability to generalize role-plays to classroom situations.
2. *Social stories*: Joe has adjusted to new situations without anxiety when presented with a social story. All current stories should be sent home so Joe's parents can review them with him.
3. *Comic strip conversations*: Joe attends well to drawings and has used conversation skills learned from previous instruction with comic strip conversations.
4. *Videotaped segments*: Joe learned his relaxation protocol by watching a videotape of himself performing it. Joe's parents would like to see this used to videotape role-plays.

Crisis Management

Joe should be provided with crisis management procedures if he becomes aggressive. Verbal and visual strategies should be used when Joe becomes anxious and, whenever possible, he should be redirected to choices for his activities and reminded of the consequences for compliance (reinforcers).

Immediately following the first kick or hit, Joe should be provided a calm, firm verbal direction such as "Stop" or "Hands down." He then should be redirected to the task at hand.

If Joe does not respond and continues the display of aggression, attempts should be made to stay out of his personal space, and his teachers should use personal safety techniques to prevent strikes or grabs.

As a last resort, therapeutic nonviolent crisis management interventions should be used by trained personnel. Staff members must take care that these techniques are not painful or punitive and are only used to hold Joe until he regains control. Any physical crisis intervention strategies may only be used by trained personnel and when Joe is continuously aggressive (defined as striking or grabbing others) or in imminent danger of being hurt, hurting others, or when damaging property and at risk for injury.

Throughout the crisis, it is critical that staff members:

- attempt to stay out of Joe's personal space as much as possible;
- remain calm and quietly directive when Joe is aggressive;
- isolate the situation and reduce the audience as much as possible;
- use physical interventions as a last resort—when Joe is in danger of hurting himself or others; and

- employ a team approach, involving at least two people, to maintain the safest, most effective crisis management procedure.

CONCLUSION

Our goal in writing this book has been to share some ideas for helping teachers and parents work effectively with children who have a diagnosis of ASD. We believe every child can learn and that the speed and quality of the child's progress depends significantly on the teacher's skill and choice of methodology.

We often end our presentations with this adapted version of "The Whale Story," by Charles Coonradt (1996) to emphasize the effectiveness of using positive approaches to achieve success:

Have you ever wondered how the whale trainers at Sea World get Shamu to jump out of the water and perform tricks? And, can you imagine the typical approach to this situation? We would put that rope 22 feet high, get a bucket of fish, and give our direction. We would lean over from our high and dry perch and say, "Jump Whale!" We wouldn't pay the whale unless the whale performed. And the whale would stay right where it was.

The trainers at Sea World arrange the environment to make sure the whale can't fail. They start with the rope below the surface of the water, in a position where the whale can't help but swim over it. Every time the whale goes over the rope, it gets fed fish and gets played with and patted.

But what happens when the whale goes under the rope? Nothing. No constructive criticism, no developmental feedback, and no warnings in the personnel file. Whales are taught that their negative behavior will not be acknowledged.

As the whale begins to go over the rope more often than under, the trainers begin to raise the rope. They raise it slowly enough so that the whale doesn't starve, neither physically nor emotionally.

Most people today are doing things right most of the time. Yet, we spend the majority of our time giving feedback on the things that we don't want repeated and didn't want to happen in the first place. We need to set up circumstances so that people can't fail. (pp. 66–67)

We believe this story provides an example of how we should best work with children today. We need to start with tasks they can do and provide positive feedback to shape their skills into more complex achievements. We need to take responsibility when children fail and adjust our expectations and approaches until we find a place in which they can succeed. We want to celebrate successes with these children, as Figure 66 shows.

FIGURE 66. A teacher and child celebrating success!

We believe the future is bright for children diagnosed with ASD and that much of the hope lies in the experience and skills of teachers. We began the book with a quote from a parent. To end the book, we want to acknowledge the importance of developing partnerships with parents who play a crucial role in the education of their children. Working together, we should, as Coonradt (1996) said:

+ Over Celebrate
+ Under Criticize
+ And Know How High to Raise the Rope! (p. 67)

REFERENCES

Alberto, P., & Troutman, A. (2009). *Applied behavior analysis for teachers* (7th ed.). Upper Saddle River, NJ: Merrill Prentice Hall.

American Psychiatric Association. (2000). *Diagnostic and statistical manual of mental disorders, text revision* (4th ed.). Washington, DC: Author.

Autism Genome Project Consortium. (2007). Mapping autism risk loci using genetic linkage and chromosomal rearrangements. *Nature Genetics, 39,* 319–328.

Ayers, A. J. (1979). *Sensory integration and the child.* Los Angeles, CA: Western Psychological Services.

Baer, D. M., Wolf, M. M., & Risley, T. R. (1968). Some current dimensions of applied behavior analysis. *Journal of Applied Behavior Analysis, 1,* 91–97.

Bandura, A. (1977). *Social learning theory.* New York, NY: General Learning Press.

Baron, M. G., Groden, J., Groden G., & Lipsitt, L. P. (2006). *Stress and coping in autism.* New York, NY: Oxford University Press.

Benoit, R. B., & Mayer, G. R. (1974). Extinction: Guidelines for its selection and use. *Personnel and Guidance Journal, 52,* 290–295.

Bereiter, C., & Engelmann, S. (1966). *Teaching disadvantaged children in the pre-school.* Englewood Cliffs, NJ: Prentice-Hall.

Billingsley, F. F., & Romer, L. T. (1983). Response prompting and the transfer of stimulus control: Methods, research, and a conceptual framework. *Journal of the Association for Persons with Severe Handicaps, 8,* 3–12.

Bondy, A., & Frost, L. (2001). The Picture Exchange Communication System. *Behavior Modification, 25,* 725–744.

Bredekamp, S. (Ed.). (1987). *Developmentally appropriate practice in early childhood programs serving children from birth through age 8*. Washington, DC: National Association for the Education of Young Children.

Bricker, D., & Cripe, J. (1992). *An activity-based approach to early intervention*. Baltimore, MD: Brookes.

Buggey, T. (1999). Look, I'm on TV! Using videotaped self modeling to change behaviors. *Teaching Exceptional Children, 31*, 27–31.

Carbone, V. J. (2002). *Teaching verbal behavior to children with autism and related disabilities*. Unpublished manuscript, Arlington, VA.

Cavallaro, C. (1983). Language interventions in natural settings. *Teaching Exceptional Children, 16*, 65–70.

Cedillo v. Secretary of Health and Human Services, No. 98-916V (U.S. Court of Federal Claims, February 2, 2009).

Centers for Disease Control and Prevention. (2008). *Autism information center*. Retrieved from http://www.cdc.gov/ncbddd/autism/faq_prevalence.htm

Cohen, H., Amerine-Dickens, M., & Smith, T. (2006). Early intensive behavioral treatment: Replication of the UCLA model in a community setting. *Journal of Developmental & Behavioral Pediatrics, 27*, 145–155.

Coonradt, C. A. (1996). The power of acknowledgement. In J. Canfield, M. V. Hansen, M. Rogerson, M. Trutte, & T. Clauss (Eds.), *Chicken soup for the soul at work* (pp. 65–67). Deerfield Beach, FL: Health Communications.

Council for Children with Behavioral Disorders. (2009a). *CCBD's position summary on the use of seclusion in school settings*. Retrieved from http://www.cec.sped.org/Content/NavigationMenu/PolicyAdvocacy/CCBD_on_Use_of_Seclusion_7-8-09.doc

Council for Children with Behavioral Disorders (2009b). *CCBD's position summary on the use of physical restraint procedures in school settings*. Retrieved from http://www.cec.sped.org/Content/NavigationMenu/PolicyAdvocacy/CCBD_on_Use_of_Seclusion_7-8-09.doc

Data Accountability Center. (n.d.). *Number of children served under IDEA Part B by disability and age group, 2006*. Retrieved from https://www.ideadata.org/arc_toc8.asp#partbCC

Dawson, G., & Osterling, J. (1997). Early intervention in autism: Effectiveness and common elements of current approaches. In M. J. Guralnick (Ed.), *The effectiveness of early intervention* (pp. 307–326). Baltimore, MD: Brookes.

Dowrick, P. W. (1999). A review of self-modeling and related interventions. *Applied & Preventive Psychology, 8*, 23–39.

Durand, V. M. (1990). *Severe behavior problems: A functional communication training approach*. New York, NY: Guilford.

Education for All Handicapped Children Act of 1975, Pub. Law 94-142 (November 29, 1975).

Engelmann, S. (1968). The effectiveness of direct verbal instruction on IQ performance and achievement in reading and arithmetic. In J. Hellmuth (Ed.), *Disadvantaged Child* (Vol. 3). New York, NY: Bruner Mazel.

Engelmann, S. (1980). *Direct instruction*. Englewood Cliffs, NJ: Prentice-Hall.

Engelmann, S., & Carnine, D. (1982). *Theory of instruction*. New York, NY: Irvington.

Fouse, B., & Wheeler, M. (1997). *A treasure chest of behavioral strategies for adolescents with autism*. Arlington, TX: Future Horizons.

Gagnon, E. (2001). *Power cards: Using special interests to motivate children and youth with Asperger syndrome and autism.* Shawnee Mission, KS: Autism Asperger Publishing.

Ganz, J. B., & Simpson, R. L. (2004). Effects on communicative requesting and speech development of the Picture Exchange Communication System in children with characteristics of autism. *Journal of Autism and Developmental Disorders, 34,* 395–409.

Gray, C. (1993). *The original social story book.* Jenison, MI: Jenison Public Schools.

Gray, C. (1995). *Social stories and comic strip conversations: Unique methods to improve social understanding.* Arlington, TX: Future Horizons.

Gray, C. (2000). *The new social story book.* Arlington, TX: Future Horizons.

Gupta, A. R., & State, M. W. (2007). Recent advances in the genetics of autism. *Biological Psychiatry, 61,* 429–437.

Guralnick, M. J. (1997). *The effectiveness of early intervention.* Baltimore, MD: Brookes.

Happé, F., Ronald, A., & Plomin, R. (2006). Time to give up on a single explanation for autism. *Nature Neuroscience, 9,* 1218–1220.

Hart, B. M., & Risley, T. R. (1968). Establishing the use of descriptive adjectives in the spontaneous speech of disadvantaged children. *Journal of Applied Behavior Analysis, 1,* 109–120.

Hart, B. M., & Risley, T. R. (1978). Promoting productive language through incidental teaching. *Education and Urban Society, 10,* 407–429.

Hazlehurst v. Secretary of Health and Human Services, No. 03-654V (U.S. Court of Federal Claims, February 2, 2009).

Hodgdon, L. A. (1995). *Visual strategies for improving communication* (8th ed.). Troy, MI: QuirkRoberts.

Hunter, M. (1980). *Teach more faster.* El Segundo, CA: TIP Publications.

Individuals with Disabilities Education Act, 20 U.S.C. §1401 et seq. (1990).

Individuals with Disabilities Education Improvement Act, PL 108-446, 118 Stat. 2647 (2004).

Iwata, B. A., Dorsey, M. F., Slifer, K. J., Bauman, K. E., & Richman, G. S. (1982). Toward a functional analysis of self-injury. *Analysis and Intervention in Developmental Disabilities, 2,* 3–20.

Koegel, L. K., & Koegel, R. L. (1999a). Pivotal response intervention I: Overview of the approach. *Journal of the Association for the Severely Handicapped, 24,* 174–185.

Koegel, L. K., & Koegel, R. L. (1999b). Pivotal response intervention II: Preliminary long-term outcome data. *Journal of the Association for Persons with Severe Handicaps, 24,* 186–198.

Koegel, R. L., & Williams, J. A. (1980). Direct versus indirect response-reinforcer relationships in teaching autistic children. *Journal of Abnormal Child Psychology, 8,* 537–547.

Krantz, P. J., & McClannahan, L. E. (1993). Teaching children with autism to initiate to peers: Effects of a script-fading procedure. *Journal of Applied Behavior Analysis, 26,* 121–132.

Krantz, P. J., & McClannahan, L. E. (1998). Social interaction skills for children with autism: A script-fading procedure for beginning readers. *Journal of Applied Behavior Analysis, 31,* 191–202.

Leaf, R., & McEachin, J. (1999). *A work in progress: Behavior management strategies & a curriculum for intensive behavioral treatment of autism.* New York, NY: DRL Books.

Let's Beat Autism Now. (n.d.). *Autism poetry*. Retrieved July 17, 2009, from http://www.letsbeatautismnow.com/Poems.html

Lovaas, O. I. (1987). Behavioral treatment and normal educational and intellectual functioning in young autistic children. *Journal of Consulting and Clinical Psychology, 55,* 3–9.

Maurice, C., Green, G., & Luce, S. C. (Eds.). (1996). *Behavioral intervention for young children with autism: A manual for parents and professionals.* Austin, TX: Pro-Ed.

McAfee, J., & Attwood, T. (2002). *Navigating the social world: A curriculum for individuals with Asperger's syndrome, high functioning autism and related disorders.* Arlington, TX: Future Horizons.

McClannahan, L. E., & Krantz, P. J. (1999). *Activity schedules for children with autism: Teaching independent behavior.* Bethesda, MD: Woodbine House.

McEachin, J. J., Smith, T., & Lovaas, O. I. (1993). Long-term outcome for children with autism who received early intensive behavioral treatment. *American Journal on Mental Retardation, 97,* 359–372.

McGee, G. G., Daly, T., & Jacobs, H. A. (1994). The Walden preschool. In S. L. Harris & J. S. Handleman (Eds.), *Preschool education programs for children with autism* (pp. 126–162). Austin, TX: Pro-Ed.

McGee, G. G., Morrier, M. J., & Daly, T. (1999). An incidental teaching approach to early intervention for toddlers with autism. *Journal of the Association for Persons with Severe Handicaps, 24,* 133–146.

McGinnis, E., & Goldstein, A. P. (1997). *Skillstreaming the elementary school child.* Champaign, IL: Research Press.

Mesibov, G. B., Shea, V., & Schopler, E. (2006). *The TEACCH approach to autism spectrum disorders.* New York, NY: Springer.

Meyen, E., Vergason, G., & Whelan, R. (1996). *Strategies for teaching exceptional children in inclusive settings.* Denver, CO: Love.

Michael, J. (1982). Distinguishing between discriminative and motivational functions of stimuli. *Journal of the Experimental Analysis of Behavior, 37,* 149–155.

Michael, J. (2007). Motivating operations. In J. O. Cooper, T. E. Heron, & W. L. Heward (Eds.), *Applied behavior analysis* (2nd ed.). Upper Saddle River, NJ: Prentice Hall/Merrill.

National Institute of Health, National Institute of Neurological Disorders and Stroke. (n.d.). *NINDS autism information page.* Retrieved from http://www.ninds.nih.gov

National Research Council. (2001). *Educating children with autism.* Washington, DC: National Academy Press.

New York State Department of Health, Early Intervention Program. (1999). *Clinical practice guideline: Report of the recommendations. Autism/pervasive developmental disorders, assessment and intervention for young children (Age 0–3 years)* (NYSDH Publication No. 4215). Albany, NY: Author.

Noonan, M. J., & McCormick, L. (1993). *Early intervention in natural environments: Methods and procedures.* Belmont, CA: Brooks/Cole.

Offit, P. A. (2007). Thimerosal and vaccines—a cautionary tale. *New England Journal of Medicine, 357,* 1278–1279.

O'Neill, R. E., Horner, R. H., Albin, R. W., Sprague, J. R., Storey, K., & Newton, J. S. (1997). *Functional assessment and program development for problem behavior: A practical handbook* (2nd ed.). Pacific Grove, CA: Brooks/Cole.

Ozonoff, S., & Cathcart, K. (1998). Effectiveness of a home program intervention for young children with autism. *Journal of Autism and Developmental Disorders, 28,* 25–36.

Partington, J. W. (2006). *The assessment of basic language and learning skills–Revised.* Danville, CA: Behavior Analysts.

Paul, G. (1967). Outcome research in psychotherapy. *Journal of Consulting Psychology, 31,* 109–113.

Perry, A., & Condillac, R. (2003). *Evidence-based practices for children and adolescents with autism spectrum disorders: Review of the literature and practice guide.* Toronto, Ontario: Children's Mental Health Ontario.

Rhode, G., Jenson, W. R., & Reavis, H. K. (1992). *The tough kid book: Practical classroom management strategies.* Longmont, CO: Sopris West.

Rosenshine, B. (1976). Recent research on teaching behavior and student achievement. *Journal of Teacher Education, 27,* 61–64.

Rosenshine, B., & Stevens, R. (1986). Teaching functions. In M. C. Witrock (Ed.), *Handbook of research on teaching* (3rd ed., pp. 376–391). New York, NY: Macmillan.

Rowe, M. B. (1972, April). *Wait time and rewards as instructional variables, their influence in language, logic and fate control.* Paper presented at the National Association for Research in Science Teaching, Chicago, IL. (ERIC Document Reproduction Service No. ED061103)

Sallows, G. O., & Graupner, T. D. (2005). Intensive behavioral treatment for children with autism: Four-year outcome and predictors. *American Journal on Mental Retardation, 110,* 417–438.

Schopler, E., & Mesibov, G. (1995). *Learning and cognition in autism.* New York, NY: Plenum Press.

Schwartz, I. S., Billingsley, F. F., & McBride, B. M. (1998). Including children with autism in inclusive preschools: Strategies that work. *Young Exceptional Children, 1*(2), 19–26.

Schwartz, I. S., Garfinkle, A. N., & Bauer, J. (1998). The Picture Exchange Communication System: Communicative outcomes for young children with disabilities. *Topics in Early Childhood Special Education, 18,* 144–159.

Shogren, K. A., Faggella-Luby, M. N., Bae, S. J., & Wehmeyer, M. L. (2004). The effect of choice-making as an intervention for problem behavior: A meta-analysis. *Journal of Positive Behavior Interventions, 6,* 228–237.

Skinner, B. F. (1957). *Verbal behavior.* Acton, MA: Copley.

Snyder v. Secretary of Health and Human Services, No. 01-162V (U.S. Court of Federal Claims, February 12, 2009).

Snyder-McLean, L., Solomonson, B., McLean, J., & Sack, S. (1984). Structuring joint action routines: A strategy for facilitating communication and language development in the classroom. *Seminars in Speech and Language, 5,* 213–228.

Sulzer-Azaroff, B., & Mayer, R. (1991). *Behavior analysis for lasting change.* Fort Worth, TX: Holt, Reinhart & Winston.

Sundberg, M. L. (2008). *Verbal behavior milestones assessment and placement program.* Concord, CA: AVB Press.

Sundberg, M. L., & Partington, J. W. (1998). *Teaching language to children with autism or other developmental disabilities.* Pleasant Hill, CA: Behavior Analysts.

Tomlinson, C. (1999). *The differentiated classroom: Responding to the needs of all learners.* Alexandria, VA: ASCD.

Turnbull, H. R., Huerta, N., & Stowe, M. (2006). *The Individuals with Disabilities Education Act as amended in 2004.* Upper Saddle River, NJ: Pearson/Merrill/Prentice Hall.

Turnbull, H. R., & Turnbull, A. P. (2000). *Free appropriate public education* (6th ed.). Denver, CO: Love.

U.S. Surgeon General. (1999). *Other mental disorders in children and adolescents.* Retrieved from http://www.surgeongeneral.gov/library/mentalhealth/chapter3/sec6.html

Washington State Department of Social & Health Services. (n.d.). Autism awareness. Retrieved September 14, 2009, from http://www.dshs.wa.gov/ddd/autism.shtml

Winner, M. G. (2002). *Thinking about you thinking about me.* San Jose, CA: Author.

Winner, M. G. (2005). *Think social! A social thinking curriculum for school-age students.* San Jose, CA: Author.

Wolery, M., & Gast, D. L. (1984). Effective and efficient procedures for the transfer of stimulus control. *Topics in Early Childhood Special Education, 4,* 52–77.

Zhao, X., Leotta, A., Kustanovich, V., Lajonchere, C., Geschwind, D. H., Law, K., . . . Wigler, M. (2007). A unified genetic theory for sporadic and inherited autism. *Proceedings of the National Academy of Sciences, 104,* 12831–12836.

ABOUT THE AUTHORS

Wendy Ashcroft is the director of field experience at Christian Brothers University in Memphis, TN. She enthusiastically teaches both graduate and undergraduate education courses and supervises practicum and student teaching experiences for developing teachers. Dr. Ashcroft's public school experience included 11 years as a classroom teacher for students with autism, intellectual, physical, and multiple disabilities, and 21 years as a special education administrator. She is known widely for her leadership of Project REACH, a Shelby County Schools program that provides support and training for school personnel and parents interested in children with autism. Dr. Ashcroft has been an active leader in the International Council for Exceptional Children and The ARC and in state and community program development for children with autism. She is an avid windsurfer, sailor, and swimmer and is raising two happy-go-lucky golden retrievers.

Sue Argiro is a special educator with more than 20 years of experience working with children with autism and other developmental disabilities. She received her master's degree in special education from the University of Memphis. She began her teaching career as an elementary school teacher before earning a degree in special education. Ms. Argiro taught special education at the elementary level for Shelby County Schools in Memphis, TN, before joining their specialized autism program called Project REACH. Currently, she works as a Student Response Team Consultant, providing support for all classroom personnel, related service providers, and administrators of children with autism and other related disabilities from preschool through high school. In addition, she provides training to parents and oversees programs conducted in the students' homes.

Joyce Keohane received her master's degree from University of Memphis and has worked in the field of special education for more than 30 years. She enjoyed 20 years as a classroom teacher for students with various disabilities. Over the past 11 years, as a consultant for Shelby County Schools, she has focused on students with autism spectrum disorders. She has been involved in training and support for teachers, parents, and administrators through Project REACH, a group of professionals that provide support within the schools and community. She has had opportunities to speak for local and international audiences concerning evidence-based strategies that are successful interventions for special needs students.